TOTAL QUALITY MANAGEMENT FOR ENGINEERS

To my parents, my wife Alweena and my children Adel and Bilal

TOTAL QUALITY MANAGEMENT FOR ENGINEERS

Mohamed Zairi,

BSc (Hons), MSc, PhD

Unilever Lecturer in TQM, European Centre for TQM, The Management Centre, Bradford University (UK)

WOODHEAD PUBLISHING LIMITED

Cambridge England

Published by Woodhead Publishing Ltd,
Abington Hall, Abington,
Cambridge CB1 6AH, England

First published 1991, Woodhead Publishing Ltd

British Library Cataloguing in Publication Data
A catalogue record for this book is available from the British Library.

ISBN 1 85573 024 3

Designed by Andrew Jones (text) and Chris Feely (jacket)
Typeset by Cambridge Composing (UK) Ltd
Printed by Billing & Sons Ltd, Worcester

CONTENTS

FOREWORD

The drive throughout the business world for greater efficiencies, reduced costs and increased productivity often falls on the shoulders of engineers. Traditional and cutting approaches, however, have failed time and time again, and it is those companies which have grasped the quality nettle that have been successful, ridden business recessions, and annihilated the competition.

Total Quality Management is creating a revolution in manufacturing and service organisations throughout the world. The impact this has had on the engineering profession may be measured by the number of qualified engineers now seeking information, courses and literature on the subject of TQM.

Clearly there is a need for engineers to understand TQM and how it may be implemented. The powerful combination of TQM logic and engineering-based technology will be attractive to all scientifically minded people and should help them achieve a substantial impact on the costs of lack of quality in their organisations.

Total Quality Management and engineering are both user driven, practical subjects which depend on a good foundation of theories and concepts. Dr Zairi's well researched book provides a guide for engineers to the theory of TQM, and will be a welcome addition to their libraries.

John S Oakland
Professor of Total Quality Management

PREFACE

---

*Quality never happens by mistake,
it is always the result of
intelligent effort.*

(unknown)

Total Quality Management (TQM) for engineers seemed to be an obvious book to write for a variety of reasons. Firstly, although the concept of quality is familiar to engineers, their treatment of it has always been narrowly focused. Secondly, many people, including engineers, are still wrestling with the difficulties associated with the concept of TQM and its application. It was therefore considered important enough to attempt presenting TQM as an approach which relates to all aspects of business organisations, including both internal and external environments. Thirdly, the role of engineers seems to be more and more positively enhanced nowadays. Their involvement is much more widely spread than previously.

As TQM tends to focus on business organisations as total dynamic systems, its portrayal in this fashion should help engineers appreciate the level of penetration and wide implications TQM has for all aspects of business organisations.

Total Quality Management is an evolutionary concept. Its nature, title, role and 'acronym designation' are all subject to changes with time. It represents current conditions for competitiveness. Organisations who wish to fulfill most, if not all, of the market conditions, will exploit TQM to their advantage by making it a necessary pre-requisite for achieving competitiveness, and a means to drive the business rather than just a loose input.

It is unfortunate that cynics who consider TQM to be just a fad, and cannot wait for the acronym to disappear, have failed to visualise the evolutionary process by which considerable growth and reliance on the role of quality has taken place. TQM today may mean Total Business Management (TBM) or Total Market Leadership (TML) tomorrow. Does it really matter?

A fad is a label, an experiment, a piece of corporate advertising. TQM is none of these. Its evolution could be traced back from the eras of mass inspection, control, assurance and management. Each of these stages reflects a change in market conditions and customer requirements. What TQM has done amongst other things is render customer input much more valuable and waste of any kind something which should be eliminated with great effort, vigour and determination.

Some cynics, such as marketing specialists, argue that TQM does not preach anything new and that the marketing function has always applied most of the ideas claimed to be essential in the TQM philosophy. First of all, TQM does not necessarily teach many new concepts. It does however, strongly emphasise the need to focus on every single aspect of the business from the point of view of adding value. Nothing is peripheral, nothing is just supportive, everything adds value. TQM does not just over-emphasise front end activities such as marketing, which is traditionally considered to be the key link in customer-supplier chains. TQM presents the customer-supplier chain in a much wider context, where meeting customer requirements becomes an overall organisational objective.

Secondly, although most of the ideas used in TQM are 'obvious', one can only refer to the following quotation, to realise why it is important to re-consider everything and every process in business organisations:

'Common sense is not so common' (Voltaire)

The obvious is always so near and yet human nature finds it more challenging to look at the furthest horizon. The clearest example is the Western approach to improvement (innovation) in comparison to the Japanese (Kaizen).

Western approach = Innovation = Complexity
Kaizen = Improvement = Practicality

Simple solutions in the West up until recent years at least, have always been discarded because their impact was not considered to be sufficient. Ideas were considered to be more acceptable if they represented a high degree of complexity.

Thirdly, TQM introduces a kind of discipline for everyday business behaviour both internally and externally. The standard tools and techniques used in the context of TQM help everyone concerned in measuring performance of the processes they own and in carrying out the necessary improvements to achieve better performance all the time. This leads to the achievement of doing everything right internally, first time and every time.

The use of benchmarking and competitive measurement also introduces discipline in assessing business performance more objectively. By continually looking for competitive gaps and adopting best practice in every aspect of the business superior performance can be achieved. This is by doing the right things externally.

Most books written on TQM tend on the whole to focus on specific aspects such as tools and techniques, Statistical Process Control (SPC) or TQM implementation guidelines. This book is unique in the sense that it has adopted a different approach by not so much prescribing, but rather trying to improve the level of awareness, knowledge and understanding of the reader about TQM. Engineers, amongst many other people, still fail to appreciate the degree of propensity and pervasiveness TQM has in shaping competitive behaviour. The book does therefore, assume that the reader may have no knowledge at all, limited knowledge, or even perhaps some narrowly focused knowledge on TQM and its implications.

The structure of the book is designed to enable the reader to gain gradual knowledge and appreciation of the nature of TQM and its wider implications on organisations. Chapter 1 examines the degree of change in the role of engineers, the reasons for these changes and the reasons for the suggested link between the role of engineers and TQM.

Chapters 2 and 3 look at the evolution of quality until the present day and define TQM in terms of philosophies, concepts and contributions from pioneers and gurus in the field of quality. Chapters 4 and 5 define TQM in terms of systems and tools for improvement respectively.

Chapter 6 presents an area which most engineers may be familiar with – the concept of Total Preventative Maintenance (TPM). This chapter highlights the importance of 'Zero Breakdown' in achieving Zero Defect. Chapter 7 is another example which engineers may be familiar with – Total Safety Systems (TSS). This chapter highlights the importance of the Zero Risk concept for achieving Zero Defect.

For TQM to succeed, it is argued that there are three essential elements which, together, contribute to changing corporate culture. This change is important for TQM to become a routinised and voluntarily accepted concept, part of everyday working life. Chapters 8, 9 and 10, therefore, tackle the essential areas of leadership, customer-supplier chains and continuous improvements, respectively.

Chapter 11 is not a fully developed argument because it is considered to be beyond the scope of this book. Chapters 1 to 10 describe how the ground should be prepared and how to plant the seeds. One is then bound to ask what happens next? Chapter 11 therefore is a brief attempt to describe implementation, quality costing and performance measurement.

This book aims to present a comprehensive approach which is intended to broaden the knowledge of engineers and others concerned with TQM and its implications on their working environment. It is also intended for students who have to wrestle with this concept in the course of their various studies.

A comprehensive reading list is included at the end of the book. This can also be considered as an opportunity for students and practitioners alike to pursue any specific arguments they may become interested in when reading the book.

The author has been greatly inspired by the various writings of authors included in the bibliography. There is no doubt that the rich ideas and views coming from the work of others have helped support the arguments presented by the author himself. Unfortunately the list is too long to mention people by name. Nonetheless, the author is grateful to all the people whose ideas have helped shed some light on specific areas of TQM and whose contribution in this field will be valued and greatly appreciated by all those who aspire to progress and advancement.

The author is also grateful to his family for their support and understanding and for putting up with his moods during the writing of this book.

1

THE ENGINEER AND TQM:
A POSITIVE LINK

INTRODUCTION

The engineering profession has evolved in a dramatic way over the past few years. Indeed, engineers are no longer confined to fulfilling specific tasks of a support nature only. Their involvement is much more encompassing and they tend to assume much broader roles with higher organisational objectives. They manage technological systems, resources and projects and contribute substantially by adding value to organisational performance. To understand the relevance of TQM to engineers, it is perhaps important to spend time discussing the evolution in the engineering profession which has brought its practitioners to the centre of business activities.

Engineers have in the past, been a difficult group to consider. They did not fit easily into the categories provided by occupational status, the power of decision-making, the visible contributions towards productivity and profitability improvements and the privileges of association and contact with power providers.

Cultural snobbery has also added little credibility to the engineering profession and its uptake as a career in academic establishments. It has often been described as dealing with 'nuts and bolts' and regarded as perhaps not much different from the contribution of semi-skilled workers and shopfloor workers generally.

It is therefore not surprising that the engineering profession for a number of years has not increased in status within organisations and has not gained any further recognition or encouragement from society as a whole.

The traumatic experiences suffered by most Western economies in the face of the competitive excellence of Japanese businesses have raised many questions on routines and old habits, particularly the role of the manufacturing function and how various tasks including those of engineers are to be redefined.

It is with this new role of engineers in mind that this chapter seeks to establish the link between the preachings of TQM and the expected role of engineers in fulfilling the required organisational objectives.

The chapter distinguishes between the traditional role of engineers as a support group to the highly valued visible contributing functions, and a new role based on integrated activities with other functions and with more visible contributions towards internal efficiency and competitiveness in the outside market.

THE ENGINEER AS A SPECIALIST

Engineering as a specialist profession has been perceived as no more than a support function which is not encouraged to contribute directly in adding value to organisational functions. The model represented in Fig. 1.1 shows the traditional view of the engineering function as a 'Non Value Adding' activity, similar to the role of personnel and finance. These functions have always been described as providing technical/legal/commercial advice and guidance without necessarily being able to influence the decision-making process.

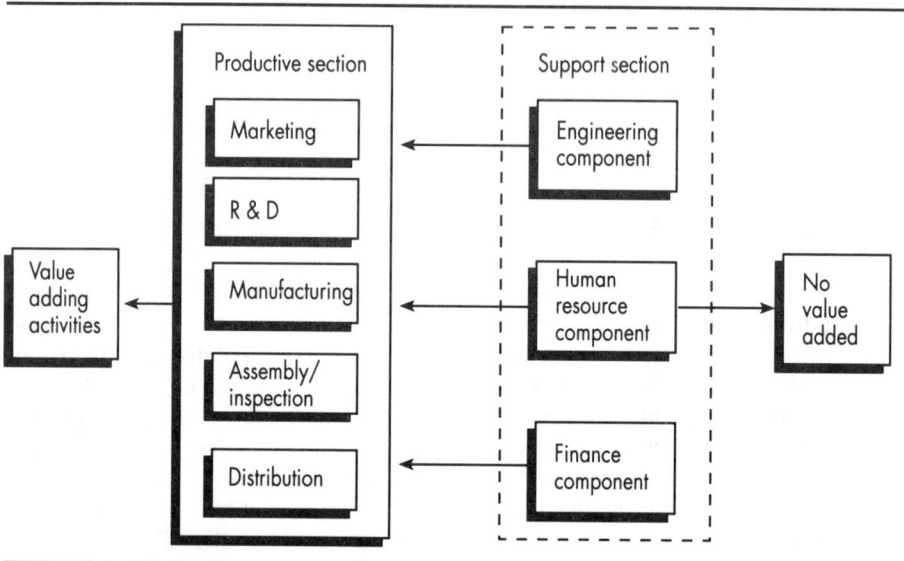

1.1 The role of engineering in the traditional organisational systems model.

The message which emerges from Fig. 1.1 is that an enclosure has been deliberately put around the engineering function to keep it as a separate component from the other functions regarded as the lifeblood of organisations. This suggests that the partitioning of the various functions and their compartmentalisation is not necessarily an infrastructural problem but one more embedded in attitudes and beliefs towards the role of engineering in industry.

The concerns over the narrowly defined role of engineers and their specialisation are widely spread. The lessons learnt from the Japanese competitors have drawn attention to the urgent need to produce knowledge workers with organisational awareness of objectives and direction. Various terminologies have been used to help redefine the role of engineers, such as 'an integrated role' and 'a systems role' amongst others.

The need to shift away from a narrowly defined role with task oriented objectives towards a more integrated role which contributes towards productivity improvements within organisations, can perhaps be expressed by the following comments.

'Our whole society is based on individualism, specialisation and entrepreneurial skills. This impedes our ability to develop an integrated inter-disciplinary team approach dedicated to optimise the whole endeavour, not its specific parts. This requires not only a broad-based technical knowledge but also business, financial and sociological acumen as well.'[7]

'As Vice President of Industrial Engineering, I want to work with IEs who have all the technical skills – who can do the analysis and produce the correct numbers, but also can integrate those skills with business strategy.'[11]

'Japanese engineers have a very broad education. It is very much seen as being industry's business to provide technology specific training. This surely raises the question as to whether the moves in the UK in recent years towards technology specific degree courses might be in totally the wrong direction. Surely we need more engineers with a much broader engineering and general educational background.'[20]

'Britain's cultural tradition is of highly specialised, narrow, in-depth education, long dominated by the particular and peculiar standards of the pure scientist. This tradition emphasises knowledge creation as distinct from its application and gives status to those who know the most about the least ... The products of these specialised courses then in industry have set up specialised segmentalist groupings which inhibit the integrative approach so necessary in manufacturing and successfully developed by our Japanese competitors.'[18,19]

THE FAILURE OF ENGINEERING EDUCATIONAL SYSTEMS: THE UK EXPERIENCE

The failure of manufacturing industry in the UK in not sustaining its strength to compete in world markets has been linked to a variety of factors including the weak role of academic institutions in not providing skills which could have enabled industrialists to compete more positively. In Britain, for example, engineering educational institutions have been blamed for their rigidity and steady-state approach towards evolution and changes in the industrial world.

Educational systems in the UK have tended to place more focus on the production of specialists in the areas of mechanical engineering, production engineering, chemical engineering, control engineering, electrical engineering, electronic engineering and aeronautical engineering.

The 'A' level curriculum in the UK has been described as a limited pool, offering narrow options to graduates (three subjects) in comparison to seven subjects in other European programmes. In terms of the quantity of graduates in engineering in comparison to pure scientists Table 1.1 shows that Britain is lagging behind when compared with Japan.[18,19]

Table 1.1 A comparison of graduate numbers between UK and Japan

Specialist options	Britain	Japan
Engineering graduates per annum	12,000	70,000
Pure science graduates per annum	22,000	10,500

These figures, albeit simplistic, indicate that there is a difference in emphasis on the engineering profession in comparison with the need for pure scientists between Japan and the UK. To highlight further the shortcomings of the British engineering educational system, reference has to be made to an important research project which was specifically conducted to assess the quality, suitability and effectiveness of existing educational systems and the various engineering options they provide.

The 'Goals of Engineering Education Project' (GEEP)[9] was commissioned by the

Council for National Academic Awards (CNAA) and the Department of Education and Science and carried out by the School of Electronic and Electrical Engineering at Leicester Polytechnic. GEEP conducted in-depth interviews with 250 mechanical, electrical and electronics graduates in 55 public and private organisations. The project also conducted interviews with 200 people with or for whom engineers worked.

The report concluded that the present British engineering educational system is rigid, inflexible and does not prepare engineers well enough to attain promotions and career development within organisations. The report goes on to say that:

'It is no surprise then to observe that the profession appears fragmented and that engineers appear to lack the will to do anything about this themselves. Though formally described as a professional, these findings suggest that the engineer is usually treated more like a technician, a hired hand, who performs a technical task without comment, and without expecting to or being expected to comment.'[9]

Table 1.2 lists extracts from some key comments made by the different respondents of the GEEP report.

THE NEW BREED OF ENGINEERS

The modern competitive nature of organisations has placed more emphasis on integrated roles and the ability to manage projects on a cross-functional basis. This is considered to be necessary for linking organisational internal strengths to the competitive market externally.

As far as engineers are concerned, their role has been broadened to cover aspects of organisational competitiveness. Macro-engineering awareness is perceived to be the element of their education/training which will enable them to understand how large systems operate including people processes, machine processes, market behaviours, suppliers, etc. Micro-engineering awareness consists mainly of their detailed engineering knowledge about the operation and design of technical processes (electromechanical systems, processing systems and computer aided engineering systems).[10]

Who are the new engineers?

Engineers have so far been described in broad terms without specifically referring to the nature of their education and training or their place within organisations. The new breed of engineers with broader education has been described in various ways such as manufacturing engineers, systems engineers or industrial engineers.

Manufacturing engineers

Manufacturing engineering is considered to be the integration of industrial engineering with electrical engineering, mechanical engineering and computer science, with the addition of business and finance.[7]

Table 1.2 The engineer and business requirements

Need for a broad education	It is effective to use engineers with a multidisciplinary background
	They need new tools because jobs and technologies change
	Engineers are inflexible, unadaptable, convergent thinkers
	A broad technical education is valuable because it presents different views
Ability to communicate	One of an engineer's biggest failures is the inability to communicate
	Widespread literacy rather than a course of communications is the answer
	Education should teach how to argue
	Communications are as important as engineering
Knowledge of the business context	Ignorance is fuelled by reluctance
	Engineers are an insular breed who consider it unnecessary to be concerned with the profitability and efficiency of the organisation as a whole
	Engineers are reluctant to justify costs as it is seen as questioning their expertise
	Engineers have had no training in alternatives. They are keen to see things relating immediately to their jobs, but are not keen on peripheral aspects, e.g. budgeting
Engineers and the decision making process	There is a tendency to insulate engineers from non-technical issues, yet these are areas of key importance
	Engineers are not allowed to manage – others make decisions for them
	Engineering is not viewed as an integral part of management
	There is an enormous gap between engineers' knowledge and that of the company

Systems engineers

Systems engineers are those people concerned with the design, commissioning and operation of:

- Machine systems (minis, micros, instruments, machines, processes);
- Computer aided engineering support systems (CAD/CAM);
- Manufacturing systems (integrated assemblies of computers, people organis- ations, systems, market interfaces and business planning system interfaces). [14–18]

Industrial engineering

The industrial engineer (IE) is sometimes referred to as the integrated engineer as the nature of the training is broad, giving general knowledge on methodology, people systems, problem solving approaches, innovativeness and the ability to link designs, products and manufacturing processes as an integrated system.

There is however a more formal definition given by the Institute of Industrial Engineers Terminology Handbook. This refers to industrial engineering as follows:

'Industrial engineering – concerned with the design, improvement and installation of integrated systems of people, materials, equipment and energy. It draws upon specialised knowledge and skills in the mathematical, physical, and social sciences together with the principles and methods of engineering analysis and design, to specify, predict and evaluate the results to be obtained from such systems.'[23]

The various definitions given above all refer to the integration of technical systems with organisational objectives and people systems. The role of engineers is seen to be pertinent in facilitating the integration of technical processes to other aspects of organisational systems with productivity improvement very much in mind and with the ability to channel 'inputs' for maximising performance, aided by the ability to measure and control performance.

The engineer as manager

It is often considered that engineers tend to aspire to a career in management once they have progressed well enough in their jobs.[22] Others have discussed the need to equip engineers with the tools and organisational knowledge to help them solve a variety of problems[3] and the need to have engineers as part of the 'product-realisation process' to create goods and services that will generate wealth.[5] It is also thought that as it is predicted that future competitiveness of organisations will more and more emphasise project teams and matrix structures, the progression of engineers to management jobs in manufacturing will become the norm.[21]

The transition of an engineering specialist from a technical role to a managerial role leads to a dramatic change in time utilisation as far as skills and knowledge are concerned. It is expected that at least 85% of the time of an engineer is spent dealing with technical aspects of his or her job. This pattern is however reversed when promotion to a managerial job takes place. 60% of a manager's job is spent making decisions and only 30% on technical matters. Managers are however expected to understand some broad concepts of the technical aspects of the operation processes they are in charge of, Fig. 1.2.

There are various descriptions which have been given to the expanding role of engineers. These refer to the involvement of engineers in the decision making process and in the achievement of organisational objectives. The following role descriptions are a good example of how an engineer is considered in an organisational system based on modern competitive approaches.

Role description 1

This example describes engineers as people who will undergo the following transitional process:[13]

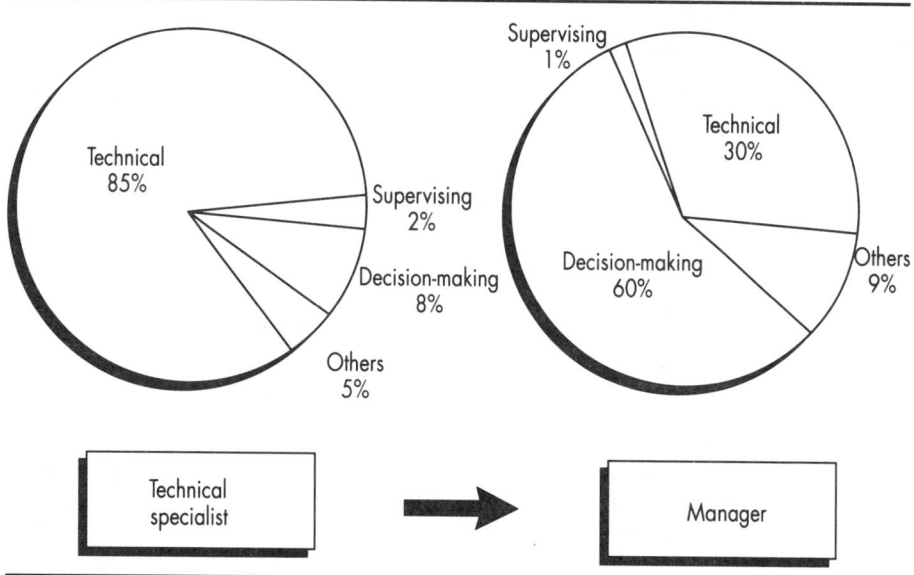

1.2 From engineers to managers: a growing role.

Step 1 Technical specialist: An individual with practical and technical training and or/experience in a given field;

Step 2 Project manager: An individual assigned the direct responsibility of supervising a given project through the phases of planning, organising, scheduling, monitoring and controlling;

Step 3 Group manager: An individual who is assigned direct responsibility to plan, organise and direct the activities of a group with a standing charge;

Step 4 Director: An individual who oversees a particular function of the organisation. This is a critical responsibility that directly affects the welfare of the organisation;

Step 5 Administrative manager: An individual who oversees the administrative functions and staff of the organisation. Responsibilities cut across several functional areas and he/she therefore must have proven managerial skills and diversity in previous assignments.

Role description 2

This model is proposed for the new breed of engineers who have to cope in a highly automated and technologically advanced environment.[8]

System integrator: The abilities necessary to ensure that the components of technology based systems in a production environment are fully integrated. This integration task could involve co-ordinating the activities of individuals, groups, vendors and projects;

Communicator: The communication skills and abilities required to develop effective communication within the organisation. The total production process performance is communicated to everyone through a manual or system-oriented channel;

Designer of systems/organisations: Knowledge of systems and methods used to design operating systems and organisation structures;

Problem-solver: Competence in the techniques of problem solving analysis and solution, ability to diagnose problems and resolve them to improve productivity and quality levels, and ensure organisational effectiveness;

Innovator: Creative judgement to maximise the effective utilisation of organisational resources. Productivity improvement techniques are applied to reduce the total cost of doing business in a high technology production environment;

Advocate and decision maker: On-going assessment and thorough understanding of the high technology production process. Knowledge of social sciences and behavioural characteristics are used for negotiation, consensus building, teamwork, acceptance criteria and action implementation in decision making;

Planner of integrated systems requirements: Knowledge of budget and control to manage the financial requirements in the high technology arena. Alternative methods and techniques for improving the effectiveness of decision making are also planned for both short and long term;

Teacher and a model style: Behavioural knowledge to influence and improve morale and motivation in the high technology environment. Coaching and negotiation skills used to help peers, superiors and subordinates in overcoming obstacles to productivity and total system effectiveness;

Change master: Acceptance leader, structured group process provider, teacher, skill developer, facilitator, data gatherer, collaborator, team member, team leader, situational leader, challenger, participative management system designer, catalyst and design team leader.

Role description 3

This model suggests that the enlarged role of engineers has to consist of conceiving, designing, implementing and operating more sophisticated manufacturing systems.[21] This new managerial role is expected to be affected by the following factors:

1   Need to deploy other skills beyond technical skills, such as computing, control, materials handling;

2   Need to design integrated systems consisting of interdependent processes rather than specifically concerned with particular tasks;

3   Need to work alongside, and refer to, other specialists and to co-ordinate all the various efforts;

4   Need to operate as project teams in the form of a matrix organisation;

5   The need to act in a 'continuity' role within project teams for the purpose of fulfilling organisational objectives rather than for the achievement of specific tasks;

6   Need to take account of a business perspective in the execution of various roles with the accommodation of labour and financial implications.

Role description 4

This model can be described in two parts which relate to the evolution in the career of an engineer from a technical aspect to a broader and managerial aspect. [14-18]

Requirements for manufacturing systems engineers: Skills and knowledge requirements in the areas of business and market strategy, process engineering, production engineering including design for packaging, control engineering and instrumentation, systems analysis, computing and information systems design, human relations, methodologies of manufacturing systems design related to range of industry types, organisation and job design, factory systems economics.

Requirements for business systems engineers: Business systems engineers are multidisciplinary engineers and have knowledge and expertise in the following areas – finance and accounting, business systems studies, strategic planning, human relations and information technology. They also need a good understanding of manufacturing systems.

There is little to distinguish between the various descriptions provided. They all highlight the need for a managerial role for engineers, by moving from purely technical skills/knowlege oriented role to a broader organisational role which encompasses additional skills/knowledge in behavioural sciences, communication, financial and strategic competences.

ENGINEERS' COMPETENCES AND THE ROLE OF TQM

TQM basically advocates the introduction and practice of a new culture. This is to be based on waste removal, maximising organisations' effectiveness and encouraging a process of innovativeness and adding value by problem solving activities. This process is encouraged by people interactions at different levels and continuous and effective communication processes which try to relay continually the need to focus on organisational objectives.

This chapter has so far tried to explain the reasons why engineers have to develop, grow and move away from a traditional culture which encourages specialism and individualistic contributions, towards a new approach based on a broader role. This role is meant to reflect the importance of considering organisations as total systems and the need to work across boundaries to achieve the objectives which will decide on the future existence of the organisations concerned.

One can see that there is a high degree of compatibility between what TQM tries to preach as a philosophy of modern competitiveness, and how the new role of engineers can fit in this scenario. The slogans such as 'world class manufacturers', 'market leaders', 'competitive organisations' are not self-advertised labels but statements which recognise the degree of success, vigour, health, progressiveness and determination that businesses such as Japanese manufacturers have earned themselves through best practice and a dedication to TQM.

THE EVOLUTION OF ENGINEERS FOR TQM

The evolution in the role of engineers was initiated by the developments and changes which took place in manufacturing industry itself. Manufacturing industry has evolved from an era which used to rely on heavy demand and people intensive processes to produce large volume and low variety products (mass production era of 1960s). The introduction of automated systems in the 1970s in the form of CNC machines and automated materials handling systems has led to more reliance on highly skilled labour and a more disciplined approach towards new product development using electronics. The 1980s is perhaps the era where marketing has emerged as the leading function in organisational systems dictating types and levels of competitiveness. This era was marked by an intensive process of introducing technological innovations both for manufacturing operations purposes and also for new product development processes (use of 3D CAD systems).

It appears that the 1990s competitive set-up is going to be heavily influenced by customer input, customer power and customer choice. It is becoming widely accepted that organisational systems have got to be more flexible to react to customer demands. They have to reduce lead times considerably and have to cut down constantly on waste and add value to customer services. The use of CAD systems linked to Computer Aided Manufacturing (CAM) systems to relate customer requirements to organisational ability to meet those requirements, and the introduction of Just In Time (JIT) philosophy and the Focused Factory approach are not accidental, Table 1.3.

Table 1.3 Changes in the manufacturing environment

	1960s	1970s	1980s	1990s
Driving force	Markets	Finance	Marketing and technological innovation	Customer power
Product development process	Incremental changes Based on experience and using simple tools	Some use of electronic power, still reliance on drafting tools	Heavy use of electronic power 3D–CAD systems	CAD systems and heavy involvement of customers
Role of manufacturing function	Mass production People intensive processes Low/basic skills	Automated systems (NC, CNC) Material handling/ assembly systems	Flexibility in automated systems Integrated manufacturing systems Computer controlled processes	Focused factory JIT philosophy Quality and productivity orientation
Role of manufacturing engineers	Traditionally skills based	Skills based and knowledge based	Knowledge based with use of computer power (systems approach)	Systems approach and integrated knowledge based role in project management form

It is the desire to achieve customer satisfaction at all levels which has prompted organisations to look more closely at the benefits of TQM and its importance as a strategy for survival, health and prosperity. The Focused Factory approach is about having slimmer manufacturing processes which are of high flexibility and capability to produce to customer specifications. The introduction of JIT philosophy aims to eliminate waste, reduce lead time and optimise efficiency levels. The use of powerful 3D CAD systems aims to design to precise customer specifications.

This new approach towards modern competitiveness using TQM as the major disciplining force to achieve the desired objectives has wider implications on people systems including the role of the engineer as has been discussed previously. The role of manufacturing engineers has evolved in parallel with evolutions in organisational systems and the relevant technological processes introduced. The engineer has become more of a knowledge based worker using powerful tools such as computers to design, implement, monitor and control and predict the performance of various sub-systems. Under the umbrella of TQM, the engineer has been developed to take a systems approach for organisational objectives and to use an integrated and broader knowledge based on participating in project management tasks.

The evolution of the role of the engineer towards an ability to fulfill tasks and contribute to problem solving, eliminating waste, adding value, being innovative and being committed towards organisational objectives can be described by the following three models.

Model 1: The basic support perspective

- The organisation is usually formal and departmentalised in its structure;
- The product line is usually well established or complex;
- A fairly strong 'we-they' stigma often exists;
- This traditional style of management has little commitment towards employee development programmes or seldom encourages participative management to be introduced.

Model 2: The multiple resource perspective

- Genuine commitment to employee involvement at the plant management level, and often at the corporate level;
- This culture in turn dictates much of the organisational philosophy;
- The company is more decentralised, and exhibits a defined planning process under which goals and objectives are regularly established for individuals and the company as a whole;
- An awareness of employee needs also represents a more progressive style of management.

Model 3: The total involvement perspective

- A family approach to doing business shows that the participative culture is a way of life in the company;
- The product line is stable and/or simple in design;
- Corporate support and funding is found at all organisational levels;
- A participative mentality is a pre-requisite for employment.

Although the three models above do not depict clear pictures about management styles and types of organisational structures one can deduct that the spirit of employee involvement and full participation for the achievement of organisational objectives can only grow if there is clear commitment from all parties especially those who have the duty to ensure the success of their organisations. TQM is the discipline which will determine the likelihood of organisational objectives turning into reality.

THE ENGINEER IN A TQM ENVIRONMENT

Organisational systems under TQM consist of a series of subprocesses which can use inputs to convert them to outputs and which, in turn, become inputs themselves for a subsequent transformation process. This repeated cycle is meant to supply both internal and external customers. The main aim of the process is to add value continually, and reduce waste and lead time, Fig. 1.3.

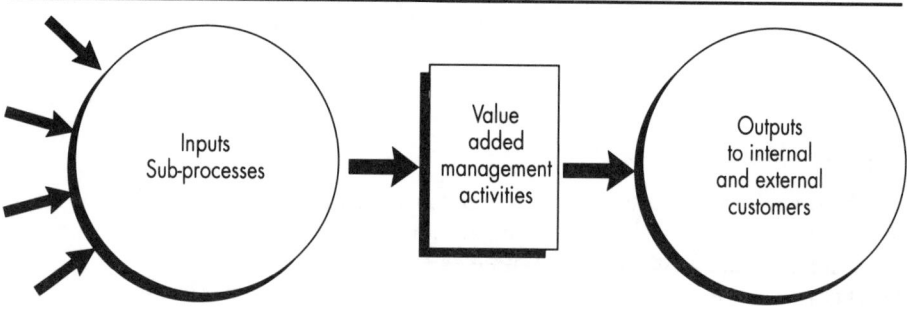

1.3 Integrated model of organisational processes.

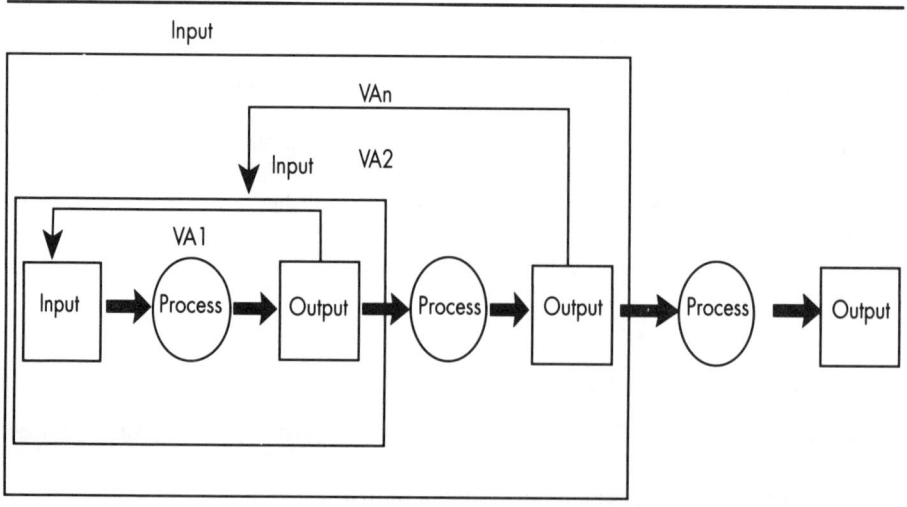

1.4 The propagation cycle for productivity improvement.

Value Added Management (VAM) therefore is not to be considered as an activity with determined dimensions, timescales and potential. It has to be perceived as a propagated process, Fig. 1.4, where TQM and its preachings become a way of life to change performance levels incrementally and/or radically.

The model in Fig. 1.5 describes the major elements of organisational systems, which are of a socio-technical nature, by which the dynamic behaviour of organisations is determined.

Component A is a major element in defining and determining the levels of competitiveness and customer needs. It has to result from effective communication inputs and processes and the positive manipulation of information.

Component B consists of a series of subprocesses defining customer-supplier relationships, task/activity processes, decision-making processes and flow of information processes. This component can be defined as 'who owns the problem?'.

Component C can be described as the 'oven' where the conversion process takes

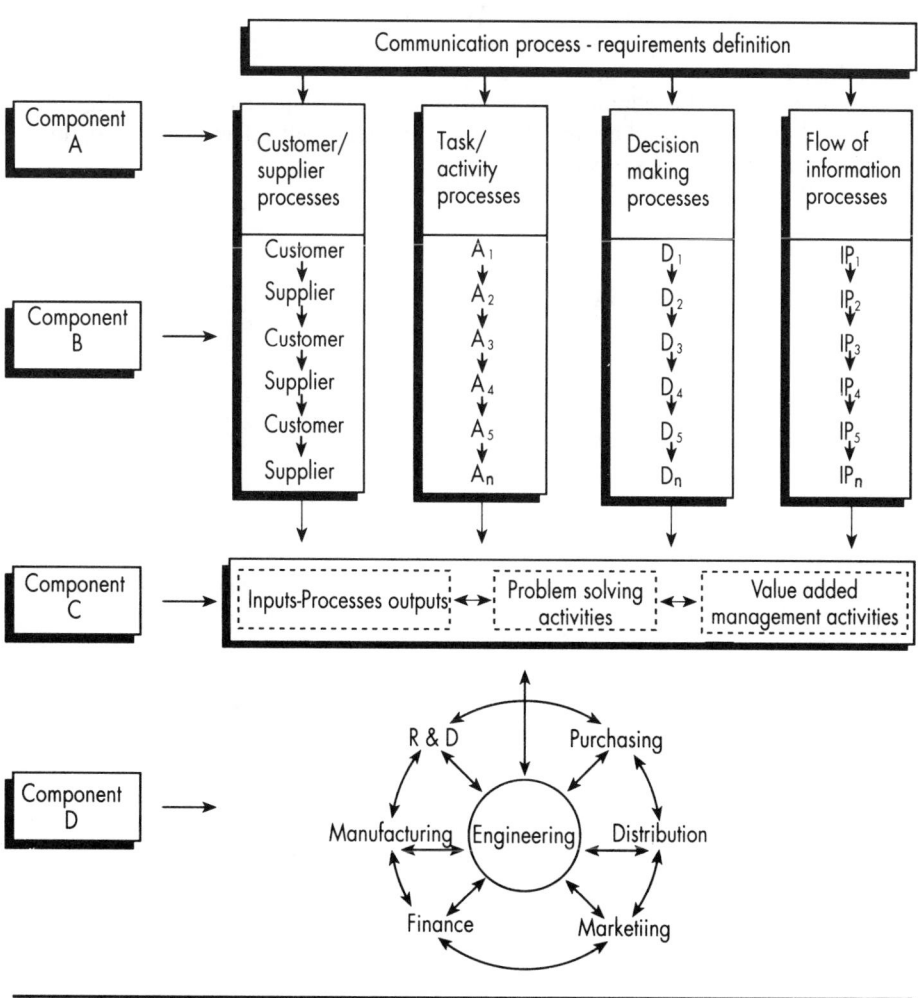

1.5 A model of the integrated role of the engineering function within organisation systems.

place to produce something of value to the customer both internally and externally. It is fuelled by the continuous input, problem solving activity and the constant desire to improve.

Component D is the 'engine' which keeps the whole system on course and relies on the integrated, supportive, collaborative, innovative, committed, co-ordinated nature of the various functions within it. The integrated approach is adopted for the achievement of a common goal/aspiration. The contribution from the engineering function has to be perceived as part of the total socio-technical process.

CONCLUSIONS

This chapter attempted to answer the questions which have crossed many minds such as 'why is TQM relevant to engineers?' Modern competitive philosophies are affecting cultures and sub-cultures at various levels. It is not just organisations which have to change internally, but also society at large is coming to terms with the wider implications of technological innovation and its impact on job creation/displacement. Educational establishments have to redesign their current curriculae more frequently and are asked to be more innovative in providing skills which industry requires. The concept of customer-supplier under a TQM umbrella will affect most educational establishments supplying skills to industry.

2

THE PIONEERS OF TQM

HOW OLD IS THE QUALITY CONCEPT?

TQM in its various forms appears to dominate business life nowadays but the crucial question to ask is whether TQM is an evolutionary concept? This chapter therefore intends to examine the various contributions to the current developments in the area of TQM and present a brief history on the various gurus of this modern approach to competitiveness.

Quality in fact has been around for quite a long time and has progressed from stages of playing a purely reactive role (inspection) to its present prominence in shaping the competitive strategy of business.

Quality did not emerge until the era of mass production, as part of Frederick Taylor's scientific management preachings. One role of supervisors was to carry out inspection of the work of their subordinates. However, the man who spearheaded the quality movement was W A Shewart, who in 1931 gave a clearer definition of Total Quality Control, how to measure and control it. Shewart argued that variability has to be accepted as a way of life and that differences between parts, peoples' skills and process parameters, lead to differences between the same (different) goods produced. Shewart debated that by using statistical and probability techniques, variability can be better understood, monitored and controlled.

Quality then underwent various stages of evolution comprising sampling (to check a limited number of items representing the whole batch to find out about overall behaviour/state of quality). The quality assurance era involved the work of pioneers such as Juran, Feingenbaum (on Total Quality Control), Reliability Engineering (checking product performance over time) and the concept of Zero Defect advocated by people like Crosby who believes that perfect quality is both technically possible and economically desirable.

The quality movement has carried on progressing until the present day, when quality has taken a central place in determining organisational objectives and competitive indices. It seems that besides the Japanese, the rest of the world has suddenly woken up from a long sleep with eagerness and a sense of urgency to be updated on all the potential benefits of quality when adopted as a way of conducting business.

WHY ARE THE JAPANESE LEADING THE FIELD OF QUALITY?

It is not usually easy to provide straight answers to such questions. However, there are a number of factors which have led the Japanese to reach their present status as world leaders in manufacturing industry and in demonstrating the way modern business should be run. The leading pioneers of the quality movement (Deming, Juran) started to promote their work in the late 1940s to early 1950s. This was a crucial time for the Japanese who, after suffering humiliation in the Second World War, wanted desperately to get on with life and re-built a new Japan which is industrially strong and respected worldwide. This happened at a time when Japanese products were suffering from poor quality and reliability standards and therefore something was desperately needed to rectify the situation. This does perhaps explain the third and most important factor, which is the level of enthusiasm, responsiveness and commitment in wanting to achieve high quality standards.

Western countries have had the same opportunities to promote quality, but seem to have ignored the powerful influence that it could have on future competitiveness. Indeed, Deming started to teach the concepts of quality in 1941, and although these were well received by engineers and industrialists, they were snubbed by managers. Ironically this happened at a time of industrial boom. The following statement from Deming[1] highlights his disappointment in not succeeding in selling the idea to management:

'The courses were well-received by engineers, but management paid no attention to them. Management did not understand that they had to get behind improvement of quality and carry out their obligations from the top down. Any instabilities can help to point out specific times or locations of local problems. Once these local problems are removed, there is a process that will continue until someone changes it. Changing the process is management's responsibility. And we failed to teach them that.'

The Japanese miracle is perhaps to be explained by a strong motivation to succeed, strong leadership, total commitment and belief in continuous improvement. Although most of the pioneers of the quality movement are American descendants (the catalyst), the Japanese are enjoying the harvest from believing that the American ideas (the seeds) are a way of life. Similarly to Deming, Juran blames attitudes and lack of commitment from management as the reason why the uptake of quality, as a way of doing business, has taken so long. He was reported to have commented that:[21]

'A segment of the Western press has come up with the conclusion that the Japanese miracle was not Japanese at all. Instead it was due to two Americans, Deming and Juran, who lectured to the Japanese soon after World War II. Deming will have to speak for himself. As for Juran, I am agreeably flattered but I regard the conclusion as ludicrous. I did indeed lecture in Japan as reported, and I did bring something new to them – a structured approach to quality. I also did the same thing for a great many other countries, yet none of these attained the results achieved by the Japanese. So who performed the miracle?'

HOW THE WEST HAS WOKEN UP TO THE IMPORTANCE OF QUALITY

For so long, Western economies have been strong advocates of doing business according to profitability returns and taking the balance sheet approach. This business culture has been highlighted by the dominance of accounts in determining business targets and in greatly influencing business progress. This approach was however identified subsequently to be full of shortcomings and deficiencies and in fact was not protecting the long term interest of business.

Is it perhaps possible that the West has learnt one useful lesson from the Japanese? Is there effective use of human resources by having great respect for their contribution in business and by not trying to look too closely at figures on paper? Indeed what the Japanese have done effectively is to blend two schools of thought. One is based on the engineering approach to work, based on Frederick Taylor's work and the other is the preachings from the human relations movements (i.e. appreciation of peoples' knowledge, respecting their pride and encouraging them to control their work environment and holding them responsible for their own quality standards).

Statistical Quality Control seems to be the most powerful tool in linking the human aspects to set quality and productivity levels and encouraging a bottom-up approach. This has been acknowledged by Drucker[19] who concluded that:

> 'In the main, the United States has lacked the methodology to build quality and productivity into the manufacturing process. Similarly, we have lacked the methodology to move responsibility for the process and control of it to the machine operator, to put into practice what the mathematician Norbert Wiener called the "human use of human beings"'.

It has therefore got to be widely recognised that the prominence of TQM today is due to a small number of people without whose contribution businesses would have still perhaps carried on making the same mistakes, with the same levels of ineffectiveness and with similar percentages of waste. As a philosophy of modern business TQM will probably carry on evolving and introducing new concepts and principles. Although this is essential in maintaining the health and positive course of businesses, the fundamental principles which have been developed by the likes of Deming, Juran, Feingenbaum and others will still play a crucial role in determining the degree of success in business competitiveness. These various philosophies are examined in the following sections.

W E DEMING

Deming was born on 14 October 1900. His main interest was in the application of statistical techniques. He was greatly influenced by the teachings of Walter Shewart who was the originator of Statistical Process Control (SPC) techniques. He was the first Western scientist to be invited by the Japanese to give a series of seminars to workers and managers on the use of control charts and statistical techniques for the control of quality. He was invited to the Japanese Union of Scientists and Engineers (JUSE) in 1950 where he encouraged the Japanese to use statistical techniques to focus on problems of variability and their causes. He also encouraged them to go beyond the utilisation of statistics and strive for continuous improvement by using what has been referred to as the 'Deming Cycle' (Plan, Do, Check, Action (PDCA)).

Deming convinced Japanese managers that the purpose of using quality management techniques is to help companies stay in business:

Reduce input costs
(i.e. people, methods, equipment,
materials, environment)

↓

Lower unit costs

↓

Increase profit

↓

Return on investment

↓

Stay in business

He also drew Japanese managers' attention to the need for using modern consumer research, conducting regular customer surveys and following closely developments and changes in the market place, in order to be able to plan and act positively. Deming stressed that the efficient use of statistical techniques ensures positive competitiveness in the market place and the obtainment of the desired returns.

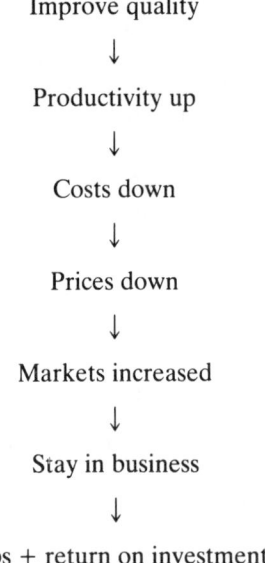

Improve quality

↓

Productivity up

↓

Costs down

↓

Prices down

↓

Markets increased

↓

Stay in business

↓

Jobs + return on investment

Deming strongly believes that quality improvement has to be management led. He sees management responsibility in two main areas:

(a) To create a positive climate for quality improvement: It is management's responsibility to make sure that work is fun and that workers must enjoy it and do it for a purpose as part of their self-esteem. Deming stresses the importance of what he calls intrinsic motivation (self-esteem, individual responsibility for what he/she does) rather than extrinsic motivation (acceptance of material rewards for work carried out). Deming believes that the present work culture in Western countries has 'destroyed workers' by depriving them of enjoying what they do and by placing emphasis on merit systems based on results.

In a recent interview, Dr Deming concluded that:

Through work, an individual should get self-esteem and joy. It should give him a feeling he is doing something useful and the position to improve it otherwise work becomes characterised by extrinsic motivation (the acceptance for a day's work), which is humiliating.'

(b) Emphasis on knowledge workers rather than rigid systems: Deming claims that many errors which occur in organisations are caused by existing systems which are impractical, too rigid and inaccurate rather than due to people's errors. Managers cannot be blamed since their job is to make the system work by trying to reduce costs and make money for their organisations. Questioning figures to achieve good results can only make things worse rather than better. For so long the West has placed emphasis on efficiency and asking people to do their best without closely questioning their degree of knowledge. Deming concludes that:

'... we would be better off if people did not do their best. People doing their best have ruined us! There is no substitute for knowledge!'

Deming's preachings [29] are summarised in Table 2.1.

Table 2.1 Deming's fourteen points

1	Create consistency of purpose toward improvement of product and service, with the aim to become competitive and thus to stay in business, and to provide jobs.
2	Adopt the new philosophy. 'We are in a new economic age. We no longer need to live with commonly accepted delays, mistakes, defective materials and defective workmanship.'
3	Cease dependence on mass inspection to achieve quality. Eliminate the need for inspection on a mass basis by building quality into the product in the first place.
4	End the practice of awarding business on the basis of price tag. Instead, minimise total cost. Move toward a single supplier for any one item, on a long-term relationship of loyalty and trust.
5	Improve constantly and forever the system of production and service, to improve quality and productivity, and thus constantly decrease costs.
6	Institute modern methods of training and education on the job, including management.
7	Institute leadership. The aim of supervision should be to help people and machines and gadgets to do a better job.
8	Drive out fear, so that everyone may work effectively for the company.
9	Break down barriers between departments. People in research, design, sales and production must work as a team, to foresee problems of production and in use that may be encountered with the product or service.
10	Eliminate slogans, exhortations and targets for the work force asking for zero defects and new levels of productivity. Such exhortations only create adversarial relationships, as the bulk of the causes of low quality and low productivity belong to the system and thus lie beyond the power of the work force.
11a	Eliminate work standards (quotas) on the factory floor, substitute leadership.
b	Eliminate management by objective. Eliminate management by numbers.

12a Remove barriers that rob the hourly worker of the right to pride of workmanship. The responsibility must be changed from sheer numbers to quality.

b Remove barriers that rob people in management and in engineering of their right to pride of workmanship. This means, inter alia, abolishment of the annual or merit rating and of management by objective.

13 Institute a vigorous programme of education and self-development.

14 Put everybody in the company to work to accomplish the transformation. The transformation is everybody's job (through company-wide quality improvement).

The fourteen points can be seen as the ingredients which organisations require to carry out the total transformation that is based on company wide quality improvement philosophy. Deming also warns about the obstacles which may inhibit the implementation of the fourteen principles. These have been referred to as the 'deadly sins' or the 'deadly diseases' and are discussed below.

The deadly diseases

Lack of consistency: Lack of consistency of purpose to stay in business by not planning to provide products and services in the future, with a specific market in mind, in order to keep the company in business and providing for joh creation;

Short term profits: Short term thinking defeats constancy of purpose to stay in business with long term growth;

Performance appraisal: The effects of performance appraisal (personal review system, evaluation of performance, annual review, etc) are devastating;

Job-hopping: Mobility of management causes instability, leads to decisions being made by people with little knowledge and understanding of business activities and who feed from their experiences in different situations;

Use of only visible figures: Management should not just refer to visible figures. Although these are important, management should learn how to manage their businesses by taking a wider and more global approach (the figures that are unknown are even more important).

The two deadly sins which Deming considers to be most important are the 'evaluation of performance – merit rating – annual review', and 'running a company on visible figures only'.

Deming is perhaps the most respected TQM guru with a tireless dedication and commitment to help businesses worldwide implement quality improvement techniques and concepts. He still considers his mission as promoting the concept of joy in work and joy in learning. He was awarded the Second Order of the Sacred Treasure which is Japan's premier Imperial honour and the Deming prize is considered in Japan as one of the highest and most important honours. The Deming Associations are formed worldwide to teach the Deming Quality Management Philosophy to senior managers worldwide.

Although the fourteen management principles are considered universally to be of paramount importance for modern competitiveness, Deming's preachings can be found in everything he has written and everything he says. His philosophy on corporate quality management can be characterised as follows:

- It is management-led;
- Everyone in the organisation has to take part;
- It is based on a continuous process of improvement;
- It is scientifically-based;
- It aims at serving the customer better all the time.

JOSEPH M JURAN

Juran has contributed as much to total quality as Deming. He raised pertinent questions on the contribution of quality in reducing costs and improving standards in 1951 in his book 'Quality Control Handbook' which has subsequently become an essential reference book. He was invited to Japan in 1954 at the same time as Deming to speak to Japanese senior managers on the importance of planning, organising and managing quality programmes. Juran is the founder and chairman of the Juran Institute, he is also the author of many books and hundreds of papers. He has acted as a consultant to major industrial organisations and governments and is still in great demand as an international speaker. He was awarded over thirty medals, fellowships, and honorary memberships in some twelve countries. He was awarded the Second Order of the Sacred Treasure by the emperor of Japan, the highest decoration given to a non-Japanese citizen for helping the development of Quality Control in Japan.

Juran's approach to Quality Control and its management is two-sided:

(i) Companies' mission in terms of fitness for use by providing products and services which conform to customer specifications, plus issues of reliability, availability, maintainability, customer service, etc.

(ii) The role of senior managers in providing leadership, in providing the required resources, in encouraging awareness and participation and in developing systems of policy, goals, plans, measures and controls for quality.

Fitness for use is achieved by a process which reflects the interplay between the various stages or organisational activities before meeting customer demands. This process which Juran terms 'the spiral of progress' [28] is represented in Fig. 2.1. The spiral of progress reflects the chain of user-supplier relationships at various stages of the process.

Quality, according to Juran, has to be controlled at each stage of the process but should not be implemented just as a mechanical process. It should be aimed at controlling:

- Sporadic problems or avoidable costs (defects and product failure, scrapped materials, labour wasted usage for re-work, repair, dealing with customer complaints);
- Unavoidable costs dealing with chronic problems (prevention and control).

The first category of problems is easily solved by using quality control techniques such as tolerance reviews, foolproofing, standard statistical techniques, charts and diagrams. The second category however requires the introduction of a new culture which is intended to change attitudes and increase company-wide knowledge. The

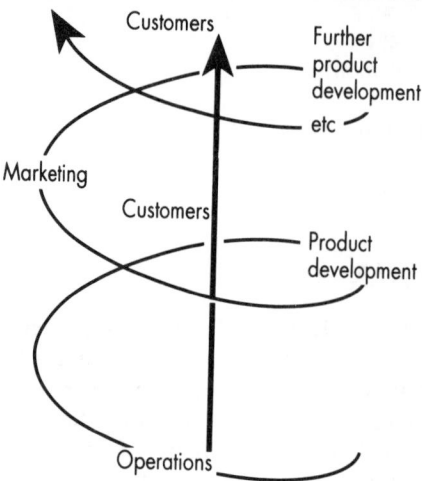

2.1 The spiral of progress in quality.

Table 2.2 The Juran quality trilogy

1 **Quality planning**
   Identify the customers
   Determine the customers' needs
   Develop product features
   Establish quality goals
   Develop a process
   Prove process capability

2 **Quality control**
   Choose control subjects (what to control)
   Choose units of measurement
   Establish measurement
   Establish standards of performance
   Measure actual performance
   Interpret the difference (actual versus standard)
   Take action on the difference

3 **Quality improvement**
   Prove the need for improvement
   Identify specific projects for improvement
   Organise to guide the projects
   Organise for diagnosis – for discovery of causes
   Diagnose to find the causes
   Provide remedies
   Prove that the remedies are effective under operating conditions
   Provide for control to hold gains

long term health of businesses is determined by a structured approach to quality which is planned, implemented and controlled according to the mission of the businesses concerned. Juran proposes that three managerial processes are necessary for the structured implementation of a total quality programme: planning, control and improvement, Table 2.2. Juran argues that the planning process is crucial for improvement to become a continuous activity. Planning therefore has to be conducted with a long term view rather than on a project by project basis. He gives the example of the manager who is surrounded by alligators:

'He (the manager) undertakes to slay alligators, one by one – a reptilian version of project by project improvement. But there will never be an end to it, because more and more alligators keep emerging from the swamp. The ultimate answer is to drain the swamp.'[28]

PHILIP B CROSBY

Crosby was a former corporate vice president for quality at ITT and is the founder of the Crosby Quality College where over 15,000 senior managers have attended courses and seminars. He is also the author of many books amongst which 'Quality is free: The art of making quality certain' is a universally adopted book. The essence of Crosby's quality drive is prevention. He argues that quality is free. The costs are only related to the various obstacles which prevent workers from producing right first time.

The major objective of organisations implementing total quality should be Zero Defect (ZD) according to Crosby. Acceptable Quality Levels (AQL) should be forbidden because they compromise the commitment towards the achievement of ZD.

There are two major problems which are the causes of poor quality in industry according to Crosby; those which are due to employee poor awareness and knowledge and others which are due to carelessness and lack of attention. The former can be easily identified, measured and solved but the latter need a long term management effort in changing culture and attitudes.

Crosby argues that if management are serious about achieving ZD they have to be serious about prevention. He proposes some guidelines for managers which he calls the 'four absolutes of quality management'.

1 Quality means conformance to the requirements: The setting of requirements is management responsibility as are the communication devices and their effectiveness. Crosby argues that if management wants people to 'do things right first time' they have to tell everyone clearly what that is;

2 Quality comes from prevention (vaccination is the way to prevent disease): The first absolute was to understand the process by which various processes are involved in producing products/services. The second is about identifying and eliminating all chances for error to occur;

3 Quality performance standard is Zero Defects: This is conformance to the requirements and should be the personal performance standard of everyone in the organisation according to Crosby and will come from a change in attitudes;

4 Quality measurement is the price of non-conformance: According to Crosby manufacturing companies spend 25% of sales doing things wrong and service companies spend about 40% of their operating costs on the same wasteful actions.

Similarly to arguments raised by Deming and Juran, Crosby thinks that companies' performance is reflected by their management's attitudes to quality. To achieve great improvements, management have to believe in the following points:

- The conviction by senior managers that they have had enough of quality being a problem and wanting to turn it into an asset;
- The commitment that they will understand and implement the four absolutes of quality management;
- The conversion to that way of thinking from the conventional wisdom that caused the problem in the first place.

Crosby argues that it takes a long time to transfer from conviction to conversion,

Table 2.3 Crosby's fourteen step quality improvement programme

1 Management commitment: Help management recognise that it must be personally committed to participating in a quality improvement programme.

2 Quality improvement team: Bring together representatives of each department to form such a team.

3 Quality measurement: Determine the status of quality throughout the company.

4 Cost of quality evaluation: Establish the cost of quality to indicate where corrective action will be profitable for a company.

5 Quality awareness: Share with employees the measurements of what non-quality is costing through training and communication material.

6 Corrective action: Bring problems to light for all to see and resolve them on a regular basis.

7 Establish an ad hoc committee for the Zero Defect programme: After a year has gone by, a Zero Defects Day will reaffirm management's commitment, to the words 'Zero Defects' and the thought that everyone should do things right the first time.

8 Supervisor training: A formal orientation of the Zero Defects programme with all levels of management should be conducted prior to its implementation.

9 Zero Defects Day: Zero Defects as the performance standard of the company is established in one day to provide emphasis and long lasting impression.

10 Goal setting: Regular meetings between supervisors and employees help people learn to think in terms of meeting goals and accomplishing specific tasks as a team.

11 Removal of error causes: Individuals are asked to describe any problems that keep them from performing error-free work. The appropriate functional group will develop an answer to those problems.

12 Recognition: Award programmes are established to recognise those who meet their goals or perform outstanding acts. Awards should not be financial; recognition is what is important.

13 Quality councils: Quality professionals and team chairpersons should meet regularly to communicate and determine actions to upgrade and improve the quality improvement programme.

14 Do it again: Set up a new team of representatives and begin again to overcome the turnover and changing situations that can occur in the year to 18 months to implement the typical quality improvement programme.

but that as soon as the transfer process begins it is a positive sign that improvement has started to take place. He concludes:

'Management have their future in their own hands. It is not the laws of probability or statistics that have kept them down, it is their own policy of "that's good enough".' (Quality Today, May 1987)

The Crosby approach to total quality is to change the culture and attitudes within organisations to implement continuous improvement. This approach is therefore more management oriented than tool oriented since it does not refer at all to the control of quality by the use of various statistical techniques. Crosby proposes a checklist with fourteen points which would facilitate the introduction of continuous improvement, Table 2.3

ARMAND V FEINGENBAUM

Feingenbaum became known to the Japanese at the same time as Deming and Juran. As head of quality at General Electric he had extensive contact with Japanese companies such as Hitachi and Toshiba. But it is really through his books on Total Quality Control that he became best known. He was the first to argue that quality should be considered at all the various stages of the process and not just within the manufacturing function.

Feingenbaum argued that the contribution of the manufacturing function in isolation is not enough for the production of high quality products. He concludes that:

'The underlying principle of the total quality view, and its basic difference from all other concepts, is that to provide genuine effectiveness, control must start with identification of customer quality requirements and end only when the product has been placed in the hands of a customer who remains satisfied. Total Quality Control guides the co-ordinated actions of people, machines, and information to achieve this goal. The first principle to recognise is that quality is everybody's job.'[12]

From a quality consideration, Feingenbaum argues that new products progress in the factory through similar stages of what he terms the industrial cycle. He refers to three categories of stages:

1 New design control;
2 Incoming material control;
3 Product or shopfloor control.

He also made a major contribution by studying quality costs. He identifies the various costs in what he calls the 'hidden plant' the proportion of the total plant capacity which specifically deals with re-work and corrections. He considers that the size of the hidden plant can amount to 15–40% of the total plant capacity.

BILL CONWAY

Conway has been referred to as the 'Deming disciple'. He considers that quality management is the management of the various stages of the development, manufacturing, purchasing and distribution processes with consideration of economic viability and a desire to improve on various activities to reduce material waste and time wastage.

He considers that quality problems are often caused by management lack of conviction and commitment. Quality improvement according to Conway has to come from a new management way of thinking and also the wide utilisation of statistical tools. He proposes a list of six guidelines, Table 2.4

Table 2.4 Conway's list of quality improvement tools

---

1 Human relations skills: Management responsibility to create a harmonious working climate built on trust, mutual respect and common goals.

2 Statistical surveys: Use the power of surveys to identify areas for improvement and to be better informed about various developments.

3 Simple statistical techniques: Use simple charts, diagrams to highlight problems, analyse them and propose various solutions.

4 Statistical Process Control: Minimise variations within various processes using control charts.

5 Imagineering: Problem solving techniques using problem visualisation with the view of identifying ways for waste elimination.

6 Industrial engineering: The use of various techniques to re-design work, methods, plant layout for the purpose of achieving great improvements.

KAORU ISHIKAWA

Ishikawa is considered as Japan's leading figure in the area of Total Quality Management. His inspiration came from the work of Deming and Juran and, to a lesser extend, Feingenbaum. He is well respected for the following contributions:

1   Quality Control Circles – he was the first to introduce this concept and to have put it into practice successfully;

2   He is the originator of Fishbone Diagrams or Ishikawa diagrams which are now used worldwide in continuous improvement to represent cause-effect analysis;

3   Ishikawa has commented that Feingenbaum's approach to Total Quality Control includes many non-specialists and therefore the input on quality problem solving may be limited. He argues that Company Wide Quality Control (CWQC) has to rely on the wide use of statistical techniques. He has classified statistical techniques in three categories, Table 2.5. Ishikawa argues that nearly 90–95% of the problems can be solved using the elemental statistical techniques which do not require specialist knowledge.

Table 2.5 Ishikawa's statistical techniques to CWQC

1 Elemental statistical techniques
Pareto analysis (vital few versus trivial many)
Cause and Effect diagram (not a true statistical technique)
Stratification
Check list (tally sheet)
Histogram
Scatter and diagram
Graph and Shewart control chart (SPC chart)

2 Intermediate statistical method
Theory of sampling surveys
Statistical sampling techniques
Various methods of statistical estimation and hypothesis testing
Methods of utilising sensory tests
Methods of experiment design

3 Advanced statistical method (using computers)
Advanced experimental design
Multivariate analysis
Operations research methods

GENICHI TAGUCHI

Taguchi worked as director of the Japanese Academy of Quality between 1978–1982. He was awarded the Deming prizes in 1960 for his contribution in developing techniques for industrial optimisation. He has developed methods for on-line and off-line quality control which form the basis for his approach towards total quality control assurance. In 1989, Taguchi received MITI's Purple Ribbon Award from the Emperor of Japan for his contribution to Japanese industrial standards. He is now an international consultant in quality control and assurance.

Taguchi's methods incorporate the use of statistical techniques. They are primarily intended for designers and engineers to optimise the settings so that products are robust. These statistical methods are intended as a trouble shooting/problem solving tool in the early stages of the product development cycle. Besides control variables which are dealt with by SPC, Taguchi methods enable engineers/designers to identify 'noise variables' which if not controlled can affect product manufacture and performance.

Taguchi defines the quality of a product as the loss imparted by the product to the society from the time the product is shipped. The loss may include various things such as customer complaints, added warranty costs, damage to company reputation, loss of market lead amongst others.

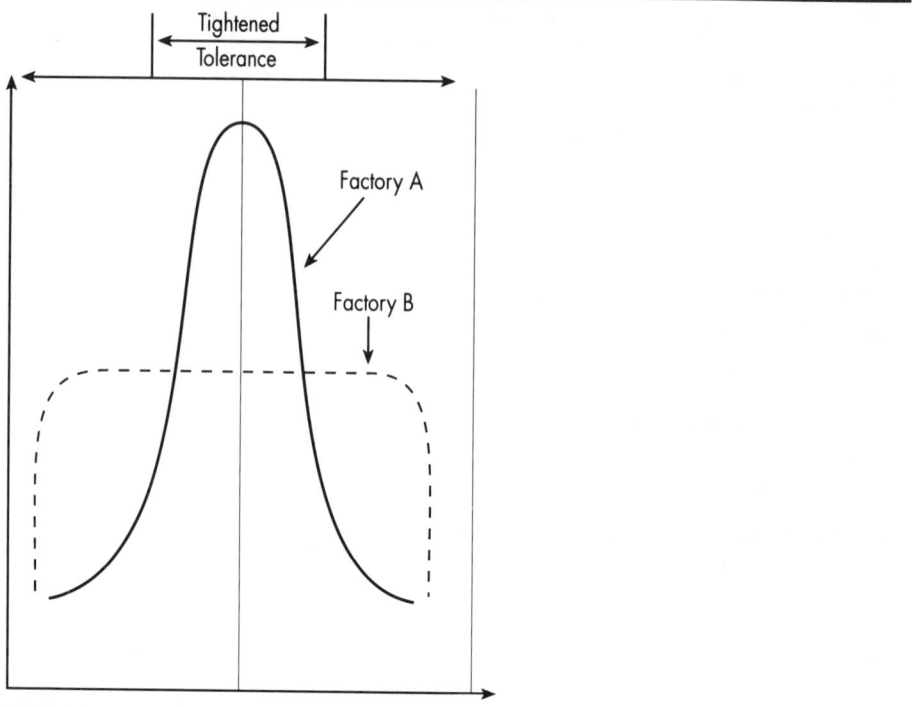

2.2 The loss function.

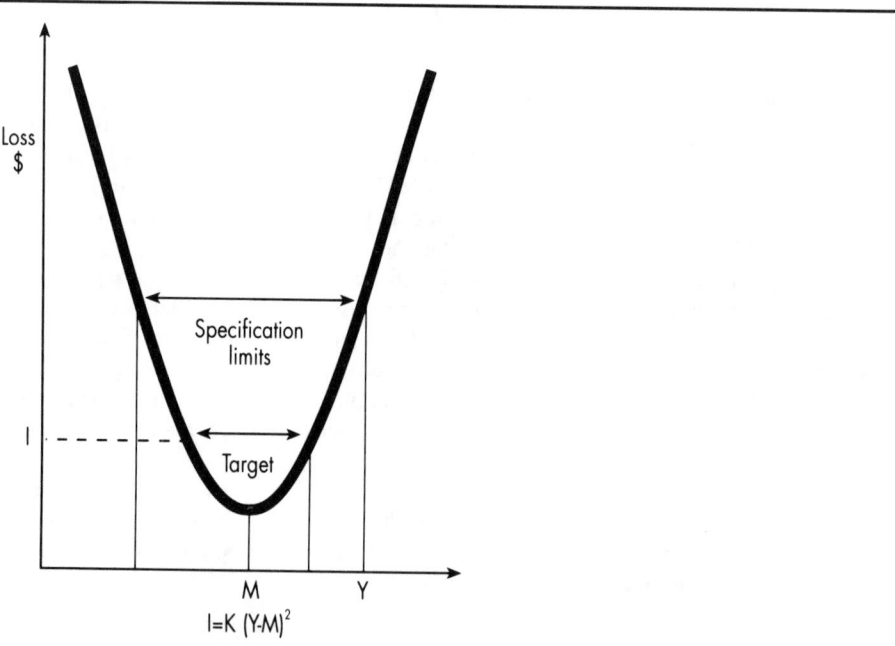

$$I = K (Y-M)^2$$

2.3 Loss as a quadratic function.

The loss function

As represented in Fig. 2.2, Taguchi argues that a product does not start causing losses until it is out of specification but more importantly when there is deviation from the target value.

Factory B runs higher risk loss costs (quality loss + factory loss). The more deviation there is from targets, the greater are the losses.

The Quality Loss Function (QLF) can also be represented by a quadratic formula $L = D^2C$ (Loss increases by the square of deviation from the target value, see Fig. 2.3).

QLF is useful because it not only warns about deviations at the early stages of new product development but can also provide managers with cost estimates.

Taguchi's methods emerged because of his disagreement about the use of Zero Defect as a principle to produce quality products. The Zero Defect principle is that robustness derives from consistency. Provided that there is a consistency in deviations, it will be quite possible to make adjustments in the target. Zero Defects does not permit scattered deviations within specifications.

Taguchi argues that product robustness comes from having consistent deviation which then makes the task of elimination much easier, Fig. 2.4. He proposed the list in Table 2.6 as guidelines to quality improvement.[10]

Table 2.6 Taguchi's quality imperatives

---

1 Quality losses result from product failure after sale; product 'robustness' is more a function of product design than on-line control, however stringent, of manufacturing processes.

2 Robust products deliver a strong 'signal' regardless of external 'noise' and with a minimum of internal 'noise'. Any strengthening of a design, that is, any market increase in the signal-to-noise ratios of component parts, will simultaneously improve the robustness of the product as a whole.

3 To set targets at maximum signal-to-noise ratios, develop a system of trials that allows you to analyse change in overall system performance according to the average effect of change in component parts, that is, when you subject parts to varying values, stresses, and experimental conditions. In new products, average effects may be most efficiently discerned by means of 'orthogonal arrays'.

4 To build robust products, set ideal target values for components and then minimise the average of the square of deviations for combined components, averaged over the various customer-user conditions.

5 Before products go on to manufacturing, tolerances are set. Overall quality loss then increases by the square of deviation from the target value, that is, by the quadratic formula $L = D^2C$, where the constant C, is determined by the cost of the counter-measure that might be employed in the factory. This is the 'quality loss function'.

6 Virtually nothing is gained in shipping a product that just barely satisfies the corporate standard over a product that just fails. Get on target, don't just try to stay in spec.

7 Work relentlessly to achieve designs that can be produced consistently; demand consistency from the factory. Catastrophic stack-up is more likely from scattered deviation within specifications than from consistent deviation outside. Where deviation from target is consistent, adjustment to the target is possible.

8 A concerted effort to reduce product failure in the field will simultaneously reduce the number of defectives in the factory. Strive to reduce variances in the components of the product and variances will be reduced in the production system as a whole.

9 Competing proposals for capital equipment or competing proposals for on-line interventions may be compared by adding the cost of each proposal to the average quality loss, that is, the deviations expected from it.

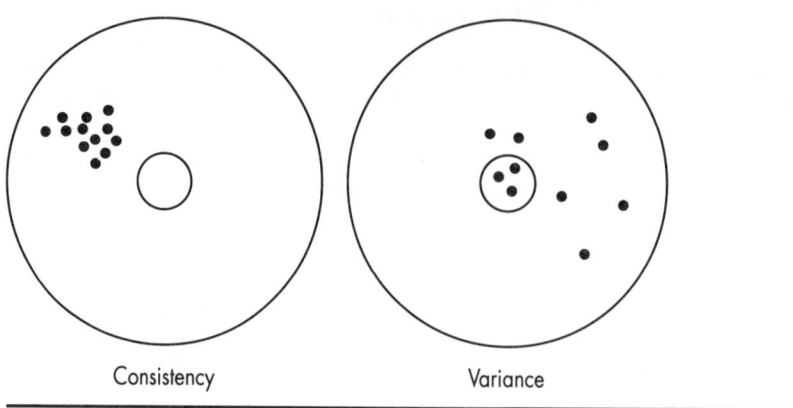

Consistency   Variance

2.4 Consistency (Taguchi) versus variance (ZD).

A note on signal to noise (deviation)

The signal is what the product, part or component is trying to deliver.

Noises are what are termed as 'interferences' which affect the signal. Noises come from two different types of factors which affect the functional characteristics of a product by affecting its performance according to the set values.

(i) Operating environmental variables (external noise factors) e.g. temperature, dust and humidity:
(ii) Internal noise factors (two types): (a) Deterioration, wear and tear of process parts; (b) Imperfections in process function, variations due to settings.

A note on orthogonal arrays

These are techniques used to set the right targets for design (by maximising signal-to-noise ratios). They are also described as a distillation mechanism whereby the effect of various factors is identified and measured.

Orthogonal arrays are useful because:

(i) They define the specific objective by choosing a realistic signal and giving an estimate of the expected noise;
(ii) They define feasible options especially for the critical design values (e.g. dimensions);
(iii) They enable companies to select the product option which provides the highest signal to noise ratio and hence products which have robust characteristics in the market place.

SHIGEO SHINGO

Shingo has pioneered the area of Zero Quality Control, by asking similar questions to those asked by Taguchi. Shingo argues that the effort put into tightening tolerances does not necessarily raise production costs significantly as is widely believed.

Shingo has been teaching concepts of production engineering to many Japanese managers and is still promoting the area of Zero Quality Control by arguing that inspection processes or the use of statistical quality control should be completely eliminated.

He believes that quality should be controlled at the source of the problem not after the problem has manifested itself. Consequently he recommends that inspection should be incorporated within the process where the problem has been identified and where it should be eliminated. He considers that Statistical Quality Control (SQC) tends to focus on the effect (subsequent errors related to operators) rather than the cause which is due to process imperfections and abnormalities.

He is the developer of a concept called Poka–Yoke (or foolproofing). Poka-Yoke means that checklists for each operation are provided so that human error is completely eliminated. It is also similar to the concept of autonomation (jikhoda) based on low-cost automated processes which stop automatically when the required operations are completed or when mistakes/abnormalities develop.

Shingo recommends the following guidelines in Table 2.7 for the implementation of Poka-Yoke.

Table 2.7 The implementation of Poka Yoke

1 Control upstream, close to the source of problem by for example incorporating monitoring devices to warn on defects in materials or abnormalities within the process.

2 Establish control mechanisms to deal with different problems to enable operators to know which problem to cure and how to cure it with minimal disruption to the operating system.

3 Take a step by step approach by taking small strides, simplifying control systems and having economic viability in mind. Efficiency, technological sophistication, available skills, work methods have all got to be carefully studied for effective usage of Poka Yoke.

4 Do not delay improvement by overanalysing: Although many manufacturers' main objective is to achieve closeness between design manufacturability, many Poka Yoke ideas can be implemented as soon as the problems have been identified with no cost at all to the companies concerned. Poka Yoke encourages interdepartmental co-operation and is a main vehicle for continuous improvement because it encourages continuous problem-solving activity.

W G OUCHI

Ouchi is famous for his work on 'theory Z' and has researched the impact of Japanese management philosophy on American businesses. Ouchi came to the conclusion that the success of Japanese businesses is mainly due to their commitment to quality and their participative style of management.

Ouchi believes that in American business great inefficiencies are mainly due to an acute specialisation problem. He concludes that:

'In the United States we conduct our careers between organisations but within a single speciality. In Japan people conduct careers between specialities but within a single organisation.'[30]

Table 2.8 Ouchi's 13 steps in theory Z

1 Understand the type Z organisation and your role.

2 Audit your company's philosophy.

3 Define the desired management philosophy and involve the company leader.

4 Implement the philosophy by creating both structures and incentives.

5 Develop interpersonal skills.

6 Test yourself and the system.

7 Involve the union.

8 Stabilise employment. Avoid layoffs and share the misfortune.

9 Decide on a system for slow evaluation and promotion.

10 Broaden career path development.

11 Prepare for implementation at the first (bottom) level.

12 Seek out areas to implement participation.

13 Permit the development of relationships (for example, promote good communication).

Ouchi proposes the guidelines in Table 2.8 for the implementation of Japanese management philosophy based on high commitment to quality and a participative style of management.

There is no doubt that further TQM ideas and concepts will be developed in the future to facilitate meeting the requirements of a business market which is ever changing. The work of the gurus discussed in this chapter will, however, always have prominence in shaping up future competitiveness.

3

DEFINING TQM: THE PHILOSOPHY

INTRODUCTION

The previous chapter touched on the relevance of TQM as a philosophy for modern competitiveness and discussed the various contributions in the area of quality management which have propelled its prominence to today's levels of competitiveness. This chapter carries the argument forward by raising questions on the various meanings of TQM, levels of ownership (user-supplier chain), the strategic link between TQM concepts and competitiveness, the productivity link, and the link between TQM and technological innovation.

WHAT IS QUALITY?

As a starting point one has to ask whether quality is a state, a condition, a feeling, an impression or reality? Linked to this is the question of whether quality has any components and if so what are they?

Quality refers to certain standards and the ways and means by which those standards are achieved, maintained and improved upon. Most definitions given to quality refer to 'fitness for use' or 'conformance to requirements'.

The standard definitions on quality have been given by various institutions such as the British Standards Institution (BSI), the American Society for Quality Control (ASQC), the European Organisation for Quality Control (EOQC) and the International Organisation for Standardisation (ISO) amongst others.[24]

'Quality therefore is the totality of features and characteristics of a product or service that bears on its ability to satisfy given needs.' (BS 4778 (1); ANSI/ASQC A3 1978).

Table 3.1 illustrates a classification of various definitions of quality based on intrinsic and extrinsic factors.[23] These various approaches highlight the wide and varied views on the quality concept. There is however growing support for quality to be closely associated with customer demands, views and perceptions. Some of the definitions which closely relate to the customer are given in Table 3.2.

The important point which emerges from Table 3.2 is the dynamic nature of the quality process. Since the customer is the driving force one would expect this process to be dynamic and therefore reflect changes in impression, taste, specifications, etc.

Table 3.1 Various definitions of quality

Transcendent definition	Quality is neither mind nor matter, but a third entity independent of the two ... even though quality cannot be defined, you know what it is.
Product-based definition	Differences in quality amount to differences in the quantity of some desired ingredient or attribute.
User-based definition	Quality consists of the capacity to satisfy wants.
Manufacturing-based definition	Quality [means] conformance to requirements.
Value-based definition	Quality is the degree of excellence at an acceptable price and the control of variability at an acceptable cost.

Table 3.2 Customer-related definitions of quality

Quality is a key attribute that customers use to evaluate products or services.[2]

Quality = everything everyone in a business does, no matter what sort of business, to satisfy the total requirements of every customer – whoever that customer (or user) may be.[18]

Quality is driven by the marketplace, by the competition, and especially by the customer.[33]

The 'Quality' concept rejects the traditional notion of quality as being the degree of conformance to a standard or measurement of workmanship. The Japanese concept of quality hinges on the product's 'fitness of use', and the degree of customer satisfaction derived from using that product. In other words, it is not the producers but the customers who determine whether or not quality has been achieved.[13]

Quality is achieving and exceeding customer expectations in order to provide business for the future. The goal is to achieve a continuous quality improvement effort that permeates every process, every product and every service in the organisation. Businesses exist to deliver quality. Customers are buyers and users of products and services. They can be external or internal.[12]

Quality is the capability of a product or service to satisfy 'knowingly' those preconceived composite wants of the user(s) that are intelligibly related to characteristics of performance or appearance, and do not cause major overt or covert reactions or actions by other people.[25]

The changes in customer quality drive have been suggested to be part of both measurable determinants and subjective criteria. The various dimensions of quality which the customers are inspired from in their determination of quality standards have been classified as both intrinsic and extrinsic factors.[34]

(i) **Intrinsic quality determinants:** design, reliability and product life.
(ii) **Extrinsic determinants:** environment, psychology of human wants, information about products and services, advertising, variety and warranties.
(iii) **Composite determinants:** price, safety, maintenance and service, and aesthetic aspects.

Other research has suggested that customers are heavily influenced by 'eight dimensions' in determining quality levels.[29,19,23] The framework presented includes the following:

(i) **Performance:** refers to the primary operating characteristics of a product.
(ii) **Features:** are the 'bells and whistles' of products – secondary characteristics that supplement the product's basic functioning.
(iii) **Reliability:** probability of a product's failing within a specified period of time.
(iv) **Conformance:** degree to which a product's design and operating characteristics match pre-established standards.
(v) **Durability:** a measure of product life, has both economic and technical dimensions.
(vi) **Serviceability:** speed, courtesy, and competence of repair.
(vii) **Aesthetics:** (subjective dimension) – how a product looks, feels, sounds, tastes or smells.
(viii) **Perceived quality:** (subjective dimension) – assessment of standards relying on indirect measures when comparing product brands.

Table 3.3 illustrates an example where customers' priorities and perceptions change with time.[9] This table shows that in the American automobile industry, customer

Table 3.3 Customer quality perceptions and priorities

Customer changes in the importance of automobile characteristics (in USA)

	1970	1975	1980
1	Styling	Fuel economy	Quality
2	Value for money	Styling	How well-made
3	Ease of handling and driving	Prior experience with the make	Fuel economy
4	Fuel economy	Size and weight	Value for money
5	Riding comfort	Ease of handling and driving	Riding comfort

Factors influencing customer perception of quality

Before purchase	At point of purchase	After purchase
Company's brand name and image	Performance specifications	Ease of installation and use
Previous experience	Comments of sales-people	Handling of repairs, claims, warranty
Opinions of friends	Warranty provisions	Spare parts availability
Store reputation	Service and repair policies	Service effectiveness
Published test results	Support programmes	Reliability
Advertised price for performance	Quoted price for performance	Comparative performance

priorities have shifted from styling in 1970 to fuel economy in 1975 and to quality design and performance in 1980. In addition Table 3.3 shows that customers' perceptions on product quality are influenced by various factors at each stage of the buying process.

SOME QUALITY CHARACTERISTICS

Some characteristics of quality are product/service related and others are process-related.

(i)   **Grade:** A category or rank indicator of products, processes or services intended for the same functional use, but with a different set of needs (ISO/TC 176 [1984]).
(ii) **Imperfection:** A departure of a quality characteristic from its intended level or state without any association with conformance to specification requirements or to usability of a product or service (ASQC A1 [1978]).
(iii) **Nonconformity:** A departure of a quality characteristic from its intended level or state that occurs with a severity sufficient to cause an associated product or service not to meet a specification requirement (ANSI/ASQC A1 [1978]).
(iv) **Defect:** A departure of a quality characteristic from its intended level or state that occurs with a severity sufficient to cause an associated product or service not to satisfy intended normal, or reasonably foreseeable, usage requirements. (ANSI/ASQC A1 [1978]).

THE QUALITY PROCESSES

Organisation – process – individual quality

It has been suggested that quality has to be looked at at three levels.[20] These include organisation quality, process quality and individual quality.

(i)   **Organisation quality:** Looking at the organisation strategy (vertical definition) and whether it is doing the right things; and looking at operational systems (horizontal definition) and whether they are doing things right.
(ii) **Process quality:** Sets of inputs and outputs, interfunctional activities which are geared towards producing the goods and services that the customer wants.
(iii) **Individual quality:** Human performance system.

Quality of design – conformance – performance

This process considers quality as a 'never ending improvement of a firm's extended process'.[31] This process starts with the customer and ends with the customer as follows:

Communication of customer needs → the continuing process to convert needs into products/services → determining how products/services are performing → finding out what new characteristics can increase customer satisfaction.

(i) **Quality of design:** This is the degree of achievement of purpose by the design itself. It starts with market research, sales input analysis and continues to the development of a product/service concept which would satisfy the customer.

(ii) **Quality of conformance:** This takes the agreed standards as a basis for measurement and control. It therefore ensures that all the inputs, conversion and outputs at each stage of the development of products and services are in compliance with customer specification:

'Quality of conformance is the extent to which a firm and its suppliers are able to surpass the design specifications required to serve the needs of the customer.'[31]

(iii) **Quality of performance:** This is the task that each organisation conducts in the market place to identify levels of performance of products/services. The investigative task relies on using customer opinions, market research input, feed back from sales representatives, the use of after-sales service, warranty claims, services such as support and back up, emergency calls for maintenance and repairs, etc.

Quality of performance is the link in the extended process and information generated can be fed back to re-examine the other two stages (i.e. design, conformance). This process is dynamic and therefore can be continually improved.

WHAT IS MEANT BY QUALITY CONTROL?

Quality Control (QC) has been defined as follows:[27]

'Operational techniques and activities aimed both at monitoring a process and eliminating causes of unsatisfactory performance of relevant stages of the quality loop (quality spiral) in order to result in economic effectiveness' (ISO 8402 1986).

'The operational techniques and the activities which sustain a quality of product or service that will satisfy given needs.' (ANSI/ASQC A3 1977).

QC is therefore the use of techniques (mainly statistical) to achieve, maintain and try to improve on quality standards of products and services. It co-ordinates the links between the following activities:[26]

● Specifications of what is required;
● Designing the products/services required;
● Production/installation/assembly of parts, components, elements of the service/ product package;
● Inspection of the product/service package to determine conformance to customer specifications;
● Monitoring usage/consumption of product/service to feed back the information for improvements wherever possible.

The principles of QC are based on the following stages:

No manufacture without measurement

↓

No measurement without records

↓

No records without analysis

↓

No analysis without feed back and corrective action

The concept of control

The concept of control includes all the activities which enable organisations to achieve their objectives efficiently and economically.[13] It is an ongoing process and based on continuously trying to rectify, improve and introduce new concepts.

There are three types of control which can be recognised:

(i) Irregular control: Spasmodic approaches to controlling quality (e.g. when a customer complains);

(ii) Routine control: Regular control by carrying out inspections at specific stages of the process of providing goods/services;

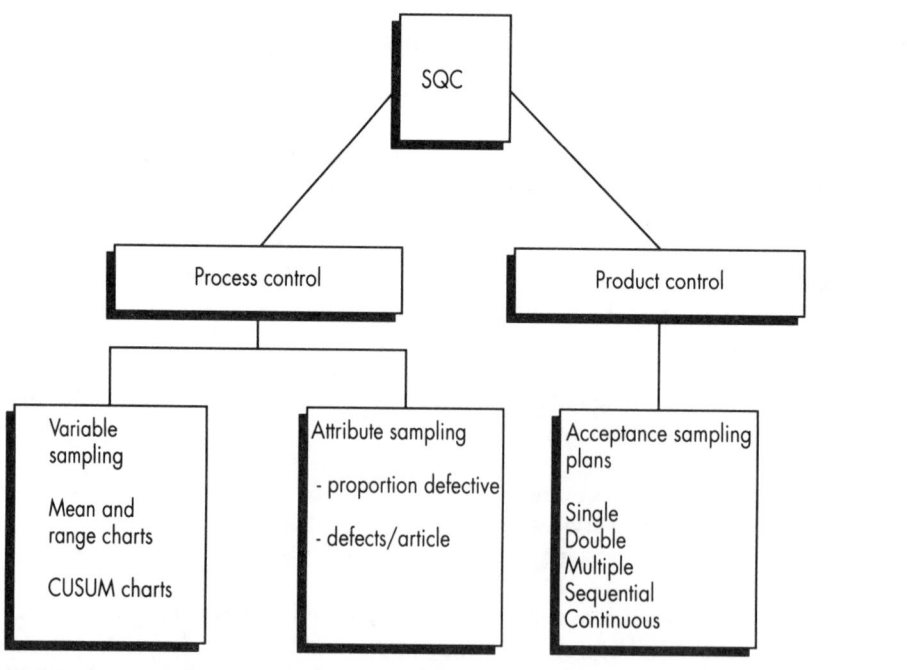

3.1 Various types of Statistical Quality Control techniques.

(iii) Scientific control: Control through measurement and analysis using statistical sampling theory. This more or less controls the process (e.g. a repetitive production process).

WHAT IS MEANT BY STATISTICAL QUALITY CONTROL?

Statistical Quality Control (SQC) is used to measure the degree of conformance of raw materials, processes and products to previously agreed specifications. It uses X and R charts for measuring variations (e.g. weight, dimensions). An X chart is used for plotting the average reading against control limits. The range (R) chart plots the difference between the largest and smallest reading. Statistical Quality Control techniques can therefore be classified into two groups: those concerned with process control and those dealing with the control of variables, Fig. 3.1.

WHAT IS MEANT BY TOTAL QUALITY CONTROL?

Total Quality Control (TQC) has been defined in a variety of ways, all of which emphasise its important role in focusing on the various activities within organisations. TQC has for example been described as:

'A management framework to ensure continuing excellence.'[11]

This management framework was suggested to include the following statements/ programmes for action:[11]

● TQC is a business philosophy which groups together manufacturing, engineering, marketing and sales amongst others, linked together by a two way flow of information;
● TQC should be considered as a mind-set to approve only criteria which lead to better than acceptable quality (via the use of continuous improvement);
● TQC is a continuous process for improvement where current standards present the opportunity for the achievement of new and higher targets (standards);
● TQC provides reliability and consistency in the delivered product/service as a check-and-balance system.

Various definitions have been given to describe TQC most of which tend to describe it as a management system. Some of the main definitions are given in Table 3.4.

Company Wide Quality Control

This is another terminology for TQC which is used in Japan. The emphasis here is once again on the total control of quality organisation wide and with the contribution of every department and every individual within the organisation. CWQC looks at the process of serving customers from the point of view of the customer-supplier

Table 3.4 Some definitions of TQC

1 The application of a number of important management principles and the statistical control of quality to all stages of planning, design, production, service, marketing, accounting and administration. It aims at achieving disruption-free, error-free activities that produce defect-free products and services at a quality cost suited to their market, and with dependable delivery.[13]

2 Problem analysis in order to develop long term solutions rather than response to short term variations. Concern with direct cost reduction and a preoccupation with efficiency are ousted in favour of the pursuit of quality through the elimination of waste and non-value adding procedures and assuring continuous improvement through the refinement and expansion of quality control systems and procedures.[17]

3 A unique concept in business management style that involves every member of any business organisation, from the top executive to the person on the lowest rung of the organisational hierarchy, in solving quality, cost and production problems. Total Quality Control is the statistical control of quality applied to the total operation of an organisation to produce dependable goods and services at a low cost suited to the market.[13]

4 An effective system for integrating the quality development, quality maintenance, and quality improvement efforts of the various groups in an organisation so as to enable marketing, engineering, production, and service at the most economical levels which allow for full customer satisfaction.

chain (both internally and externally). It therefore assumes that all the roles have to be conducted with quality, efficiency, speed of response, etc.

WHAT IS MEANT BY QUALITY ASSURANCE?

Quality Assurance (QA) means basically that Quality Control is conducted in a systematic manner. Quality Control means checking that various stages of the process of serving the customer have been conducted correctly and any defects identified have been corrected. Quality Assurance means that the process of checking, correcting and controlling is conducted in such a manner that the manufacturer/service provider is aware that all stages of the process are being conducted correctly (with the set quality standards in operation) and that what is planned is what is expected to result in terms of output. Quality Assurance also means that there is a set of documentation (a system) which demonstrates the existing standards of quality and reliability.

Quality Assurance uses what has been referred to as the 'death certificate approach'. It rejects inspection as the answer to quality problems and encourages the implementation of procedures in order to comply with set standards.

Quality Assurance has been defined as follows:

'Quality Assurance contains all those planned and systemic actions required to provide adequate confidence that a product or service will satisfy given requirements for quality.' (ISO 8402 1986) (ANSI/ASQC A3 [1977])

To make sure that products and services are in compliance to set standards, QA relies on the use of Statistical Process Control techniques. The system for the implementation, controlling and auditing in QA is often open to third party approval either by customers or government agencies.

WHAT IS MEANT BY TOTAL QUALITY MANAGEMENT?

Total Quality Management is the management of quality totally. So what is Quality Management?

> 'That aspect of the overall management function that determines and implements the quality policy. (ISO/TC 176 1984) and as such, is the responsibility of top management.' (ISO 8402 1986).

Since it has been established that quality management is a managerial responsibility, one has therefore got to link it to the destiny of businesses. It is not therefore just a question of achieving standards but one of survival and being strong all the time. Furthermore managerial responsibilities are not just concerned with focusing on one particular aspect of the business but in being fully aware and in control of all the various activities no matter how small they are. This leads to the argument therefore that TQM is an organisational concern and not the domain of any specialists or specific functions.

The question of leadership

Leadership is perhaps the most important ingredient in the TQM philosophy and has been addressed by pioneers such as Deming, Juran and Crosby. It is discussed in more detail in Chapter 8. A leader is often compared with the 'captain of a ship' who has to keep his vessel afloat, on course and guarantee its safety and the security of his crew until the planned destination is reached.

Leadership is often followed by a series of actions and initiatives which lead to positive outcomes, reflecting organisations' ambitions and desire to succeed. The following statement highlights the role of a leader in the context of TQM:[14]

> '... provide unquestioned leadership ... focus on customer results ... train all employees ... achieve and recognise employee participation ... communicate about quality both internally and externally; and, provide a quality process and quality tools.'

Leadership has to be closely associated with strategy and long term concerns. A leader should have the following strengths: [35]

- The ability to see the long term consequences of current actions;
- The willingness to sacrifice, if necessary, short term gains for long term benefits;
- The sensitivity to anticipate and adapt to changes e.g. in consumer life styles, in consumer tastes and in consumer needs;
- The commitment to manage the organisation in such a way that the leader will always be considered a welcomed and important part of the business community;
- The capacity to control what is controllable and the wisdom not to bother with what is not;

A leader is more of a 'thinker' than a 'doer'. The credibility of leaders in the context of TQM has to be in planning according to their organisations' strengths and according to where they want to be in the future. One can draw a close analogy between the role of a business leader in implementing the TQM philosophy and an army general preparing for a long and hard battle.

'Most battles are won – or lost – before they are engaged, by men who take no part in them; by their strategists' (K von Clausewitz).

The question of attitudes

It is now widely accepted that quality is a behavioural question and that the major task for senior managers is in changing people's attitudes and understanding the meaning and importance of quality. Most of the published literature seems to be concerned with broader issues such as the implementation of TQM, the utilisation of useful statistical techniques such as SPC and the benefits of encouraging a problem-solving approach towards doing business. Research however points alarmingly towards the total ignorance of understanding of what TQM is really all about at various levels of business organisations.[11] It is therefore not just about achieving certain standards of competitiveness or introducing new techniques, concepts, methodologies and technologies. It is about changing attitudes and behaviour towards doing business where parameters of competitiveness and requirements are set by the customer or negotiated with the customer. This issue of TQM and attitudes has been addressed by many writers.[32] A joint paper including the author in 1987[36] concluded that:

'Managing quality is the job of each and every member of an organisation, not solely of its managers. In this sense, managers as well as shopfloor workers must shape the environment which is most propitious for such an achievement and be given incentives to ensure that it becomes, in the routine tasks of everyday life, a reality.'

TQM – the systems question

Another way of defining TQM is in its concern to integrate various aspects of the organisation's activities and produce a total mass driven by the same commitment, beliefs and with similar objectives in mind. This system of TQM could be defined as follows:

'The agreed companywide and plantwide operating work structure, documented in effective, integrated technical and managerial procedures, for guiding the co-ordinated actions of the people, the machines, and the information of the company and plant in the best and most practical ways to assure customer quality satisfaction and economical costs of quality.'

Activities which could be integrated for organisational objectives are represented in Fig. 3.2.

TQM – continuous improvement

TQM has been defined as a philosophy based on the quest for progress and improvement. In this sense TQM looks for continual improvement in the areas of cost, reliability, quality, innovation, efficiency and business effectiveness. The main driving force is belief and commitment (quality driving force) with strategic and operational objectives as the outputs. TQM is certainly not an outcome of blueprints

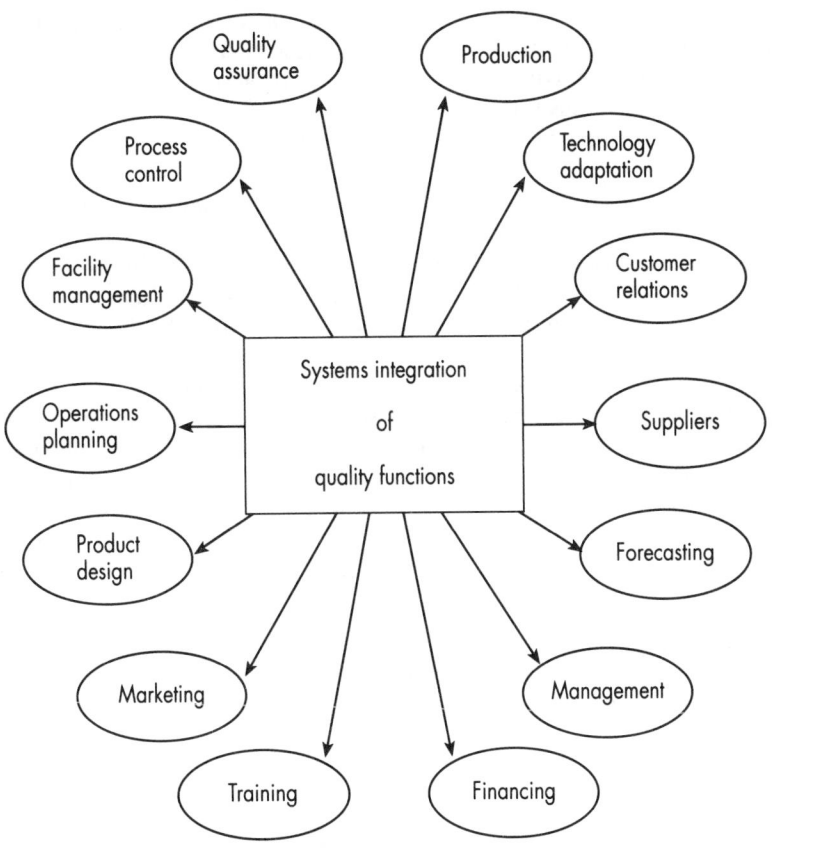

3.2 TQM: an integrated organisational system.

and simulated business performance. It is a dynamic way to perform with a determination to improve in all areas.

The following are some definitions which clearly emphasise the continuous improvement ethos:

'TQM is a fundamental shift from what has gone before. The systematic analysis, pre-planning, and blueprinting of operations remains essential, but the focus switches from a process driven by external controls through procedure compliance and enhancement to a process of habitual improvement, where control is embedded within and is driven by the culture of the organisation.'[17]

'TQM is an approach for continuously improving the quality of goods and services delivered through the participation of all levels and functions of the organisation.'[1]

TQM – customer-supplier chains

This approach to TQM looks at the whole business cycle of any organisation in terms of chains and interplays between different activities. The whole business cycle relies on incremental interconnected contributions which gradually convert customer demand into goods and services to the total satisfaction of the customer. This approach relies on adding value throughout the cycle. Each part of the organisation plays a dual role as a receiver/converter → supplier. This approach is propagated throughout the organisation thus forming a chain.

The business cycle is divided into two types of processes:

(i) **Internal process:** This relies on activities within the organisation and their relationships. It is for example through the activities of marketing that the innovation activity adds changes (incremental – radical) to existing products/ services, which are handled subsequently by an operations productive system which determines the capability of producing innovative products, the flexibility to deal with volume and variety changes;

(ii) **External process:** The business cycle is not complete if it does not deliver to the customer what was required, the time at which it was needed, to the right quality/specification standards and at the agreed price. Furthermore the suggested business cycle is dynamic. It considers a positive interaction between the internal process and the external process throughout. This therefore suggests that the customer is involved throughout and that the customer-supplier chain is strengthened by this approach to TQM, Fig. 3.3.

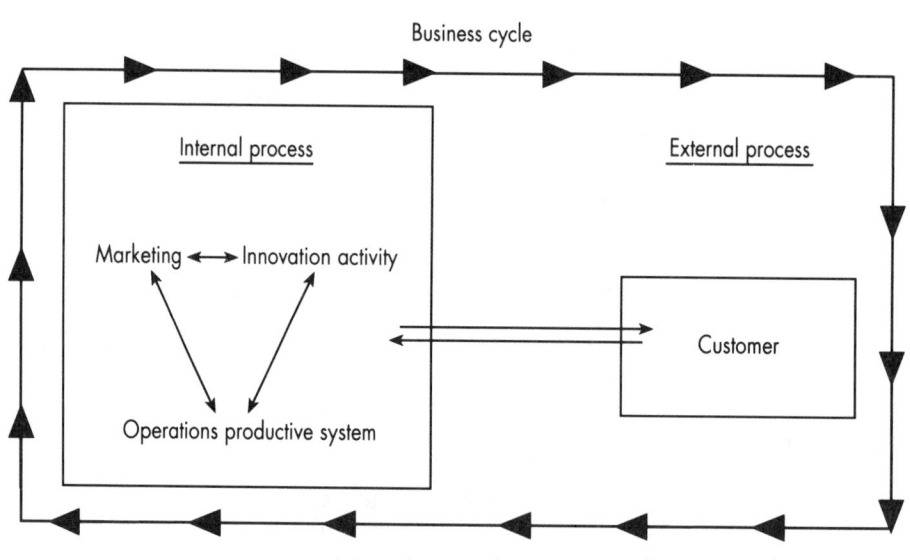

3.3 TQM: customer supplier chains.

SOME EXAMPLES OF TQM MODELS

TQM has been represented in a variety of models as a philosophy reflecting modern competitiveness. Some of the following models are a clear illustration of TQM as an organisational dynamic system based on the following:

(i) A mission to succeed by working very closely with customers and meeting their requirements with an intended commitment to better the standard and levels of service(s) all the time;

(ii) TQM has to be driven by champions at the highest level possible. Senior management commitment is a major prerequisite for success;

(iii) Organisations have to be lean and fit for the external battles of changes in the market place. This is achieved by quality systems which introduce discipline and monitor performance;

(iv) Reliance on the human machine and people's creativity in order to succeed.

The Oakland Model of TQM

The Oakland Model[30] which is represented in Fig. 3.4 defines TQM as a pyramid representing five distinct components.

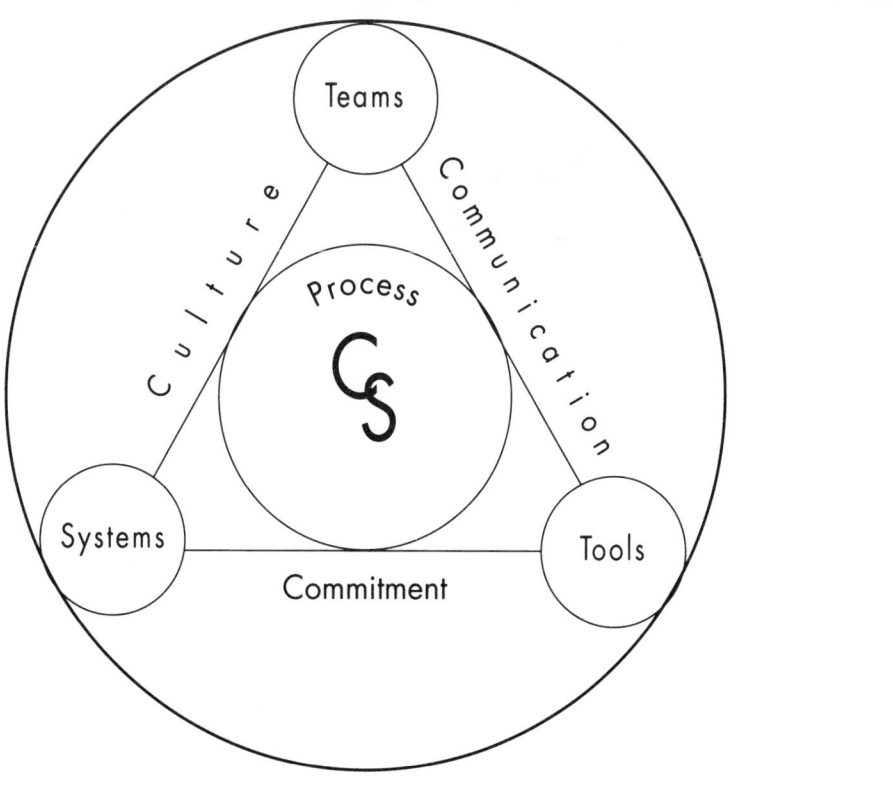

3.4 The Oakland Model on Total Quality Management.

● Management commitment: This identifies that the role of leading and introducing change has to stem from the senior management team. Their commitment has to be reflected by the levels of investment in the required area and the amount of risk taken for the achievement of success;

● Customer-supplier chains: This component is at the heart of the Oakland

45

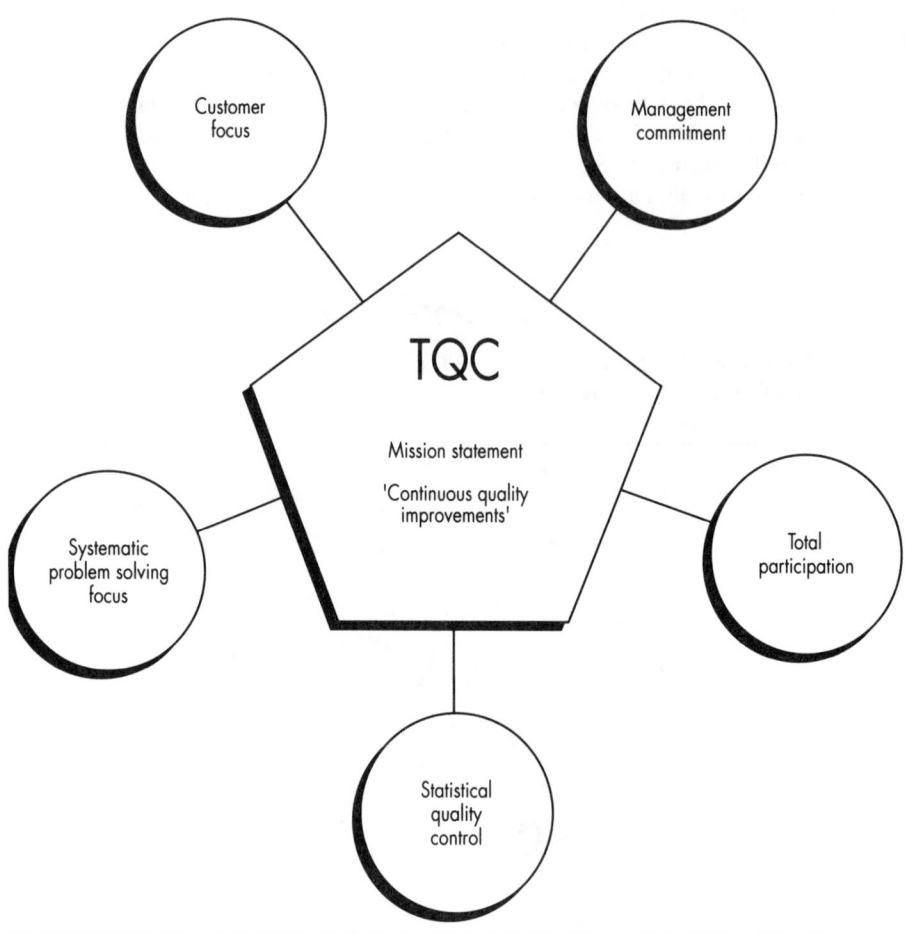

3.5 An integrated TQM model based on actions approach.

pyramid. It reflects process ownership, process management and process improvement propelled throughout the chain.

● Systems: The approach of having documented sets of procedures and standards of doing things right first time and every time.

● SPC Tools: One of the important aspects of TQM is the need to continuously measure and control conformance to customer requirements and agreed standards and to correct quickly defective measures and keep performance on track;

● Team work: This component means that a culture based on continuous improvement has to be instigated, encouraged and implemented throughout the organisation.

The Oakland model is discussed further in Chapter 11.

An integrated model based on actions approach

The integrated model[13] proposes that continuous improvement in quality has to come from an integrated approach of controlling quality via action plans in different operations of the business cycle. The model discusses quality in terms of TQC rather than TQM but control in this instance means the management of quality at various stages of the process. There are five important elements in this model, Fig. 3.5.

● Customer focus: The customer may be the ultimate consumer external to the organisation or an internal user receiving an internal service. Customer focus therefore means that all individuals in the organisation have to focus on the quality of the process in delivering services to the customer (internal and external);
● Management commitment: Commitment can be in the form of changing attitudes and expectations and establishing systems for quality measurement and control. Commitment can also be in the form of setting goals which are achievable and challenging to the organisation's future and in providing the right resources, skills, etc;
● Total participation: People at the grassroots level produce the goods and services that benefit the end customer. It is therefore workers who best understand the problems associated with the product/service delivery cycle and should be the ones to be encouraged to improve the process. Participation is also a means by which intangibles such as morale, sense of belonging and responsibility can be improved;
● Statistical Quality Control: Use of various statistical techniques to analyse collected data and solve various problems;
● Systematic problem-solving process: Based on the customer focus element and relies on the Plan-Do-Check-Action (PDCA) cycle to improve the whole business process. Information is also obtained from customer feedback, surveys and other information.

A model on the eight components of successful TQM

This model[14] looks at organisational and human resource factors more closely than at techniques, systems and standards, Fig. 3.6.

● Changing organisational culture: It is agreed here that the power of organisations should be distributed to instigate a sense of belonging and feelings of loyalty and commitment throughout. It is suggested that changing organisational culture involves five points:

(i)   Making management commitment genuine and evident;
(ii) The process has to be kept serious, but people should be allowed to have fun;
(iii) Every aspect of the process should be made positive. If it is punitive, it will go underground;
(iv) Every level of management and supervision has to be made fully conversant with the notion of how to achieve quality;
(v) The requirements have to be made explicit to be easily understood by all parties.

● Involving the employee: Employee involvement depends very much on changing organisational culture. The role of employees can be seen as 'the glue which

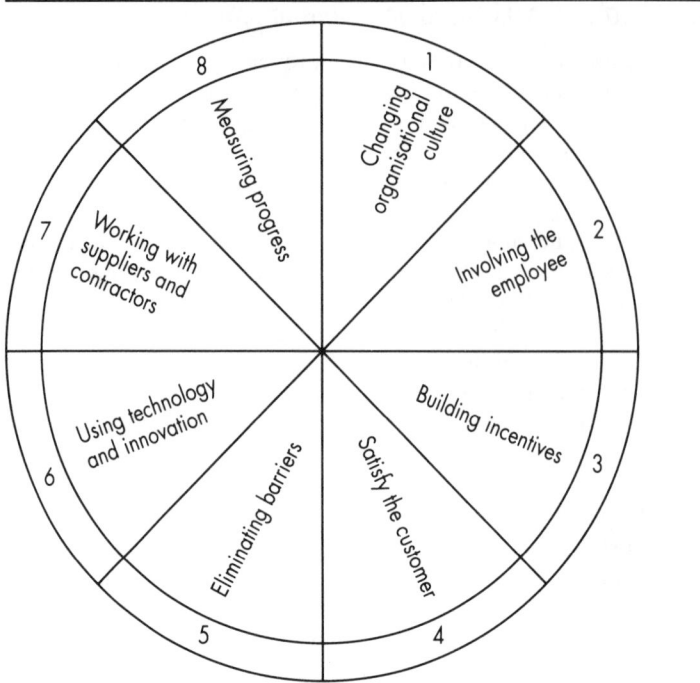

3.6 A model on the eight components for successful TQM.

holds an organisation together'. They should play a role in decision-making, their advice has to be sought, they should be encouraged to state their opinions, forums and gatherings between management and workers are to be encouraged, etc;

● Building incentives: To strengthen the organisation's overall productivity and quality, various employee incentive programmes should be introduced. Other incentives can be based on modified/improved suggestion systems, profit sharing programmes, autonomous work groups, etc;

● Satisfying the customer: Developing a culture based on working hard to improve the quality of operations by improving the system rather than blaming individuals;

● Eliminating barriers: Eliminate bureaucracy, focus on the processes, control mechanisms and make sure that lines of authority and responsibility are a means of facilitating the implementation of TQM rather than hindering it;

● Using technology and innovation: Technology is often at the forefront of improving quality. The product/service has to be provided in any standard or form the customer requires. Technology can also provide organisations with flexibility to react to changes and can ensure a continuous flow of information and therefore improve the communication processes vital for the life of any business;

● Working with suppliers and contractors: Good supplier-customer relationships facilitate the process of discussing various aspects of customer service and client problems. The evaluation of causes of errors leads to the elimination of systemic problems. These links should be conducive to positive product (service) development/customer set-up;

● Measuring progress: TQM measurement can only be related to how good organisations are being controlled and led. In order to strive for quality and productivity improvements, some yardsticks have to be present in the following areas:

(i)   A good understanding of the organisation as a system and its various processes/activities;
(ii) The various goals and objectives for performance improvement have to be clearly defined and identified;
(iii) Progress has to be recorded, analysed and measured in all aspects of the organisation.

Total Quality Management: The building blocks

The model represented in Fig. 3.7 is proposed by the author and looks at TQM at three levels. This model argues that TQM depends on various building blocks which

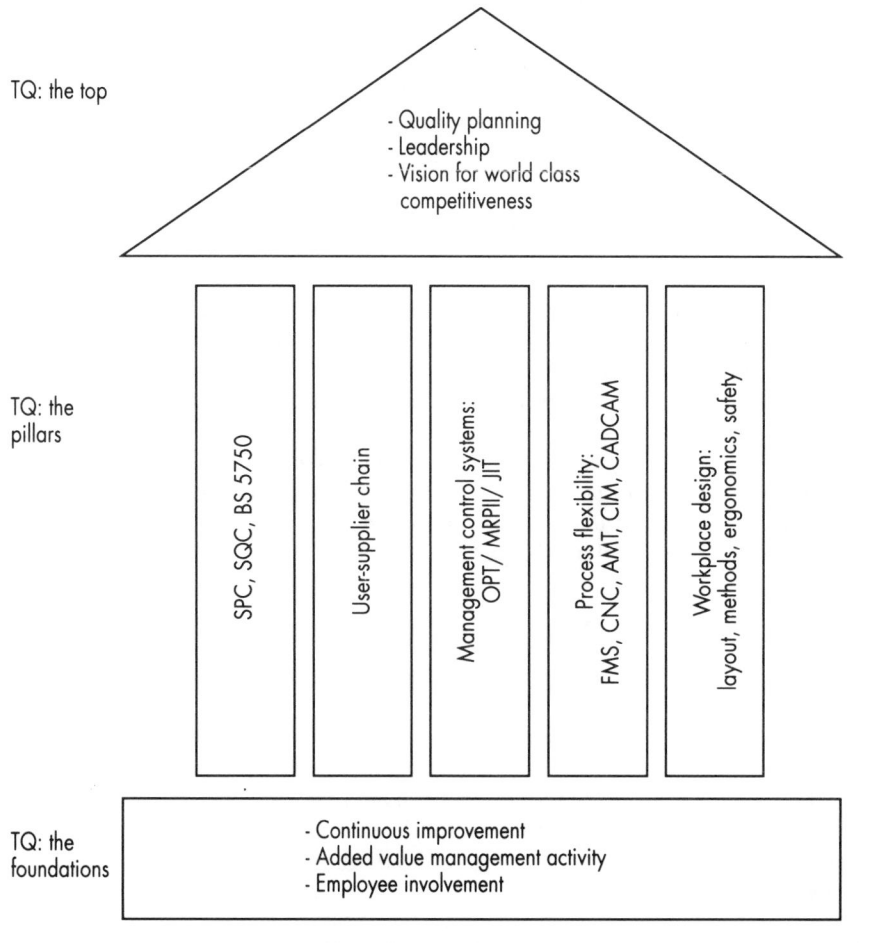

3.7 Total Quality Management: The building blocks.

together determine the strength and safety/security of the organisation. It argues that a weakness in one area will have a disastrous effect on the TQM programme as a whole and therefore proposes that organisations need to focus their TQM implementation strategy on every aspect of the business.

(i) Total Quality – The foundation: It can be argued that the ethos of TQM is eternal improvement, introduction of change, flexibility and adaptability. At the heart of any successful TQM programme are the people the organisation employs or the 'human creativity machine'. People, if nurtured in the right way, if provided with the right tools, if put in the right work environment, and if given the required flexibility to contribute can tirelessly add value to their own tasks and organisations' objectives and can solve various problems via a continuous improvement approach.

(ii) Total Quality – The pillars: The pillars of any TQM programme are the means by which the human creativity inputs can be channelled through and converted into outputs which benefit the end customer. The pillars are represented by various quality systems which represent procedures, documentation, recording and analysis mechanisms, the use of statistical techniques, workplace design, ergonomics, technological innovation, computerised management control systems and the strength of customer-supplier chain (both internally and externally). The strength of each pillar increases the strength of the whole organisation and therefore management should be interested in strengthening and adding extra pillars.

(iii) Total Quality – The top: Similarly to the roof of a building this is perhaps the most important part since it shields the organisation from adverse external factors and protects it all the time. This part has therefore got to be weather-proof (not affected by adverse changes in the market place) and should not deteriorate (organisations are dynamic in nature and have to adapt to new market patterns). Steady-state management or inertia resulting from previous successes can lead to an erosion and deterioration in the organisations concerned. The activities of senior managers therefore, in planning for quality, having a vision for the future of their organisations and in aspiring for world class competitiveness, are crucial in this respect. The top of TQM has to be supported by quality systems which again, will depend on how deep rooted the philosophy is in the organisation. Quality planning/senior management vision can only be converted into reality via a bottom-up approach and an interlink between the various building blocks.

TQM – A BOARDROOM PLACE

TQM is an evolutionary concept and as such has not appeared overnight. It is in the midst of intense competitiveness and tightening market shares that more and more organisations have started to realise that a fresh approach to competitiveness has to be introduced. The lessons learnt from world class competitors such as the Japanese suggested that TQM is at the heart of successful performance.

The evolution of quality has moved from two extremes:

(i) **From control driven to culturally driven quality:** This era has meant that quality has moved from a 'bolt on' component at the end of the business cycle, traditionally controlling production and product/services standards to an era where quality is the driving force of the whole business cycle spreading throughout the various stages and processes of the business cycle and also starting and ending with the end customer.

(ii) **From controlling in to managing in quality:** This era has meant that emphasis has gradually shifted from mechanisms and methods of measuring and controlling quality of products and processes at the operational level, to total management of quality throughout the business cycle with flexibility to react to changes, an ability to innovate and more importantly with a commitment to improve quality standards continually and meet customer demands more successfully all the time, Table 3.5.

Table 3.5 TQM evolution

	Control-driven quality	Culture-driven quality
TQM as organisational system	Low	High
	Controlling-in quality	**Managing quality**
TQM as strategic component	Low	High

The evolution of TQM was classified elsewhere as the outcome of four major eras of development.[29] Table 3.6 illustrates the evolutionary processes where quality has moved from a stage of inspecting, sorting and correcting standards which are nonconforming, to an era of developing quality manuals and controlling process performance. The third stage was to develop systems for third party certification, more comprehensive manuals including other areas of organisations than production and to use statistical techniques such as SPC. The present era of TQM is primarily strategic in nature and is based on continuous improvement as the driving force. Quality planning here is at the strategic level, with employee involvement and overall performance measurement as the key objective.

TQM AND PRODUCTIVITY – A LINK

Although TQM is more and more accepted as a strategic tool for modern competitiveness, there is still ample evidence to suggest that attempts to link its importance to productivity are still weak. It is generally believed that giving quality top priority will lead to a negative impact on productivity levels. Some attempts have been made at identifying the reasons behind the sceptic thoughts on the impact of quality on productivity[41] such as:

● Too much emphasis on quality will have a detrimental effect on costs and productivity;
● Difficulties in obtaining data concerning costs are attributable to poor quality;
● More immediate results can be achieved by cutting costs;

Table 3.6 The four major quality eras:

Stages of the quality movement

Identifying characteristics	Inspection	Statistical Quality Control	Quality Assurance	Strategic Quality Management
Primary concern view	Detection	Control	Co-ordination	Strategic
Emphasis	Product uniformity (PU)	PU with reduced inspection	Entire production chain	Market and consumer needs
Methods	Gauging and measurement	Statistical tools and techniques	Programmes and systems	Strategic planning, goal setting
Role of quality professionals	Inspection, sorting, counting, and grading	Troubleshooting and the application of statistical methods	Quality measurement planning, programme design	Goal setting, education, training, consultation
Who has responsibility for quality?	Inspection department	Manufacturing, engineering departments	All departments	Everyone in organisation and leadership from senior management
Orientation and approach	Inspects in quality	Controls in quality	Builds in quality	Manages in quality

- The perception that there are very few opportunities by which quality could improve productivity.

Other studies have argued however that if quality is considered at the strategic level, then the process of benefit quantification will become much easier. This is because quality deals with organisational objectives overall and does not focus on specific returns in specific areas.

It is widely accepted that quality has to be part of overall strategic planning and in some cases, it is the means by which high standards of competitiveness can be achieved, as stated below:[39]

'(quality) is cost effective, profitable and promotes corporate longevity'.

TQM as a strategic component affects levels of profitability by affecting the costs and market share.

Impact on costs

- Reduces scrap, rework and extra labour;
- Reduction of work in progress (WIP), inventory levels, material handling and excessive capital equipment;

● Improves the utilisation of tools and equipment;
● Reduces customer complaints, warranty and liability claims.

Impact on market share

● Changes in product/service quality have a strong relationship with changes in market share;
● Advertising has a weak relationship with market share;
● Price has no relationship with market share.

TQM has a long term focus and does not look for short term returns. It is for this reason that companies competing on the strength of offering low prices will not survive very long because this advantage can easily be matched by competitors. As has been stated:[41]

> The benefits of lower prices are short-lived as competitors quickly match price decreases. Quality improvement, on the other hand, is much more difficult to match; it requires more time, money, and creativity. High quality gives firms a competitive advantage that is much more likely to help them increase their market share than is a price war.'

Performance characteristics and competitive strategy

Companies tend to compete under the banner of cost efficiency, quality, dependability, flexibility.

Cost efficiency: looks for overheads reduction, high utilisation capacity, materials utilisation optimising, high productivity closely linked to wage rates etc.

Quality: standards, systems, skills, attitudes, problem-solving, creativity, effectiveness of communication systems, etc.

Dependability: delivery reliability, effectiveness of scheduling system, equipment reliability, etc.

Flexibility: capacity, changes, dependability of suppliers, degree of skills flexibility, effectiveness in control of work flow, flexibility in customer-supplier chain, etc.

It is the ability of an organisation in getting the order of priority right in the above competitive indices which determines its effectiveness in the market place. There is an inter-dependence between the four categories but this is not often recognised. It has been argued that companies in the West tend to consider that although the achievement of cost efficiency and high quality standards are desirable business objectives, they require different approaches. As Fig. 3.8[40] shows, because both cannot be achieved at the same time, the companies concerned tend to look for trade-offs. The same applies for the flexibility and dependability competitive indices.

The Japanese however tend to approach the achievement of various competitive advantages under the banner of quality improvement. Quality improvement could be in an area where quantification can be carried out such as production, or it could

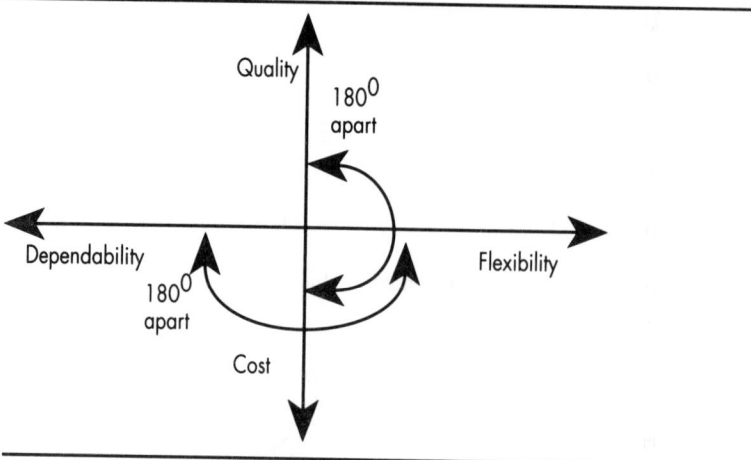

3.8 The Western approach to strategic competitiveness.

be in an intangible area such as attitudes and commitment towards a certain objective. Figure 3.9 illustrates the Japanese approach.

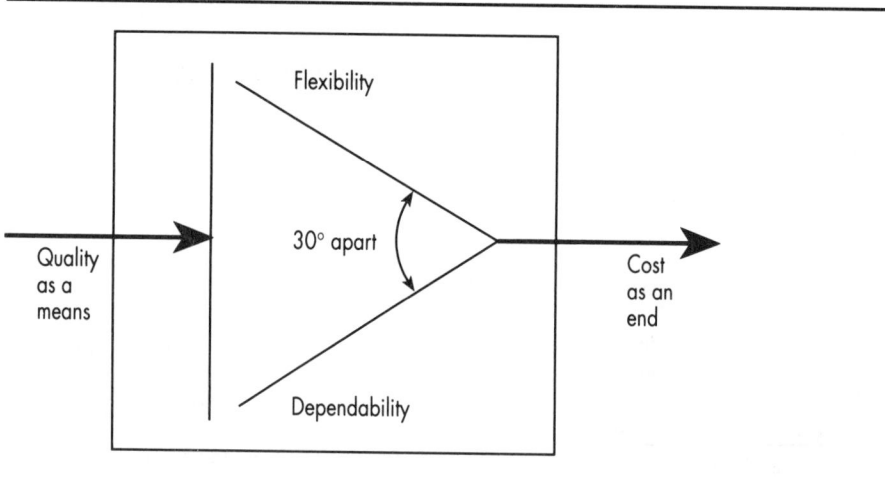

3.9 The Japanese approach to strategic competitiveness.

It is therefore important to look more closely at the link between quality and productivity. TQM has to be part of a competitive strategy as the means by which any desired objective can be achieved (ends). The measure of profitability/productivity has to be related to how customers value the standard, worthiness of products and services provided. The value and expectations of customers change with time and are directly proportional to quality and indirectly proportional to price criteria.

$$Value = \frac{Quality}{Price}$$

TQM AND ADVANCED MANUFACTURING TECHNOLOGY – A LINK

Advanced Manufacturing Technology (AMT) has been defined in a variety of ways where on the whole the use of computer technology has always been mentioned.[42–47] Other definitions have given a broader description of AMT which covers various aspects of business operations.[48–51]

Although on the whole AMT places great emphasis on the use of technological innovation, this, however, has to be part of an overall picture which reflects the long term desire to improve and discipline in improving on existing standards, applying new methodologies and providing an organisational climate based on adding value and problem-solving for world class competitiveness.

It is for this purpose that a more global definition of AMT has been proposed by the author:

'A total socio-technical system where the adopted methodology defines the level of technology to be incorporated. The nature of this socio-technical system requires continual review, re-adjustment and the inclusion of change which is necessary to counter pressures from the competitive environment. In addition to flexibility and adaptability, this system is characterised by an ongoing quest for progress.'

It is through various hard and soft technological innovations, either methodology-driven or computer-driven, that AMT seeks to make an impact in areas such as flexibility, speed of response, productivity levels and business performance effectiveness, Fig. 3.10.

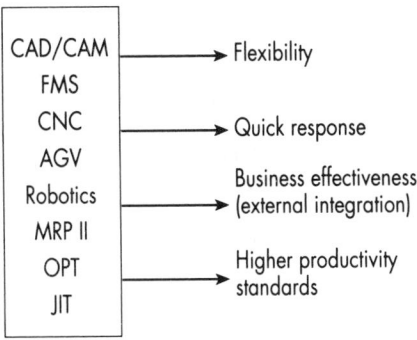

CAD/CAM → Flexibility

FMS

CNC → Quick response

AGV

Robotics → Business effectiveness (external integration)

MRP II

OPT → Higher productivity standards

JIT

3.10 Competitiveness and Advanced Manufacturing Technology.

TQM has already been thoroughly discussed in the previous sections. For the purpose of this section, a broad definition of TQM has been proposed:

'Total Quality Management is the combination of socio-technical processes aimed towards doing the right things (externally), everything right (internally), first time and all the time, with economic viability considered at each stage of each process.'

It is through a combination of quality systems, modern statistical techniques, the belief that customers have to be involved at various stages of the product/service delivery system, and through continuous improvement programmes that TQM seeks to influence business competitiveness in the areas of cost reduction, and adding value to customer products and services, Fig. 3.11.

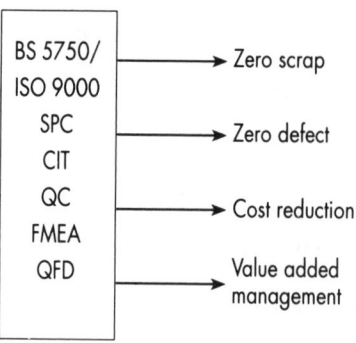

3.11 Competitiveness and Total Quality Management.

What is the link between AMT and TQM?

AMT, through the utilisation of technological innovations such as CAD/CAM, FMS, CNC, AGVs, robotics, MRP II, OPT, JIT is intended to give organisational systems the **DETERMINATION** to compete on flexibility, speed of response, effectiveness (external integration) and higher productivity standards (internally).

TQM, on the other hand, through the introduction of concepts, techniques and systems such as BS 5750/ISO 9000, SPC, continuous improvement teams is intended to help organisational systems achieve the required **DISCIPLINE** to compete positively by establishing a culture of waste reduction/elimination, cuts on lead times, problem solving and value adding activities.

It is the combination of AMT (DETERMINATION) and TQM (DISCIPLINE) that will lead to the following criteria, required for world class competitiveness:

● Effectiveness
● Innovativeness
● Competitive advantage
● Fitness to compete, Fig. 3.12.

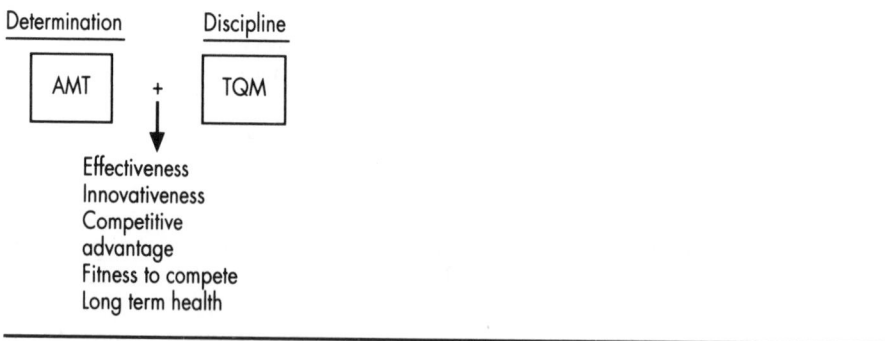

3.12 The link Between AMT and TQM.

Superior performance has to be measured on a moving scale, the levels of which are determined by customer requirements, the continued effort to exploit technological innovation and the discipline to eliminate waste and maximise value.

4

DEFINING TQM: THE SYSTEMS

THE MEANING OF QUALITY SYSTEMS

Quality systems can be perceived as the part which converts statements of objectives into real outcomes. It is the means by which customer-supplier chains are created, strengthened and maintained, Fig. 4.1.

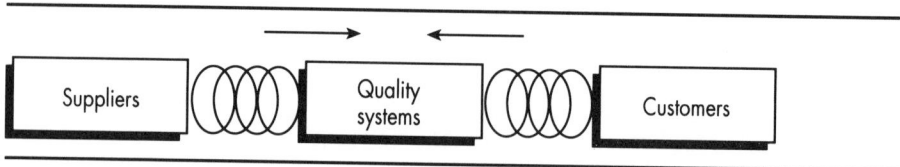

4.1 Quality systems = Creating customer supplier chains.

The implementation of TQM has to start with clearly defined objectives based on an accurate assessment of companies' strengths and weaknesses and the desired competitive gains. This approach should also define the role of TQM as a means in achieving the desired objectives.

Before proceeding in the implementation of a TQM plan, it becomes necessary therefore to communicate the strategic intentions of the organisation to all the employees. This has to be in a participative-consultative way with the possibility of reviewing the plans. TQM will be worthless if it does not carry commitment from everyone inside the organisation. This is why communication is a crucial stage and has to be conducted with a lot of care and devotion.

Quality systems therefore are intended to implement the desired objectives and make quality part of every activity within the business and everyone's responsibility. The system will rely on defining the objectives of each activity and setting appropriate procedures and documentation which will help everybody conform to requirements. Quality systems also rely on internal and external control mechanisms which are intended to meet customer requirements continuously and improve on existing performance levels by adding value in various forms to customers. In a sense quality systems are the means by which customer-supplier chains are forged and strengthened.

Quality systems have to be reviewed regularly if activities, work flow and new methods, have been incorporated into the organisation. They have also got to be reviewed against company objectives and the quality strategy, Fig. 4.2.

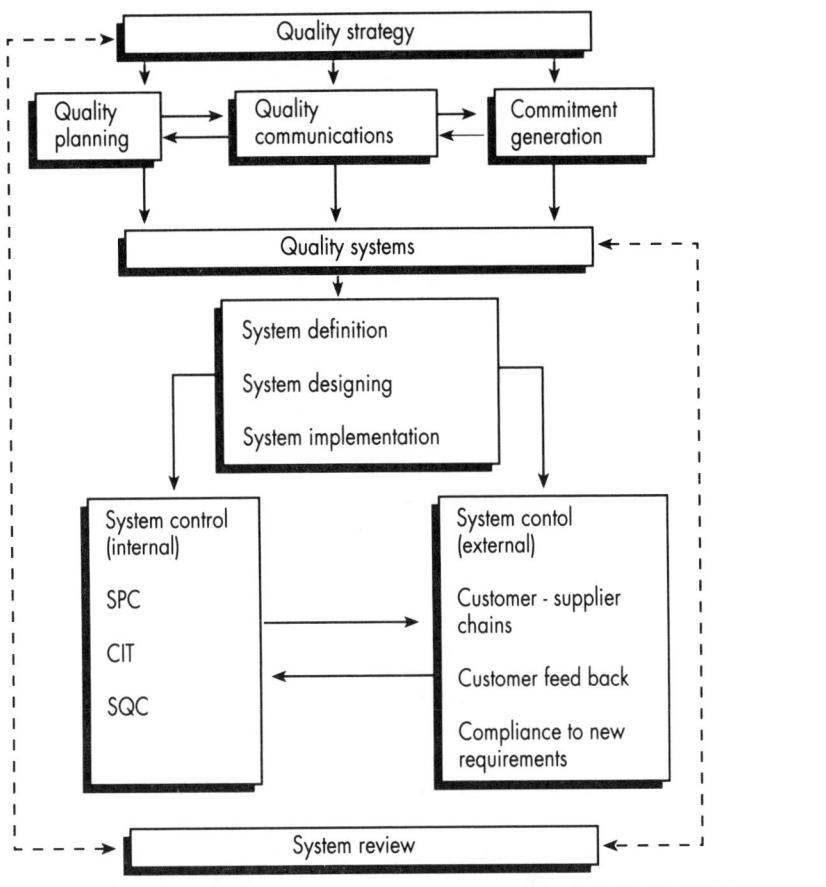

4.2 Defining quality systems.

Quality systems are about ASSURANCE and making sure that organisations reach their intended destination safely. If one takes the analogy of a vehicle, Fig. 4.3, quality assurance systems form the part of the engine (OPERATIONS). Quality planning/strategy represents all the CONTROLS in the car and quality improvement can be represented by the PROGRESS of the car. A sound TQM strategy therefore depends on a healthy engine to drive it and the former two depend in turn on good wheels to make the necessary progress towards the intended destiny.

The following are some of the definitions given to quality management systems:

'A quality assurance system entails interrelated procedures directed towards accomplishing predetermined goals. The purpose and goal of a quality management system are to ensure and attain the desired and specified quality of products and services.'[1]

'Quality assurance is a structured approach to business management and control, which embraces the ability to consistently provide products and services to specification, programme and cost.'[2]

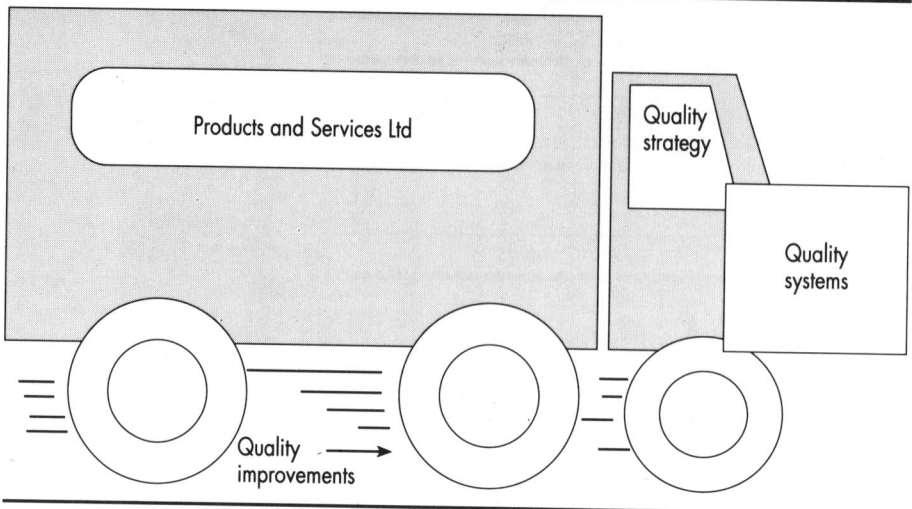

4.3 Quality systems in a dynamic context.

WHY ARE QUALITY ASSURANCE SYSTEMS NEEDED?

Figure 4.3 illustrates the point on the relevance of quality assurance systems accurately. A vehicle without an engine is useless since the controls for the destination cannot function without it and the wheels are unable to turn. Similarly, a quality policy is meaningless if it is not accompanied by a quality system which in turns needs to rely on continuous improvement for the realisation of set objectives.

This is perhaps the major justification for having quality systems. There are however a host of other reasons including the following:

(i)   If Zero Defects, Zero Risk, Zero Breakdown and Zero Defections are the goal, then quality systems are the means by which compliance to customer requirements and the achievement of customer satisfaction can be obtained by linking the internal part of the chain to the external part;

(ii) Modern competitiveness relies more and more on a TQM driving force to achieve a mix that the customer desires. It is therefore by NECESSITY that quality systems are implemented;

(iii) Quality management is its CONTROL. To control quality companywide, there has to be an implemented quality system;

(iv) Quality systems are necessary for auditing and measurement purposes;

(v)   More and more customers are demanding that their suppliers have quality systems implemented. There is therefore no excuse or justification in not having them;

(vi) The existence of various international standards and various government help offered to facilitate their implementation, makes it once again difficult for any organisation to avoid;

(vii) Widely published benefits resulting from the introduction of quality assurance systems makes them quite attractive to implement;

(viii) There is more and more evidence to suggest that TQM leads to organisational growth. It is therefore important for organisations to have mechanisms by which waste is identified and removed and errors are detected and eliminated before they can propagate;

(ix) TQM is people related. Company growth can only take place via continuous improvement and the encouragement of problem solving activity. Quality systems are the 'torch' which enables each worker to see what is required of them and where they are heading. Systems are documented procedures and techniques, they are not merely management instructions;

(x) For any organisation to benchmark its own activities against the best competitors, it has to introduce various standards which help it aspire to world class competitiveness.

THE ROLE OF QUALITY STANDARDS

Quality standards are not mandatory requirements and are issued as guidelines to be implemented by any organisation. They are therefore generic models which can

Table 4.1 Contents of a typical quality systems standard

1 Scope
2 Definitions
3 Requirements
   a Quality assurance programme
   b Organisation
   c Audits
   d Quality programme documents
   e Verification of quality
   f System functions
     – Contract review
     – Design assurance
     – Document control
     – Measurement and testing equipment
     – Purchasing
     – Incoming inspection
     – In-process inspection
     – Final inspection
     – Inspection status
     – Identification and traceability
     – Handling and sorting
     – Manufacturing and construction
     – Special processes
     – Preservation, packaging and shipping
     – Quality records
     – Non-conformance
     – Customer supplied items
     – Corrective action

be applied by the smallest organisation to a multinational one. Most standards are multi-stage processes and follow the procedure of SORTING – VERIFYING – REACTING – PREVENTING. Table 4.1 illustrates the contents of a typical quality systems standard.[1]

The most widely used model for the implementation of quality assurance systems is the ISO 9000 series developed by the International Standards Organisation. This model contains the following parts:

ISO/9000   Quality management and quality assurance standards and guidelines;
ISO/9001–3 Quality systems (three models); Assurance models encompassing design, development, production, installation and servicing capabilities;
ISO/9004   Guidelines.

ISO/9004 contains the most widely used guidelines internationally, Table 4.2.

Table 4.2 International standards guidelines

1 Introduction
2 Scope and field of application
3 References
4 Definitions
5 Management responsibility
6 Quality systems principles
7 Economics – quality-related cost considerations
8 Quality in marketing
9 Quality in specification and design
10 Quality in procurement
11 Control of production
12 Product verification
13 Control of measuring and testing equipment
14 Non-conformity
15 Corrective action
16 Handling and post-production functions
17 Quality documentation and records
18 Personnel
19 Product safety and liability
20 Use of statistical methods

THE DIFFERENT STAGES OF A QUALITY ASSURANCE SYSTEM

A sound quality assurance system has to scrutinise dynamically each and every aspect of organisations' activities, so that conformance to established standards is prevalent all the time. A good quality assurance programme should contain the following stages:

(i) **Evaluation:** This stage should be intended to evaluate specifically the adequacy of existing plans, procedures, guidelines and standards. Not only has the evaluation stage got to make sure that there is an adequate system of procedures which control the various operations of the organisation, but it has also got to relate the former closely to organisational goals and objectives;

(ii) **Measurement:** A good quality assurance system should be able to measure performance and output levels at each stage of each process, to make sure that operations are being run efficiently, economically and with conformance to customer requirements;

(iii) **Reporting:** It is vital that a good quality system has a reporting stage so that action can take place. The reporting stage becomes the responsibility of those people who would take direct action to correct the identified problem and monitor the progress of the implemented solutions;

(iv) **Reviewing:** A good quality system is one which questions the viability of solutions all the time, the logical approach of doing things, the value of each function to organisational effectiveness and whether procedures are in line with recent changes and additions to the organisational productive system. Figure 4.4 illustrates a model which represents a dynamic quality assurance system

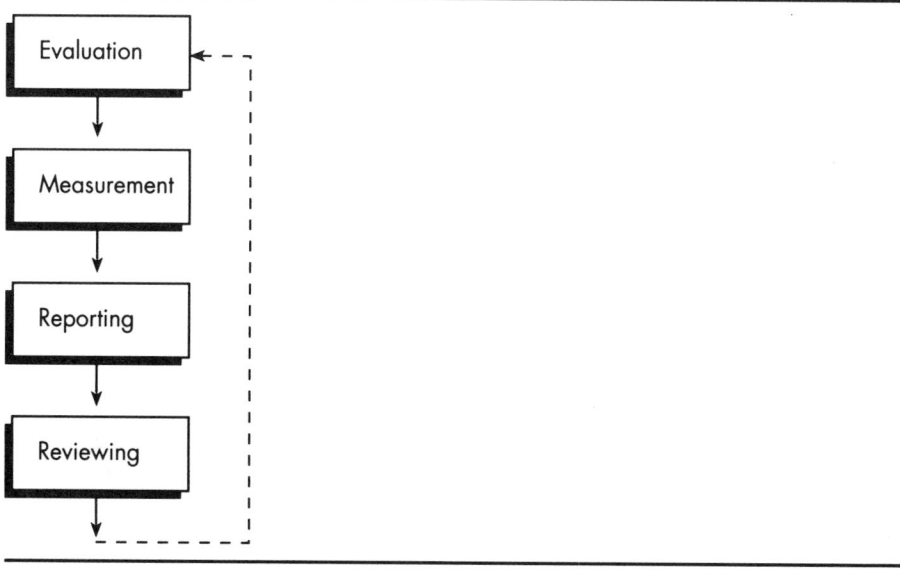

4.4 The steps in Quality Assurance programmes.

capable of updating and redirecting organisational activities so that the level of competitiveness is always positive.

The role of any quality assurance system is in fact the provision of information to the right levels so decisions are made. The role is also in making sure that implemented solutions are not forgotten, but become themselves sources for the provision of data which are investigated to provide information and the cycle goes on, Fig. 4.5.

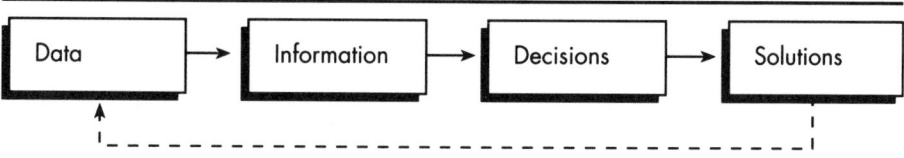

4.5 Quality systems = Managing information systems.

THE IMPLEMENTATION OF QUALITY SYSTEMS

The implementation of a good quality assurance system has to be conducted without any time constraints and also has to have the various essential building blocks of climate, readiness, resources and commitment. This section describes a step by step approach which can be used towards the implementation of a good quality system.

Overall responsibility for the quality system programme

A good quality assurance system has to have the full backing and support of the company chairman, chief executive or whoever is in charge. There has to be a commitment towards ensuring that the proposed programme succeeds and this should be demonstrated by the allocation of the right resources and by the preparation of the right climate for this to happen. In addition, there has to be clear conviction that a quality system is the means by which the company should operate for it to achieve the desired levels of performance in the market place. At no time should it be considered that the implementation of a quality system is a financial burden without clear benefits;

(i) **What are the key objectives in mind?** An organisation exists to satisfy customer requirements in a variety of ways, for example by providing goods and services which the customer demands and is willing to pay the right price for. The usefulness of quality systems has therefore got to be closely related to the former objectives. In addition, a good organisation is one which dynamically tries to improve in its various aspects to become more and more effective in serving its customers and therefore in gaining a competitive edge. Once more there has to be a link between organisational effectiveness and the role of quality systems.

(ii) **What is the cost of quality?** Quality has to be costed in all aspects of organisational activities. The costs of implementing a quality assurance system have to be related to the major outcomes and benefits. It has to be established that the outcomes from a sound quality system outweigh the initial costs involved in its implementation. This is illustrated in Fig. 4.6.[4]

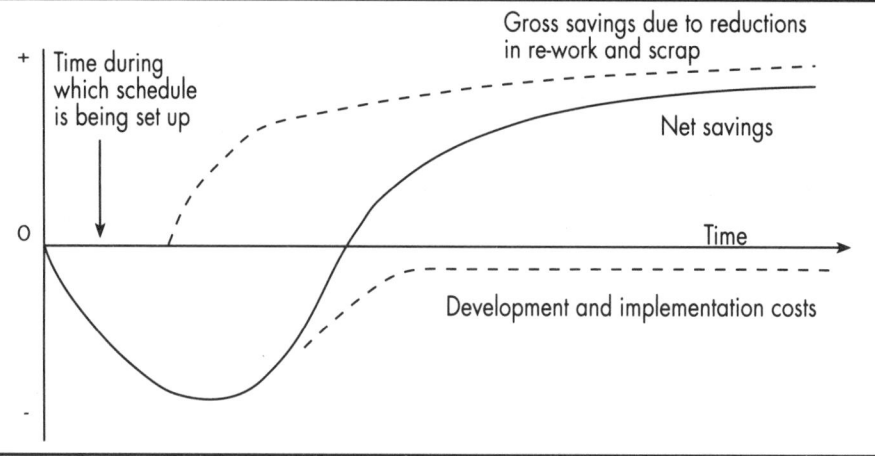

4.6 Costs and benefits of implementing quality systems.

(iii) **Who is responsible for each stage?** The responsibility of implementing a quality system has to be distributed throughout the organisation to include various management layers and all the workers to be accountable for their tasks and activities. Information providers are those people who have been doing the job for a long time and who have a good understanding of the problem areas. The lower management layers can play a role of co-ordinating and facilitating the implementation process.

(iv) **How should the quality system plan be communicated?** This stage should not be treated in a cavalier manner, since a quality system will only succeed if it carries the support and commitment of all the employees and managers. There has therefore got to be a sound strategy of sending the message across convincingly, inviting and encouraging participation and involvement. A quality system with overall commitment is unlikely to fail.

Commitment: The policy statement

The policy statement is essentially a declaration of intent that the organisation concerned is committed to quality. This declaration has to be signed by the chief executive to show that commitment comes from the very top of the organisation and that the statement is followed by a comprehensive implementation programme to convert the statement into real outcomes. The policy statement is then communicated internally to all employees and externally to all customers, suppliers and other third parties.

The quality manual

The quality manual has to be considered as a tool of paramount importance for the implementation of a quality system. It can serve different purposes, some of which are reviewed in the following section:

(i) **Describes the task:** A quality manual is the 'proof of the pudding' as far as quality systems are concerned. It is a transformation of the policy statement into procedures and guidelines for all the activities within the organisation;

(ii) **Management decision-making tool:** The quality manual, at any time, can provide management with information on various aspects of the organisation's intentions to improve quality in order to meet customer requirements. This information is therefore vital for making accurate and effective decisions;

(iii) **Productive workforce:** This is perhaps one of the main advantages of having a quality manual. Each worker is provided with guidelines on how to perform their jobs and also given standards which the company is confident that they can achieve. This therefore reduces the learning curve, increases morale and motivates the employees to increase productivity levels;

(iv) **Enhances company image:** In the eyes of customers, a quality manual illustrates how determined and serious the supplying organisation is about quality and how it is striving to achieve better performance levels for the benefit of the customer. It is also a powerful tool for making suppliers follow the example and conform to the standards of the customers;

(v) **Objective performance:** A quality manual provides information based on facts and figures and therefore organisations no longer have to depend on subjective input. Bottlenecks are more easily identified and action is taken much more quickly as a result;

(vi) Powerful training tool: A quality manual does not rely on any particular individual's contribution in the implementation of a training programme. In addition, a quality manual, because it is kept up to date all the time, enables organisations to carry out training programmes which are relevant, with up to date practices and which rely on current principles and techniques.

The key point of the quality manual is its effectiveness rather than its format. Generally speaking, a typical quality format will be represented by three main sections, Table 4.3.

Table 4.3 Different sections of quality manual

Company quality policy	Policy statement
	Statement on quality objectives
	Statement on allocation of responsibility and authority
	Details on quality implementation programme
System outlines	Outlines of primary functions of quality programme as determined by company objectives and in response to customer requirements
Procedures index	All procedures and guidelines for all systems representing quality assurance in all the functions

The quality manual has to be concise and kept as simple as possible. It is a document of intent and therefore should only reflect the broad approach the organisation is taking in relation to the implementation of quality systems. Detailed information has to be avoided as much as possible, particularly in areas where there is updating to be carried out on a regular basis. In these cases extra documentation can be prepared with the necessary detail. On the same lines, functions should be referred to in terms of descriptive names rather than individual names, because there are more likely to be changes in individual's responsibility and status within the organisation than to the functions themselves.

Procedures

Procedures are the hard evidence that quality systems are a reality. Each activity within the organisation has therefore got to be fully documented to reflect the various stages involved and the information obtained has to reflect existing procedures which are up to date, practised and with the desired standards. It is suggested that procedure development should follow the approach below:[4]

● Review current practice;
● Analyse current practice;
● Develop a draft procedure;

- Release draft for comment;
- Review comments;
- Revise and issue procedure for acceptance;
- Obtain approval;
- Issue for use;
- Implement;
- Monitor and review.

Procedures have to have some degree of uniformity and the adopted format should cover purpose, scope, references, definitions, actions and documentation. In addition, procedures have to be written with maximum clarity to be effective in giving guidelines to the end user.

The role of auditing

Auditing is an important activity in quality systems to ensure that compliance with set procedures and agreed standards takes place all the time at all stages of the productive/organisational process. As such, auditing can be defined as:

'A planned and documented activity performance in accordance with written procedures and check-lists to verify by investigation, and the examination and evaluation of objective evidence, that applicable elements of a quality programme or plan have been developed, documented and effectively implemented in accordance with specified requirements.'

The process of conducting auditing is illustrated in Fig. 4.7.

Basically the routine function is to make sure that the quality manual and procedures are up to date and operating according to specified procedures and standards. The aim is therefore to keep asking the question is there compliance? In the event that there is compliance the auditor has to terminate the investigative process and write a report. If there is non-compliance, the auditor has to look at the problem from the point of view of non-adherence to set procedure (in which case corrective action is taken). If there is a procedural problem, the procedure involved is reviewed, revised and included in the quality manual. In all cases the process of auditing terminates with writing a report once there is satisfaction that there is 100% compliance.

Auditing for conformance versus auditing for effectiveness

The role of the auditor in the former section is purely and simply to make sure that there is full compliance to agreed procedures and set standards. The auditor is not expected to challenge the limitations in the process or the feasibility of alternatives. This is why auditing for conformance has been referred to as static auditing.[7] Dynamic auditing on the other hand has been defined as the activity which is oriented towards change, adaptation and improvement.

This therefore begs the question as to whether one expects an auditor to conduct both types of auditing, or whether alongside an auditor training for checking compliance to standards one should include a value analysis specialist who will weigh up the merits of each function to optimise benefits and reduce costs and

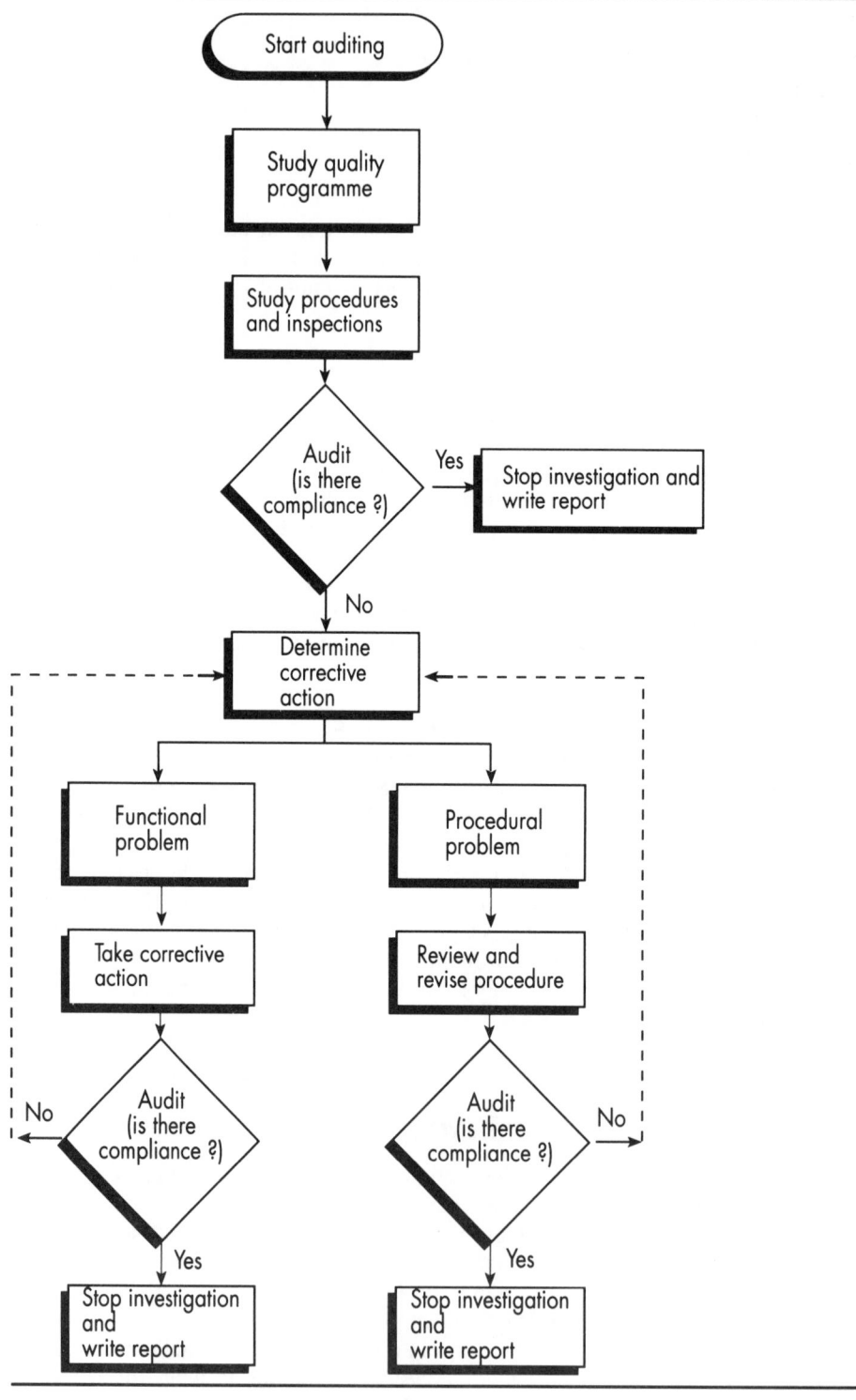

4.7 The process of auditing quality systems.

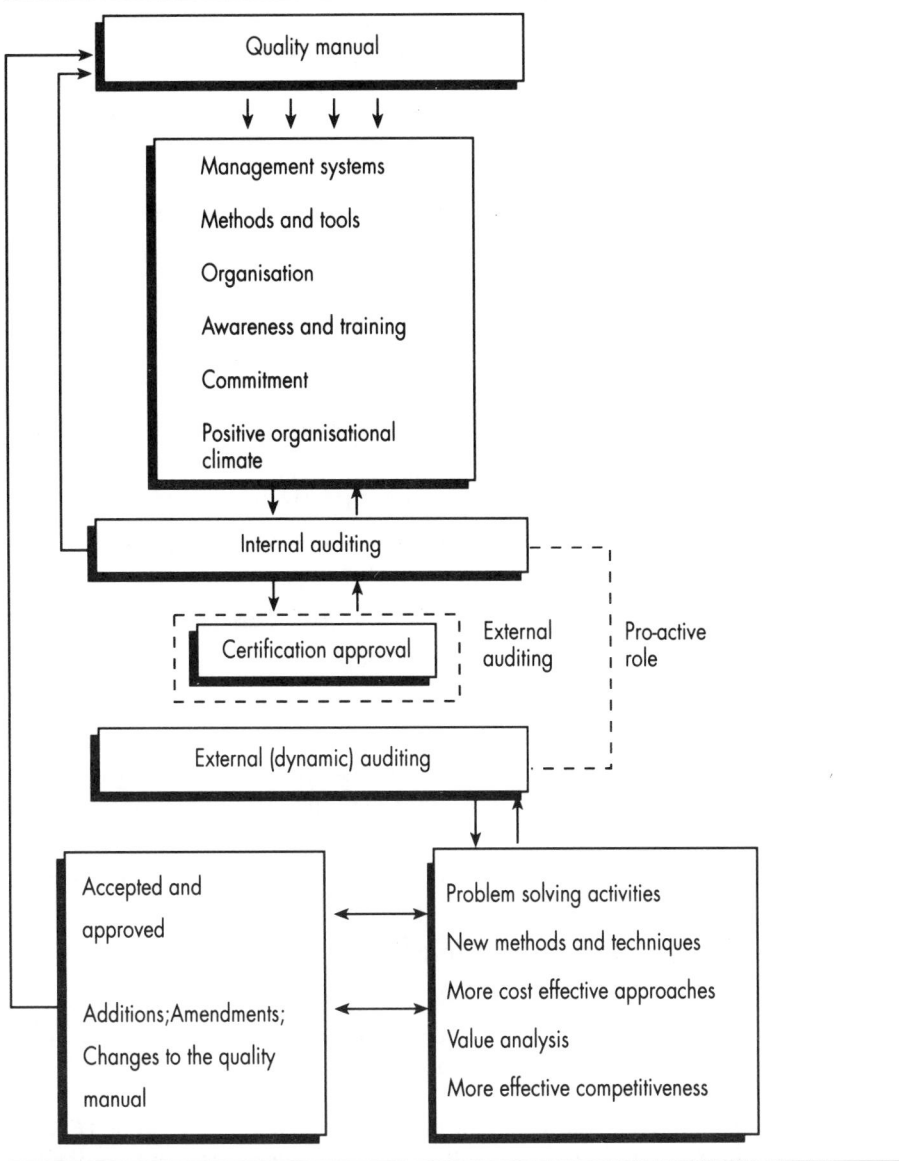

4.8 A pro-active role for auditing.

increase quality levels? This is perhaps one question that organisations have to consider, particularly in a climate of continuous improvement, where emphasis is placed on positive motion and making change as part of the corporate culture.

Figure 4.8 depicts the relationship between the internal auditing (static auditing), the auditing for certification approval, and pro-active auditing which questions the way procedures are arrived at, their economic viability and their viability as best solutions under the changing organisational circumstances.

Table 4.4 A comparison of static and dynamic auditing

Static auditing	Dynamic auditing
Reduces the scope of audits	Enhances acceptance of audits and reduces fear
Enhances cost effectiveness	Informs management and staff more adequately
Simplifies auditing and auditor qualification	Identifies opportunities for quality improvement
Allows for employing less qualified staff	Disseminates new knowledge and experience in quality assurance
Confirms meeting of standards	Induces innovations
Recognises adequate performances	Enhances 'cultural change' in the company
Suffices for quality programme registration	Encourages delegated decision making, integration, and co-operation
	Reviews all procedures and standards
	Provides greater challenge and recognition for auditors and auditees
	Enhances the role and status of quality assurance

Table 4.4 compares both types of auditing systems (derived from reference 7). Both are important. Static auditing needs to be conducted to make sure that organisations are responding to their customers' needs and requirements on an everyday basis. Dynamic auditing on the other hand has to be conducted so that companies are positively pursuing improvement in their competitive aspirations.

The challenge of auditing: A tool for quality improvement

Auditing for compliance has its usefulness and therefore is intended to scrutinise the whole business process to ensure that standards are met and procedures are fully applied. There are however various problems with this approach:

- First of all, as an approach towards encouraging the implementation of TQM it is too rigid and structured. Consequently, it restricts innovation and the implementation of change and new ideas;
- It relies heavily on the objectiveness of the auditor, his/her knowledge, impartility and reasonableness. Decisions made as a result of the published reports by the auditor have to depend on the objective criteria and the ethical nature of the auditor;
- TQM seeks to foster a climate of co-operation, team work and organisational objectives. In most cases the auditee plays a small role in assessment and recommending changes. This is because the auditor considers that the recommendations fall outside the criteria of the standard or that the auditee's views are discarded because the auditor thinks he/she knows best;
- Reports resulting from an auditing exercise can result in high costs, particularly if they recommend changes which are unnecessary or if they have not closely

considered various options of bringing about changes, with economic viability in mind. In addition, auditors (involuntarily) can lead to friction, low morale and poor employee co-operation which is vital for continuous improvement;

● Many reports tend to look at one aspect of the application of quality systems only. For example policy audit looks at written procedures and policies and weighs them up against standards (office job); practice audit checks actual practices against standards; product audit checks the productive system as a whole and carries an on-field evaluation exercise. It is therefore necessary for the auditor to be fully aware of the company's intention, its written procedures and how the various stages of the production process take place.

The dynamic auditing approach which was discussed in the previous section is therefore an ideal opportunity for conducting improvement programmes. Besides seeking to establish compliance, the auditors are encouraged to question existing practices, methods and techniques and to weigh up the potential benefits to the organisation in terms of savings in comparison with what is practised. Enough flexibility has therefore got to be allocated to the evaluating team so that a total quality climate can be spread. The reports have to emphasise synergy, integration and providing a quality organisation based on the customer-supplier chain and where progressiveness is via continuous improvement rather than by predetermining targets. Dynamic auditing has also got to rely on an equal involvement of the auditees themselves and any recommendation by the auditing team must have full approval and support of the auditees concerned.

Table 4.5 derived from Reference 15 illustrates the difference between the desired outcomes of auditing for compliance (static) and dynamic auditing (for quality improvement).

Table 4.5 Outcomes from auditing for compliance versus auditing for improvement

Objectives	Compliance	Improvement
Aims of evaluation	Formality Hard evidence Objectivity	Informality Perceptions Subjectivity
Reporting intentions	Report all discrepancies Impose corrections Ignore positives Explore in depth	Focus on key issues Suggest solutions Give more compliments Explore in breadth
Auditee response	Animosity Defensiveness Secretiveness	Co-operation Acceptance Openness

Auditors' selection and training

Success in the implementation of quality systems hinges on the professionalism, personality, knowledge, objectiveness and rationality of the auditor. It is therefore of paramount importance that the selection procedure be based on the above criteria and training has to be adequately carried out. There are many issues related to auditors of concern to business organisations having to undergo an evaluation procedure. The following are only some of the many points which have been raised:

(i) Many of the investigative tasks conducted by auditors try to establish 100% compliance to specifications by being more interested in results rather than the activities themselves, the degree of complexity in the various tasks and the work environment itself;

(ii) Some auditors can cause resentment and a climate of nonco-operation in the host organisations they visit. It could be that through their attitudes and negative approach, the eagerness, commitment and drive to implement a climate of TQM can be badly damaged;

(iii) Auditors could be influenced by practices and procedures they have come across elsewhere and therefore could be biased in their approach;

(iv) Auditors could feel uneasy about their evaluation, particularly when they do not come across anything wrong. Some people may wish to lengthen the investigative procedure more than necessary in the hope that they may come across a problem;

(v) Auditors have to have the right attitudes and temperament. They should avoid entering into fierce arguments and have the patience and ability to listen. They also have to be honest and compliment the host organisation if there is 100% compliance.

THE ISO 9000 QUALITY SYSTEM

The ISO 9000 series standard was developed by the Technical Committee 176 of the International Standards Organisation (ISO) in 1987. There are five standards in the ISO 9000 series – ISO 9000; ISO 9001; ISO 9002; ISO 9003 and ISO 9004.

ISO 9000 contains general guidelines, ISO 9001 and 9002 are quality assurance standards intended to inform customers and third parties that a particular organisation is working according to specified requirements. ISO 9003 and 9004 lead to the establishment of a total quality system based on customer-supplier chain and striving for world class competitiveness.

ISO 9000 standard is increasingly being applied, so much so that the American National Standards Institute (ANSI) and the American Society for Quality Control (ASQC) have modelled a system based on the ISO 9000 series, called the Q90 series (Q90; Q91; Q92; Q93; Q94). Table 4.6 illustrates an international comparison of quality assurance standards. It can be seen that most of the countries are basing their quality systems on the ISO 9000 series.

The European Community as part of its integration plans is encouraging wide use of the ISO 9000 series. In the EC quality strategy there was the commission's mandate to establish a European standard amongst the member countries. The European Committee for Standardisation (CEN) was given the task to develop a common standard based on the ISO 9000 series. This resulted in the EN 29000 series which is now being enforced in all EC member countries, although different countries are at different stages of implementation. The UK for example is well ahead of the other countries. It is reported[23] that there are well over 10,000 businesses registered under ISO 9000.

ISO 9000 standard as a total quality system

Most of the organisations applying for registration under the ISO 9000 standard, are doing so to comply with customer and third party requirements. To achieve a climate of competitiveness under total quality management however, businesses will have to implement the guidelines of the total ISO 9000 standard. To implement a TQM philosophy using the ISO 9000 standard as the tool, businesses will have to comply with the following:

(i) Technical input using the guidelines of ISO 9000, introducing SPC, using the Just In Time (JIT) philosophy, introducing problem-solving activities and measurements;

(ii) Introducing a quality policy which is widely communicated to all workers, and which can be implemented, by providing back up and support and allocating the right resources for its success;

(iii) Management must lead attitude changes by example. Their commitment must be unquestionable, and they have to foster a climate of openness, trust, co-operation and employee care and loyalty. The quality drive must not be seen as a one-off exercise but rather as a new way of working life.

(iv) Progress in competitiveness can be achieved if the implementation of the ISO 9000 standard is followed up by regular auditing exercises to ensure compliance. This happens by making sure that management study closely outcomes of audit reports and act upon recommendations and by making sure that quality systems become a strategic weapon and a means by which positive competitiveness can be achieved. Quality systems have therefore got to be incorporated in the planning processes of organisations.

(vi) TQM is often defined as the establishment of a customer-supplier chain. The ISO 9000 standard is an important tool which can be used to develop links with suppliers and establish long term partnerships.

BRITISH STANDARD BS 5750/ISO 9000

Origins of the standard

BS 5750 (1979) originated in the 1970s from the AQAP's standards (Allied Quality Assurance Publication) for the defence procurement and from their subsequent modification to standards MOD 05–21, 05–29 series. It was following requests from the Confederation of British Industry (CBI) that guidelines were published in 1974 to have standard BS 5179 parts 1, 2 and 3. The Warner report in 1977 called for the establishment of a common standard in view of the fact that various industries started to develop their own guidelines and standards.

BS 5750 (1979) had some shortcomings however, and as a result of pressures applied from the Society of Motor Manufacturers and Traders led by Ford Motor Company in particular, an International Standards Organisation (ISO) was formed and this led to the introduction of the ISO 9000 series in 1983–84. The reasons for this were that for world class competitiveness there has to be one common standard internationally. BS 5750/ISO 9000 was introduced in July 1987.

Table 4.6 An international comparison of Quality Assurance standards

Standards body	Quality management and Quality Assurance standards: guidelines for selection and use	Quality systems model for Quality Assurance in design/development, production, installation, and servicing	Quality systems model for Quality Assurance in production and installation	Quality systems model for Quality Assurance in final inspection and test	Quality management and quality system elements: guidelines
ISO	ISO 9000: 1987	ISO 9001: 1987	ISO 9002: 1987	ISO 9003: 1987	ISO 9004: 1987
Australia	AS 3900	AS 3901	AS 3902	AS 3903	AS 3904
Austria	OE NORM-PREN 2900	OE NORM-PREN 29001	OE NORM-PREN 29002	OE NORM-PREN 29003	OE NORM-PREN 29004
Belgium	NBN X 50-002-1	NBN X 50-003	NBN X 50-004	NBN X 50-005	NBN X 50-002-2
Canada	–	–	–	–	CSA Q420-
China	GB/T 10300.1-88	GB/T 10300.2-88	GB/T 10300.3-88	GB/T 10300.4-88	GB/T 10300.5-88
Denmark	DS/EN 29000	DS/EN 29001	DS/EN 29002	DS/EN 29003	DS/EN 29004
European Community	EN 29000-1987	EN 29001-1987	EN 29002-1987	EN 29003-1987	EN 29004-1987
Finland	SFS-ISO 9000	SFS-ISO 9001	SFS-ISO 9002	SFS-ISO 9003	SFS-ISO 9004
France	NF X 50-121	NF X 50-131	NF X 50-132	NF X 50-133	NF X 50-122
Hungary	MI 18990-1988	MI 18991-1988	MI 18992-1988	MI 18993-1988	MI 18994-1988
India	IS: 10201 part 2	IS: 10201 part 4	IS: 10201 part 5	IS: 10201 part 6	IS: 10201 part 3
Ireland	IS 300 part 0/ISO 9000	IS 300 part 1/ISO 9001	IS 300 part 2/ISO 9002	IS 300 part 3/ISO 9003	IS 300 part 0/ISO 9004
Italy	UNI/EN 29000-1987	UNI/EN 29001-1987	UNI/EN 29002-1987	UNI/EN 29003-1987	UNI/EN 29004-1987

Malaysia	–	MS 985/ISO 9001-1987	MS 985/ISO 9002-1987	MS 985/ISO 9003-1987	–
Netherlands	NEN-ISO 9000	NEN-9001	NEN-9002	NEN-ISO 9003	NEN-ISO 9004
New Zealand	NZS 5600: part 1-1987	NZS 5601-1987	NZS 5602-1987	NZS 5603-1987	NZS 5600: part 2-1987
Norway	NS-EN 29000: 1988	NS-EN 29001: 1988	NS-ISO 9002	NS-ISO 9003	–
South Africa	SABS 0157: part 0	SABS 0157: part I	SABS 0157: part II	SABS 0157: part III	SABS 0157: part IV
Spain	UNE 66 900	UNE 66 901	UNE 66 902	UNE 66 903	UNE 66 904
Sweden	SS-ISO 9000: 1988	SS-ISO 9001: 1988	SS-ISO 9002: 1988	SS-ISO 9003: 1988	SS-ISO 9004: 1988
Switzerland	SN-ISO 9000	SN-ISO 9001	SN-ISO 9002	SN-ISO 9003	SN-ISO 9004
Tunisia	NT 110.18-1987	NT 110.19-1987	NT 110.20-1987	NT 110.21-1987	NT 110.22-1987
United Kingdom	BS 5750: 1987: Part 0: section 0.1 ISO 9000/EN 29000	BS 5750: 1987: part 1: ISO 9001/EN 29001	BS 5750: 1987: part 2: ISO 9002/EN 29002	BS 5750: 1987: part 3: ISO 9003/EN 29003	BS 5750: 1987: part 0/ISO 9004/EN 29004
USA	ANSI/ASQC Q90-1987	ANSI/ASQC Q91-1987	ANSI/ASQC Q92-1987	ANSI/ASQC Q93-1987	ANSI/ASQC Q94-1987
USSR	–	40.9001-1988	40.9002-1988	–	–
West Germany	DIN ISO 9000	DIN ISO 9001	DIN ISO 9002	DIN ISO 9003	DIN ISO 9004
Yugoslavia	JUS A.K 1.010	JUS A.K 1.012	JUS A.K 1.013	JUS A.K 1.014	JUS A.K 1.011

Part 0, sections 0.1 and 0.2 of the system are powerful additions to the previous standard. They provide quality management guidelines for business organisations regardless of industry type and they can be interpreted according to strengths and objectives of individual organisations. Parts 1, 2 and 3 provide guidelines for quality systems. These guidelines have however got to be specifically applied to each organisation and are not open to interpretations. Table 4.7 illustrates the difference between the various parts and their intended applications.

Table 4.7 BS 5750/ISO 9000: different characteristics

Parts/sections	Intended use	Type of organisation	Aims/desired outcomes
Part 0, section 0.1 and 0.2	Non-contractual	All organisations	Quality management to strengthen competitiveness
Part 1, 2, 3	Contractual	Selected quality system elements required by customer	Quality assurance-desired quality cost effectiveness

Table 4.8 illustrates parts 1, 2 and 3 of the standard

Requirements

There are twenty requirements for part 1 and eighteen for part 2. The eighteen sections are identical in wording in parts 1 and 2. The only difference however is that design control and servicing are excluded from part 2. Sections 4.1 and 4.2 refer to overall management; sections 4.5, 4.8, 4.12, 4.13, 4.14, 4.16, 4.17, 4.18 refer to requirements/activities with company-wide implication; sections 4.3, 4.4, 4.6, 4.7, 4.9, 4.10, 4.11, 4.15, 4.19, 4.20 refer to specific requirements.

Management responsibility (4.1)

- Define and document policy and objectives;
- Must be understood, implemented and maintained at all levels;
- Organisation: responsibilities, authorities and interrelationships;
- Identify verification resources and personnel;
- Assign management representative;
- Review the system at appropriate intervals.

Quality system (4.2)

- Preparation of documented quality system;
- Effective implementation of documented quality system.

Contract review (4.3)

- Review each contract to ensure:
  (a) requirements are defined and documented

Table 4.8 Requirements of BS 5750-1987

Type of requirement	Part 1	Part 2	Part 3
Management responsibility	4.1	4.1	4.1
Quality system	4.2	4.2	4.2
Contract review	4.3	4.3	–
Design control	4.4	–	–
Document control	4.5	4.4	4.3
Purchasing	4.6	4.5	–
Purchaser supplied product	4.7	4.6	–
Product identification and traceability	4.8	4.7	4.4*
Process control	4.9	4.8	–
Inspection and testing	4.10	4.9	4.5
Inspection measurement and test equipment	4.11	4.10	4.6
Inspection and test status	4.12	4.11	4.7
Control of non-conforming product	4.13	4.12	4.8
Corrective action	4.14	4.13	–
Handling, storage, packing and delivery	4.15	4.14	4.9
Quality records	4.16	4.15	4.10
Internal quality audits	4.17	4.16	–
Training	4.18	4.17	4.11
Servicing	4.19	–	–
Statistical techniques	4.20	4.18	4.12

* Part 3 excludes traceability

    (b) differences from tender requirements are resolved
    (c) supplier has capability to meet contractual requirements;
● Maintain records of reviews.

Design control (4.4)

● Design and development planning;
● Design input;
● Design output;
● Design verification;
● Design changes.

Document control (4.5)

- Document approval and issue;
- Document changes/modifications.

Purchasing (4.6)

- Assessment of sub-contractors;
- Purchasing data;
- Verification of purchased product.

Purchaser supplied product (4.7)

- Product supplied by customer for building into the product: procedures needed for verification, storage and maintenance.

Product identification and traceability (4.8)

- Identify the product from drawings, specifications, etc, during all stages of production, delivery and installation.

Process control (4.9)

General

- Work instructions;
- Suitable production equipment and environment;
- Compliance to reference standards/codes and quality plans;
- Monitoring during production;
- Approval of process and equipment;
- Criteria for workmanship.

Special processes

- Continuous monitoring.

Inspection and testing (4.10)

Receiving inspection and testing

- Inspect incoming product against documented procedures/instructions;
- If released for urgent production purposes ensure identification for recall, if needed.

In-process

- Inspect, test, identify as required by procedures;
- Use of process monitoring and control methods;
- Hold product until inspection/tests have been completed (or recall system).

Final inspection and testing

● Ensure all inspections and tests have been carried out.

Inspection and test records

● As per (4.16).

Inspection, measuring and test equipment (4.11)

● Select appropriate equipment;
● Identify, calibrate and adjust at prescribed intervals;
● Document calibration procedures;
● Ensure equipment is capable of the accuracy and precision necessary;
● Identify equipment to show status (indicator or record);
● Keep records of calibrations;
● Ensure environmental conditions are suitable;
● Handling, preservation and storage;
● Safeguard inspection, test facilities, including test hardware and software, from adjustments which would invalidate calibration;
● Fixtures, templates, patterns are included in above.

Inspection and test status (4.12)

● Identify whether passed, failed, or waiting inspection;
● Use markings, stamps, tags, labels, routing cards, inspection records, location or other means.

Control of non-conforming product (4.13)

● Identify;
● Segregate (where practical);
● Disposition;
● Notify other functions concerned;
● Document;
● Non-conformity review and disposition.

Corrective action (4.14)

● Investigate causes;
● Analyse all processes, work operations, concessions, quality records, service reports and customer complaints;
● Initiate preventative actions;
● Ensure corrective actions are effective;
● Implement and record changes resulting from corrective actions.

Handling, storage, packaging and delivery (4.15)

Handling

● Prevent damage.

Storage

- Prevent damage and deterioration;
- Authorised receipt and despatch to and from stores;
- Assess stored product at appropriate intervals.

Packaging

- Control packaging, preservation and marking processes.

Delivery

- Protect after final inspection and test;
- Protect during delivery to customer (where contractually specified).

Quality records (4.16)

- Procedures for: identification
  collection
  indexing
  filing
  storage
  maintenance
  disposition of records;
- Include pertinent supplier/sub-contractor records;
- Must be: legible and identifiable
  retrievable;
- Specify retention.

Internal quality audits (4.17)

- Planned and documented;
- Scheduled (based on status and importance of activity);
- Carried out in accordance with procedures;
- Document results, notify personnel responsible;
- Management personnel responsible for areas/deficiencies to take timely corrective action;

Training (4.18)

- Identify, provide and record;
- Personnel performing assigned tasks shall be qualified (education, training or experience).

Servicing (4.19)

- Where specified in the contract;
- Verify servicing meets requirements.

Statistical techniques (4.20)

Where appropriate

● Identify;
● Verify process capability and product characteristics.

Issues associated with implementation

There are various issues associated with the implementation of BS 5750/ISO 9000 some of which are discussed in the following section.

● In the wake of 1992, it is expected that market forces will intensify and therefore BS 5750 will become a prerequisite in doing trade;
● The values from the implementation of BS 5750 can only be appreciated if it is used as a total quality system rather than for minimal requirements of products/ services compliance;
● BS 5750 is customer driven. It is therefore important to involve customers at all stages of the product/service development process. Standards are those agreed upon at the onset;
● BS 5750 starts with clear planning, and a company policy on implementing quality standards. It also aims to spread in all areas of any business organisation;
● BS 5750 depends heavily on management commitment and changing worker attitudes. People have to be involved at all stages and all the time, otherwise continued compliance will cease;
● BS 5750 is a generic framework. It is easily adaptable to any situation and different business contexts. It is therefore flexible and allows interpretations by the prospective organisation;
● Auditing is an important aspect of the implementation of the standard, and continual monitoring, review and action is necessary to maintain positive competitiveness;
● BS 5750 has to be implemented with cost effectiveness in mind. Organisations have to look for the most economical solutions and changes which meet requirements and would not affect companies' strength. Other changes can be carried out incrementally after certification approval;
● BS 5750 emphasises people issues such as training. Continued compliance can only be successful if people's skills are upgraded every time there is a change in their job design or in some aspects of their tasks.

Benefits and problems associated with implementation

Benefits

● Ensuring customer satisfaction by having quality built in at each stage of the business productive system;
● Various cost savings by having uniform working methods and by using auditing in a pro-active way, continuous improvement can lead to further substantial savings;
● Waste reduction/elimination by using knowledge work and simplifying processes;

- Speed of response is increased because lead time is cut dramatically in view of doing things 'right first time';
- Problems are identified and solved at early stages before products/services reach the customer;
- More accurate and quality decisions are made because BS 5750 places emphasis on information availability;
- The administrative system identifies the organisations' strengths and weaknesses so that improvement can become realisable;
- Customers and suppliers as a result of BS 5750 are driven by similar aspirations and common goals. Good communications and clear understanding of requirements and expectations can lead to long term partnerships.

Problems

- BS 5750 as a quality system costs a substantial amount of money to implement without any definite financial returns to the organisation concerned;
- BS 5750 is replacing what has always existed and has been perceived as not as good as previous standards;
- In many cases BS 5750 does not lead to a reduction in auditing and inspection as originally intended and has led to asking more and more questions without clear solutions;
- BS 5750 in many cases had to be introduced reluctantly for fear of losing customers and contracts. This is usually because customers insist on supplier certification to BS 5750;
- Often BS 5750 was introduced without clear management commitment who still perceive quality to be the responsibility of someone else;
- BS 5750 in some cases has been 'bolted-on' to existing cultures based on conflict between management and workers. This has often led to lack of interest by employees who may think that BS 5750 is another management exercise to gain more control over them.

REGISTRATION AND ACCREDITATION IN QUALITY SYSTEMS

What is certification?

- Certification = conformance to a standard;
- Standards are nationally/internationally recognised for specific aspects of products and services;
- There are approximately 40 certification bodies in the UK for product and quality control systems (e.g. British Standards Institution's Quality Assurance Scheme and Lloyds);
- Registration leads to adding companies names in the 'Register of Quality Assessed United Kingdom Manufacturers';
- Inclusion in the register can only be achieved through third party certification by an approved body such as BSI and in compliance with standards such as BS 5750;
- Certification bodies have to comply to certain criteria such as:
  – National/international recognition;
  – Have to balance the interests of user and supplier;

– Full documentation;
– Provision of a clearly defined appeal procedure.
● Certification schemes are generally voluntary;
● BSI conducts quality systems certification and the assessment leads to any of the following three outcomes:
– Unqualified registration;
– Qualified registration;
– Non-registration.

Firms which have been qualified are allowed to use the BSI registered firm symbol (Fig. 4.9).

4.9 BSI symbol for registered companies.

What is approval?

● Certification only looks at compliance to standards and therefore does not place any emphasis on whether products are fit for their intended purpose;
● Approval is still given by associations and agencies which use their own criteria or an industrywide standard if there is one available;
● Two major symbols operated by the British Standards Institution are often used to mark that the products have been tested and are certified as capable of meeting the widely accepted standard. These are the Kitemark and Safety mark (Fig. 4.10 and 4.11 respectively).
● Some of the major organisations which deal with product approval are:
– The British Board of Agreement (BBA);
– The Associated Office of Technical Committee (AOTC);
– The British Electrotechnical Approvals Board for Household Equipment (BEAB);
– The International Wool Secretariat;
– The Design Council;
– BSI Quality Assurance Services;
– Pressure Vessels Quality Assurance Board;
– Lloyds Register Quality Assurance Ltd (LRQA);
– Civil Aviation Authority (CAA).

4.10 BSI kitemark.

4.11 BSI safety mark.

The National Accreditation Council for Certification Bodies (NACCB)

- NACCB was set up in 1984 in the UK to carry out accreditations on behalf of the Department of Trade and Industry (DTI);
- NACCB was born as a result of a drive by the British government to encourage more positive competitiveness of UK businesses (a white paper was produced in 1982 which looked at standards, quality and international competitiveness);
- The accreditation of certification bodies such as BSI, Lloyds Register Quality Assurance (LRQA) is given according to the following criteria:
  - Integrity;
  - Technical competence;
  - Impartiality.
- There are four certification categories which include:
  - Quality management systems;
  - Product conformity;
  - Product approval;
  - Personnel engaged on quality verification.
- Accredited institutions can use the official seal of recognition, the National Accreditation Mark (Fig. 4.12).
- The process of registration takes place as follows:
  - NACCB accredits agencies such as BSI;
  - Suppliers apply to BSI for certification;

4.12 National Accreditation Mark.

– BSI makes resources available and selects appropriate assessors;
– Assessors conduct on-site audit;
– A report makes recommendations based on outcomes of assessment;
– Registration is granted/not granted;
– Twice yearly audits are conducted to ensure maintained compliance.

An illustration of the accreditation process is given in Fig. 4.13.[22]

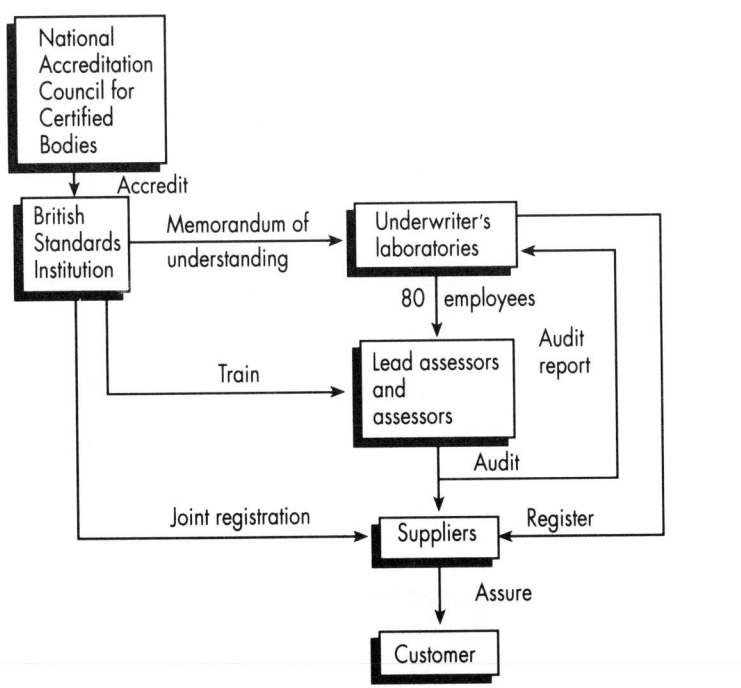

4.13 The accreditation process.

The registration of lead assessors

● The process of registering lead assessors is illustrated in Fig. 4.14;[22]

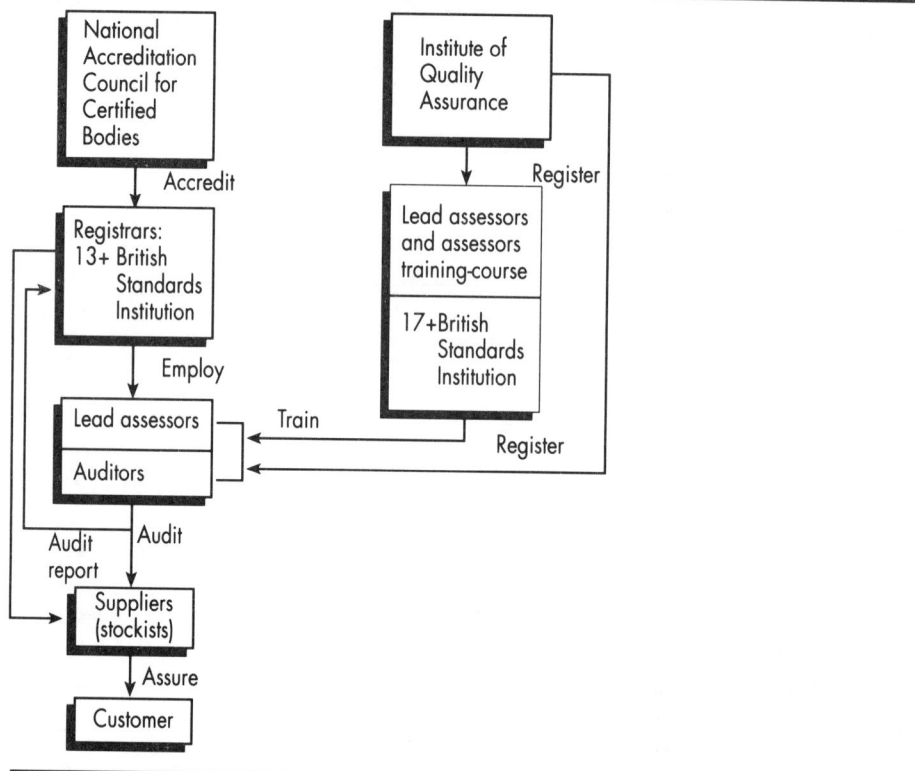

4.14 Lead assessor registration process.

● This role is assumed by the Institute of Quality Assurance (IQA) set up with government support in 1984;

● Since 1984 approximately 400 registrations took place (25% of which are staff working at BSI);

● The IQA scheme is primarily intended to establish the competence, integrity and ability to assess quality management systems and to review the work of assessment teams;

● The registration is for an initial period of three years, after which the lead assessors have to reapply;

● The IQA maintains a register of lead assessors who are expected to observe a code of conduct;

● The selection process is based on adequate training in assessment procedures, the way the assessment has to be conducted and the in-depth knowledge of standards such as ISO 9000 series;

● Candidates have to attend a training programme for lead assessors at the end of which they are expected to pass a test. They are also expected to conduct five third party assessments as a lead assessor within 12 months of finishing the training course;

● The assessments conducted by lead assessors are closely supervised and reviewed by a respected leading authority on assessment, such as BSI.

5

DEFINING TQM:
TOOLS AND TECHNIQUES

INTRODUCTION

Continuous improvement in TQM, the achievement of Zero Defect, the use of Deming's PDCA cycle and meeting customer requirements, come from the use of tools and techniques which help solve problems, generate new ideas and help organisations compete under the banner of TQM.

The use of tools and techniques is essentially intended to dissect processes, understand them better, know about the activities involved and propose solutions which can be implemented, controlled and monitored.

The purpose of measuring, recording, analysing, implementing and controlling within processes is to achieve superior performance. Tools and techniques generate data which can be analysed to provide valuable information that can help managers make much more accurate decisions. In a sense, for businesses to be managed well, their operations have to be managed well. For the latter to happen, information has to be available.

TQM is about the control of processes business wide. This takes place, generally speaking, through constantly measuring and recording. As John Oakland[1] explains, control can only take place if there is good understanding of what the processes are and where measurement can take place confidently. In relation to the former point, Oakland concludes:

'Processes operated without measurement are processes about which very little can be known. Conversely, if inputs and outputs can be measured and expressed in numbers, then something is known about the process, and control is possible.'

Measurement is therefore a necessary continuous activity if a good understanding of business strengths and weaknesses is to be established. And even more importantly, measurement is the vehicle by which customer requirements can be achieved. As explained by Juran,[2] measurement is 'the mission of establishing customer needs in units of measure'. Juran has defined measurement from two perspectives:

(i) **A unit of measure:** A defined amount of some quality feature which permits evaluation of that feature in numbers;
(ii) **A sensor:** A method or instrument, which can carry out the evaluation and state the findings in numbers, in terms of the unit of measure.

Tools and techniques are therefore the sensors which can be used in every process of business to establish the standard of quality at each stage of each process by ensuring that there is total compliance with customer requirements. The word measurement defined below,[3] is essential to every employee of every organisation because it leads to the generation of information which is vital for enabling managers to make the right decisions for the achievement of positive competitiveness.

'Measurements are the yardsticks that tell us how we've done and motivate us to perform.'

This chapter aims to answer questions such as why do we use tools and techniques? How do we define processes? How can we get to know our processes? What are the techniques available? Why are statistical techniques so important? What are the issues related to the implementation of tools and techniques? What are the reported gains/advantages resulting from the utilisation of tools and techniques?

WHY USE TOOLS AND TECHNIQUES IN TQM?

Businesses are complex systems involving a wide variety of processes which are inter-related and which are constantly changing since bringing in positive change in methods and techniques is an important management activity. To assess the true effectiveness of TQM on the whole business system various measurements have, therefore, got to be carried out. Furthermore, TQM tools and techniques are the ON-LINE methods of finding out if customer requirements are met both internally and externally.

Tools and techniques can be used in two different ways:

(i) **Reactive role:** A problem has been identified and a process seeking to solve it is carried out;
(ii) **Proactive role:** The continuous search for improvement by isolating possible bottlenecks and seeking to solve them through a process using TQM tools and techniques.

TQM places much emphasis on continuous improvement. ON-LINE problem solving is therefore essential if superior performance is to be achieved. Once a culture of problem-solving activity is established, it is therefore expected that a pro-active approach rather than a reactive one will take place.

What are the stages of problem-solving activity?

The process of solving problems using TQM tools and techniques has to go through various important stages which should include the following, Fig. 5.1:

Problem selection: It is vital that the right problem is selected, i.e. the one which causes most concern and not one that we have imagined. It is therefore important in the problem solving process, to ask very much earlier on, whether the right problem has been selected.

Data gathering: This is a very important aspect. Enough data has to be collected using various means. The data has to include various aspects of the business and

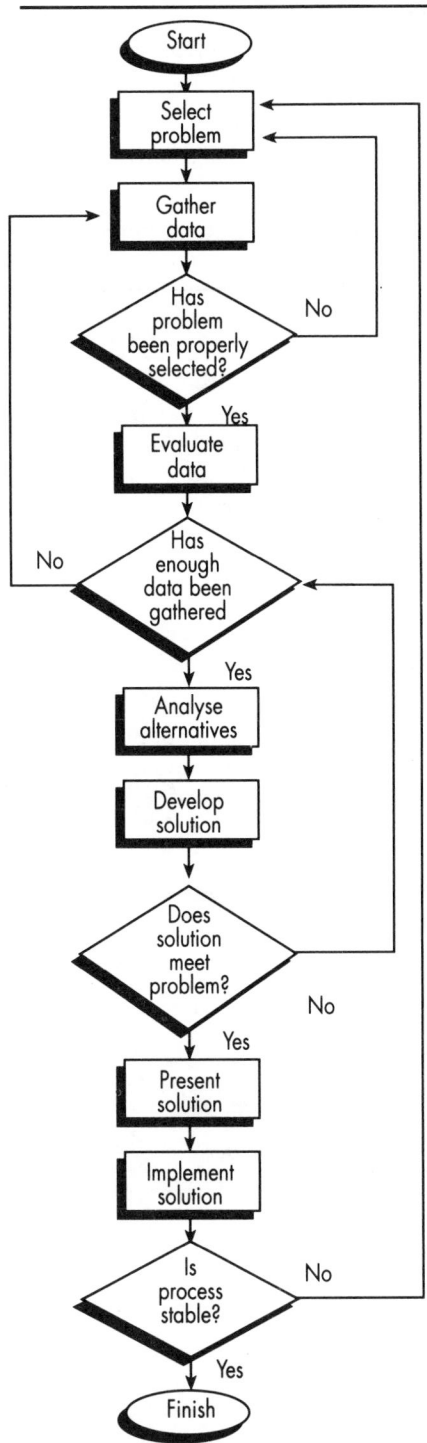

5.1 The problem solving process.

should not just be confined to the process under scrutiny itself. It may be that the solution to the problem lies in some peripheral aspects of the business, which under normal circumstances, would not have been considered to be important.

Fact evaluation: This is a stage which intends to quantify the various data collected and its appropriateness to the problem being considered. It is also a stage where it can be decided whether more data ought to be collected.

Data analysis: This stage tries to relate each piece of data collected to one aspect of the problem and basically tries to put the jig-saw together. It ponders over each solution, its potential, limitations, consequences on other activities and so on.

Solution development: The most effective, practical, economically viable solution is selected, discussed and presented to management.

Solution implementation: The implemented solution has to be monitored and controlled. If further hidden problems have been isolated linked to the same process, then review of the problem selected and data gathered, has to take place. If the solution has been implemented successfully and the process is stable, the problem-solving activity can be moved to another area.

HOW DO WE DEFINE PROCESSES?

Traditionally, processes have been defined as series of transformations of inputs into outputs, Fig. 5.2. The inputs can be referred to as 'causes and conditions' and the outputs as 'outcomes'.[37] The key characteristics of this description of a process is that transformation means adding/creating value in one of three forms:[25]

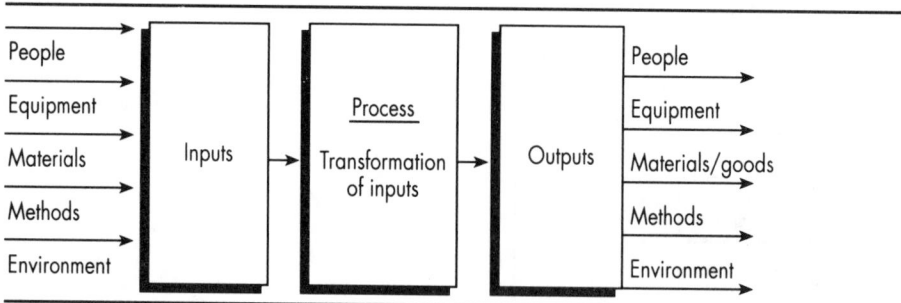

5.2 A traditional model of a process.

● Time value: Products/services are provided when required;
● Place value: Products/services are provided where required;
● Form value: Products/services are provided how required.

This traditional view of 'a process' has got many shortcomings however. It fails to identify, amongst others, the following key points:

- How can a typical process be determined?
- Where does the value added activity start and where does it finish?
- Where does process management and control take place?

In manufacturing industry, processes have always been linked to the physical transformation of raw materials during the production of goods. Consequently, any other activity was perceived as a 'static input' without any link to the value added effort. This perception has therefore meant that process control was confined to shopfloor activities, in particular those which are directly transforming raw materials into end products.

In the context of TQM, this traditional model is unacceptable since it is 'activity focused' and does not value the contribution of all aspects of organisational systems. It is therefore suggested that a process is any activity/task, which has the following features:

- Converts a set of inputs into useful outputs for internal and/or external use;
- Consumes a set of inputs to provide useful outputs for internal and/or external use;
- Provides a visible link in the customer-supplier chain;
- Its effort is geared towards the achievement of organisational objectives;
- Inputs and outputs are based on a mixture of socio-technical elements;
- Resulting outputs are amplified throughout the organisation through a synergistic effort.

Process documentation

Each activity (process) has to be properly documented to include the following:
- Process ownership should be clearly defined with responsibility for improvement already determined;
- Boundaries for each process should be clearly identifiable;
- The flow of each process has to be well understood;
- Process objectives should be clearly identified;
- Process performance should be measured against its objectives;
- Process performance measures should be checked for validity.

Process documentation by answering the above questions is vital if organisations are to achieve superior performance based on TQM philosphy. This effort (documentation) will reflect three main points:

- That strengths and weaknesses of the organisation are well understood. This means that competitive objectives are realistic and tangible;
- That control over activities is tight, since process ownership/responsibility has been allocated throughout the organisation;
- That performance measurement is a distributed activity thus reflecting the overall effort in adding value.

Once organisations have clearly defined all their activities in terms of inter-related processes whose performance can be measured, the next challenge is process improvement.

Process improvement

This is an essential activity and an integral part of TQM philosophy which is based on continuous improvement and the quest for progress to achieve and sustain superior performance. So how can we define process improvement?

Process improvement can be considered as the continued effort of transforming organisational weaknesses into strengths which will contribute towards the achievement of superior performance. Process improvement therefore comes from an investigative effort into the identification of causes and effects. A definition based on cause-effect analysis is the following:[37]

'Process improvement is the continuous endeavour to learn about the cause-and-effect mechanisms in a process to change the process to reduce variation and complexity and improve customer satisfaction. Improvements are

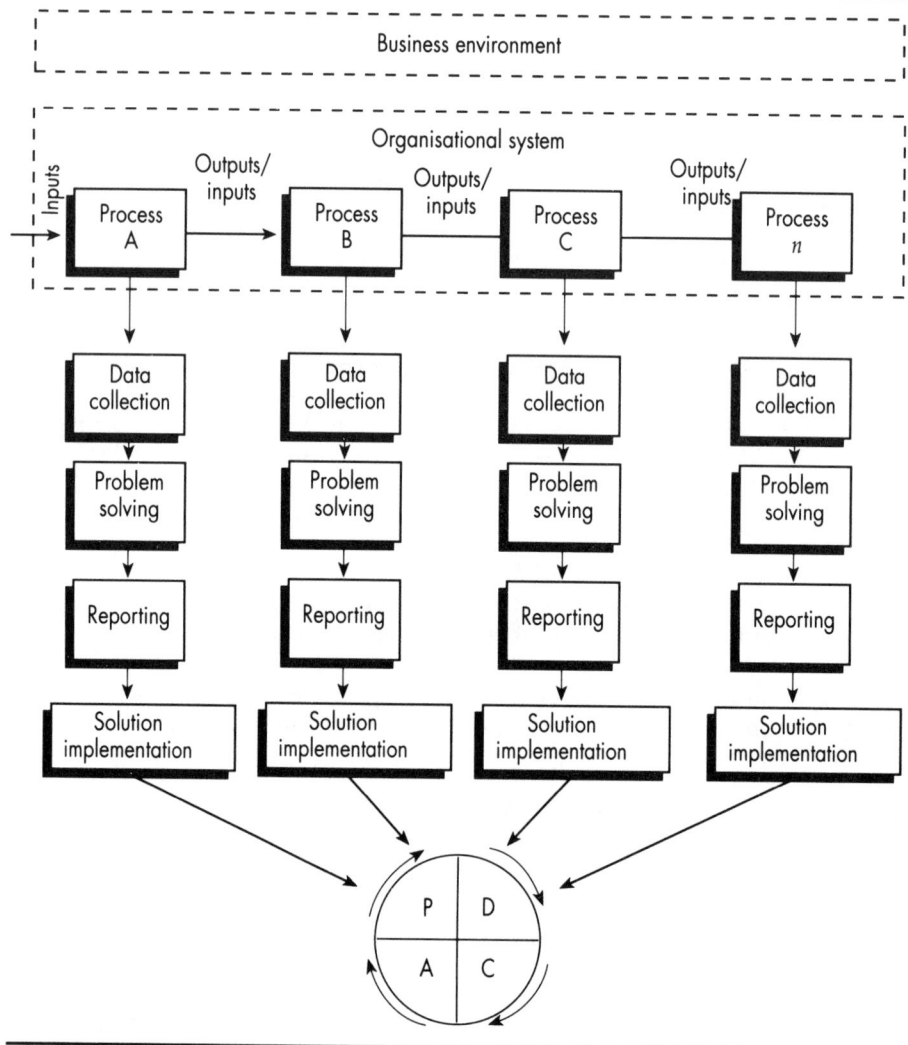

5.3 A model of a process based on TQM.

made through actions that are based on a better understanding of the cause system that affects process performance.'

There are two key words which are mentioned in the above definition – COMPLEXITY and VARIATION.

Complex processes are those which are not well understood. Consequently process improvement in this instance means that the ultimate aim is waste reduction through prevention, appraisal and correction activities (both internal and external).

Simple processes on the other hand, are those which are well understood. The purpose of simplifying processes is waste elimination through doing only what is required and making everything visible within the business environment. In this instance, principles of Zero Defects, Right First Time and Right Every Time are the driving force of the businesses concerned.

In process improvement, activities based on Deming's improvement cycle (Plan, Do, Check and Act) are carried out all the time at each level of organisational systems. Problems are identified, data is collected, problems are solved, solutions are presented in written reports, solutions are implemented. Figure 5.3 represents a dynamic model of process improvement based on TQM philosophy.

Improvement can only be appreciated through measurement. Measurement as has been described,[30] is the key to understanding. Understanding leads to action. Action means positive impact on productivity improvement/business performance. Measurements take place at two levels, Fig. 5.4:

- Macro process measurements measuring organisational collective effort (degree of effectiveness) in fulfilling customer requirements;
- Micro processes measurements measure process dynamics in the overall internal effort of adding value towards satisfying customer demands.

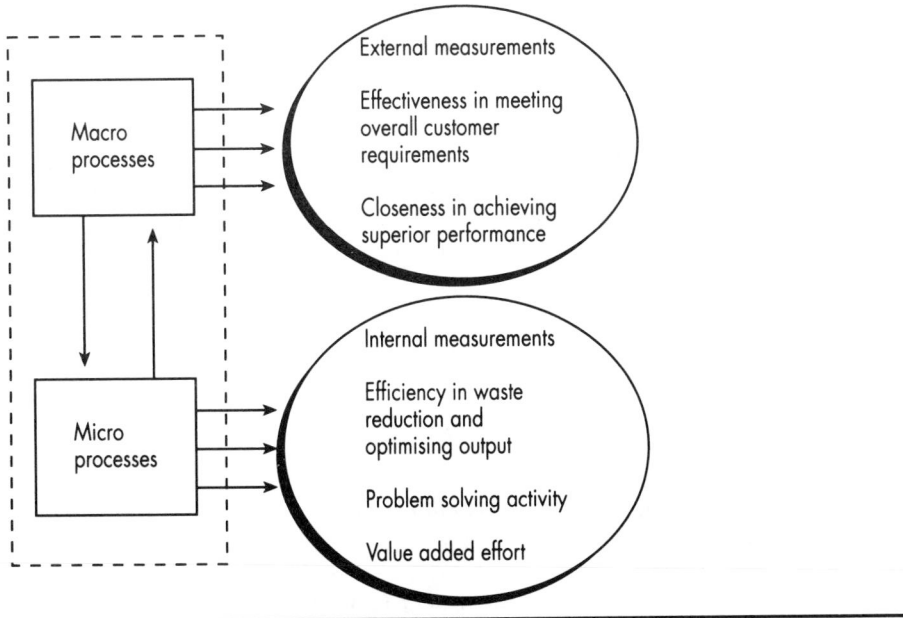

5.4 Organisational systems as a series of sub-processes.

Measurement of process improvement activities can be carried out using a wide range of techniques which can be used both as evaluation tools and methods for improving the processes concerned. Techniques such as process performance checks, process performance evaluation, process capability studies, process improvement programme evolutionary operations and simulation experiments[31] are briefly described in Table 5.1. They tend to tackle issues such as past/existing process performance and true process capability. They can also pinpoint where urgent improvement efforts need to be concentrated and the relative contribution of each variable within the processes. In the context of this chapter we will discuss process capability studies only.

Table 5.1 Process improvement evaluation and improvement techniques

Type of technique	Description
Process performance checks	Quick check procedure using small amount of data at a specific point in time (synoptic picture)
Process performance evaluations	Requires more data, checking period is approximately 1 month (looks at past behaviour of process)
Process capability studies	Studies current production process based on current data. Establishes true capability of process running under control
Process improvement programme	To be undertaken only after a process capability study has been completed. Ultimate goals are to establish a stable and in control process, with uniform output and low degree of waste
Evolutionary operations (EVOP)	To determine the set of optimal manufacturing process conditions required for the achievement of highest quality level
Simulation experiments	To understand the impact of each variable in a process – helps to conduct experiments to look at process variables, process methods

The effort of understanding and simplifying processes is to establish stable processes which can be controlled reliably and confidently. This is not always easy however because of factors internal and external to business organisations, which tend to be difficult to control and cause a phenomenon called VARIATION. This is examined in the next section.

PROCESS VARIATION AND ITS CAUSES

It is widely accepted that variation is inherent in every aspect of life. Processes within business organisations are no exception and are often subject to variation. To understand it one can ask many questions. Is variation the opposite of stable and predictable? Is it something that we can control and eliminate? How long has it been known for, and why hasn't something been done about it?

First, to understand the concept of variation better, one has to refer to two types of causes of variation – common causes and special causes. So what are they?

Common and special causes of variation

Common causes of variation are inherently part of the system (process). They affect everyone associated with the process and tend to act on the system in a predictable manner over time. They are also called random causes. Some examples include:

● Procedures and methods used;
● Education and training given;
● Passing traffic;
● Machine movement;
● Temperature changes.

Special causes are unrelated to the intended design of the process. They do not affect everyone and only arise because of specific circumstances. They are unpredictable and temporary. They are also called assignable causes. Some examples include:

● Tool wear;
● Material variation;
● Poor maintenance;
● Operator performance;
● Electric power surge;
● New methods, procedures;
● Inexperienced or untrained operators.

The use of control charts is a useful way to distinguish between the two types of variation, Fig. 5.5. If it was identified that the process is only limited by common (random) causes, and that the output is not satisfactory to customer requirements, then the only option available is to design a new process.

A process which is only affected by common causes is a stable process, that is a process which is statistically controllable since changes and variations can be predicted over time. The percentage of variation will ultimately determine the acceptability of the process in fulfilling customer requirements. On the other hand, a process which is affected by both special and common causes is unstable regardless of the degree of variation.

Figure 5.5 shows that special causes (assignable) tend to lead to a drift in the

Table 5.2 Different approaches to the interpretation of variation

	Variation that indicates good or bad performance	**Variation that results from common or special causes**
Focus	Outcomes of the process (product of service)	Causes of variation in the process
Aim	Classify outcomes as acceptable or not	Provide a basis for action on the process
Basis	What the customer wants or needs	What the process is actually delivering
Methods	Specifications, budgets, forecasts, numerical goals, other tools for judging performance	Control charts

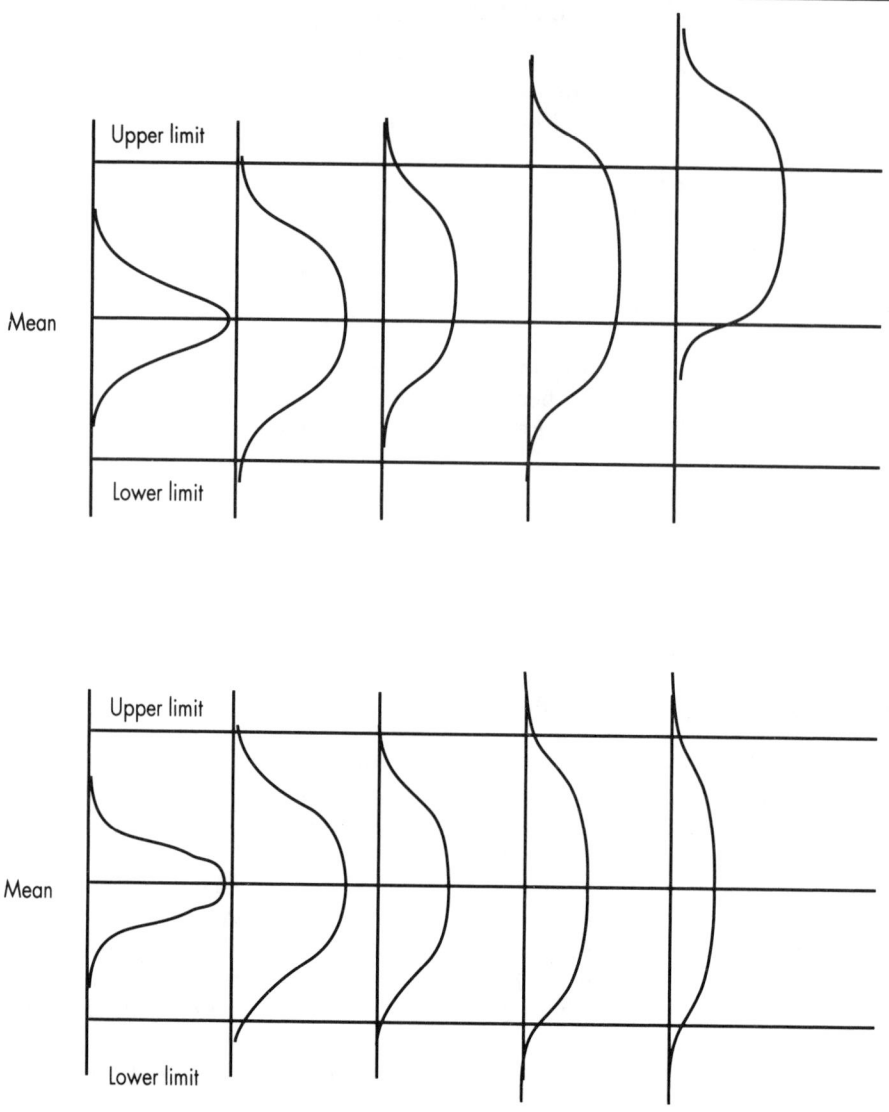

5.5 Special versus common causes of variation.

normal distribution curve from its central position. Common causes show a wide spread in the normal distribution where a continuous effort is required to fine tune the process to minimise waste. This effort of fine tuning means that additional expenditure has to be incurred each time, in order to achieve the required standard of quality levels.

Common and special causes of variation have to be differentiated from the traditional view of variation. The latter is based on a static and mechanistic approach towards making decisions on process/output acceptability. The former is based on a dynamic approach where the intention is to improve quality levels of performance/

output continuously. The latter approach is based on inspection and the former on prevention principles. Table 5.2 illustrates the difference between the two interpretations of variation.[17]

It is clear from this table that study of variation seeks to establish a quest for progress and improvement by asking questions on process limitations and how to tackle them. Performance based on 'good or bad' practice does not unfortunately seek to establish causes of variations. The notion of improvement is non-existent and performance targets are loosely defined.

One is bound to ask the question why business organisations did not implement the study of variation in their processes a long time ago? Is the study of variation a new concept?

The implications of variation

Before the uptake of TQM as a new philosophy of competitiveness, quality was regarded as an END OF LINE function where attention was given more to the end product than the process(es) themselves. INSPECTION was the way variation was studied through a decision making process based on 'acceptable' or 'unacceptable' standards. To some extent this view towards variation tended to reflect a business 'culture' based on interest in output optimisation and profit making objectives at any cost.

The 'hidden' impact of variation was only made visible because TQM calls for processes to be rendered simple and visible so that improvement can become a realistic target. Variation was previously hidden by what has been termed 'buffers'[40] in every single aspect of organisations. Since activities tended to be highly departmentalised, buffers were incorporated in all activities to absorb variation. This therefore meant that high costs had to be incurred for a long time by a large number of business organisations.

Buffers are time and resource based. They affect areas such as:

Schedules: Since there are variations in quality of output;

Lead times: Since quality cannot be controlled adequately, increases are incorporated in set up times, change over times and inspection times;

Inventory levels: The acceptance of waste means that higher inventory levels than necessary have to be carried;

Order quantity: Order quantities have to be increased to accommodate an 'accepted' percentage of waste;

Overtime: Since schedules are not accurately determined, organisations have to compensate for the lack of flexibility in time availability by encouraging overtime activity thus adding extra unnecessary costs to the organisation.

The wider implications for organisation are of course poor knowledge on internal strengths and weaknesses thus leading to a mis-match with a targeted competitive market and more importantly increased customer dissatisfaction and customer defection because of poor quality products/services.

Internally morale may be affected by portioning the blame on people for problems which are beyond their control, by taking peripheral actions with little impact on the real causes of the problem, by 'rocking the boat' whilst the answer may be a simple one.

Benefits of studying variation

Benefits from studying variation can perhaps be analysed at three levels:

Strategic benefits

- Closeness between competitive objectives and organisational capability: organisations will be able to compete on realistic grounds rather than in the land of 'make believe' as has been the case for the majority of organisations and for a long time;
- Ensuring that customer requirements can be achieved through thorough knowledge of strengths and weaknesses: Modern competitiveness under the banners of TQM places a lot of emphasis on SATISFYING customers or even more lately by ENLIGHTENING them. The latter objective can only happen if quality of goods and services can be optimised;
- The pro-active nature of studying variation means that improvement is a means of progressing. Gaining competitive advantage and enhancing business performance should therefore result from the continuous effort in solving problems that tend to de-stabilise organisational processes.

Operational benefits

- Understanding processes means better management control and therefore better quality decisions;
- By establishing identity for each process, the task of integrating various business activities becomes a more realistic one. This effort is of paramount importance if TQM philosophy is to be implemented successfully, since by definition TQM calls for the creation of socio-technical organisational systems performing as a 'mass' with common organisational objectives;
- Value added activity becomes de-centralised showing that improvements can take place in every single aspect of the organisation. This, therefore, will remove the myth that only production adds value and stops distinguishing between what traditionally has been referred to as SUPPORT activities and LINE activities;
- Performance measurement will spread through every single activity of the organisation using both macro and micro indices;
- Great reductions in costs should result through removal of waste, simplifying processes and rendering everything visible;
- Doing what the organisation needs to do rather than ought to be doing;
- Financial quantification becomes based on realistic and true measures of performance rather than on theoretically established measures based on poor knowledge and understanding of organisation's capability.

Organisational benefits

- Continuous flow of information based on provision of required information, FACTUAL information so that accurate decisions and actions can take place;
- Organisational climate based on team work, group effort and organisational objectives;
- A new culture based on localised control of processes, customer-supplier chains and valued contribution at every level;

● Knowledge work, flexibility and the encouragement of creative output in terms of quality rather than quantity.

There can be many more advantages resulting from the study of variation. Depending on the level of commitment and determination to incorporate process improvement at the heart of business activities, the degree of benefits achieved will vary from organisation to organisation.

WHAT ARE THE TOOLS AND TECHNIQUES FOR TQM?

There are two categories of tools and techniques used in quality improvement – Ishikawa's seven tools and the seven new tools for managing quality.

Ishikawa's tools for quality improvement

Ishikawa's tools and techniques are based on statistical techniques. This is because he argues, like many others, that quality cannot be managed and improved upon without use of statistics. He has categorised the statistical techniques which can be used in the area of quality improvement in three categories:[41]

Elemental statistical techniques

● Pareto analysis;
● Cause and effect diagram;
● Stratification;
● Check sheets;
● Scatter diagram;
● Graph and Shewart control chart.

Intermediate statistical techniques

● Theory of sampling surveys;
● Statistical sampling inspection;
● Various methods of statistical estimation and hypothesis testing;
● Methods of utilising sensory tests;
● Methods of experiment design.

Advanced statistical method (using computers)

● Advanced experimental design;
● Multivariate analysis;
● Operations research methods.

The seven elemental statistical techniques are perhaps considered the most widely used tools. Ishikawa recommends their use to everyone in the organisation. His experience shows that 95% of the encountered quality problems can be solved by using the seven elemental techniques. It is important, according to Ishikawa, that everyone learns how to use the basic techniques from operator level, to the CEO. He argues that the reason for the competitive gap between Japan and the West is that the latter tended to leave the area of quality control to a minority of people within the organisation, considered to be specialists in statistical analysis. In Japan however, because quality is everybody's responsibility, statistical techniques tend to have a much wider usage.

Why are statistical techniques important in TQM?

It is strongly believed that modern competitiveness is largely based on the tight management and control of information. Indeed, the quality of decision-making on an everyday basis and various levels of organisational systems is indicative of the quality of information being constantly communicated. With this argument in mind, statistics are a means by which quality information can be obtained and communicated. They are a language, the means of creating and communicating quantitative concepts and ideas.[34] They are concerned with the collection, analysis and interpretation of information contained in data.

By following an iterative process following steps such as hypothesis formulation – deduction (of its consequences) – experimentation – data analysis – induction (from the results) – formulation of new hypothesis, new knowledge can be gained, which will help in two different ways:

(i) By providing a better understanding of process characteristics;
(ii) By measuring the reliability of observations made and data collected through pinpointing what the real problem is, and how one should go about solving it.

Statistics therefore do not only help control existing processes by ensuring their stability. They are the best means by which quality improvements can be achieved. By using techniques such as experiment design, processes/products performance can be optimised and variation greatly reduced/eliminated.

The seven new quality improvement techniques

In addition to Ishikawa's statistical techniques, there are seven new tools (although, it is claimed that they originated in 1972 in Japan).[29] These techniques are thought to have been developed for the purpose of 'creative output' or 'quality thinking'. They are reported to help by providing the ability to lead to the following:

● Process verbal information;
● Complete tasks;
● Eliminate failure;
● Assist in the exchange of information;
● Dissemination of information to concerned parties;
● Provide a complete history of actions to promote improvement (as an incentive to ensure continued motivation to improve).

Table 5.3 illustrates the seven new tools of quality improvement.[29]

Table 5.3 The seven new tools of quality

Name	Description
The relations diagram method	Used to relate complex Cause and Effect relationships
KJ method: affinity diagram	Gives some order to verbal data by collation into similar categories so that it can be systematically analysed
The systematic diagram	Helps planning effectively so that objectives are achieved. It does this by showing the sequencing and inter-relationships so that the resulting actions are error-free
The matrix diagram method	Helps clarify problems through multidimensional thinking. It studies the relationships between elements by showing the strength/weakness of factors' influence thus helping understand problem better
Matrix data analysis	Requires complex mathematical skills, relies on systematic organisation and presentation of data so that relationships can be examined
PDPC (Process Decision Programme Chart) Method	Helps select best processes to use to obtain the desired results. It not only evaluates existing progress but also looks at alternatives through newly gained knowledge. So it is a dynamic approach
The arrow diagram method	Helps establish most suitable daily plan for a project and also controls its progress. Uses arrows to define all the tasks required for the project, takes into account timing for each task

This chapter only considers the seven elemental statistical techniques which Ishikawa strongly recommends and which are the most widely used techniques for quality improvement.

Flowcharts

To be able to study a process and measure its degree of variation/stability, one has to understand it. Flowcharts therefore are a means by which processes can be represented pictorially. A typical flowchart is represented in Fig. 5.1 at the beginning of this chapter. Flowcharts are usually built by using six symbols, Fig. 5.6. The

○ Process start

□ Processing/operating symbol

▱ Data/information input symbol

◇ Decision symbol

——▶ Flowline symbol

⬭ Process ends

5.6 Flowcharting symbols.

symbols can lead to an accurate and up to date representation of the process being considered and are the best means by which complex aspects can be simplified and communicated.

There are two types of flowcharts:

(i) Systems flowcharts represent the behaviour and interplay of various operations. This type of flowcharting represents DYNAMIC processes and usually includes feed back loops;
(ii) The second type of flowcharting represents current layout of work and location of equipment and machinery. It is designed to improve on floor space and simplify work flow. It is not therefore dynamic but only DESCRIPTIVE of current work flow.

Flowcharts for the study of processes have various advantages.[25] Table 5.4 illustrates some of the key benefits of using flowcharts.

Table 5.4 Advantages of using flowcharts

Advantage	Description
Communication tool	Best means of representing complex operations and illustrating inter-relationships between various activities
Planning tool	The detail obtained from building a flowchart can be used for changing or building new processes
Provides an overview of the system	Removes unnecessary details and represents exactly what is happening
Defines roles, determines inter-relationships	Facilitates inter-departmental, inter-functional co-operation by showing existing relationships
Promotes logical accuracy and troubleshooting	Enables people to identify errors and inaccuracies and thus helps in process optimisation
Documents a system	The best means by which processes can be understood and thus properly documented

Flowcharting cannot be carried out in an ad-hoc manner. There are some simple rules to be followed.[13,25]

1 It is necessary to involve the right people who are directly or indirectly involved in the design, operation, maintenance, control or supply of the process. Thus all customers and suppliers in the particular part of the chain have to be involved;

2 Involvement means encouraging people to participate by providing details and information on that part of the process which they are directly involved in;

3 Participation for process flowcharting has to be based on the collection and provision of data and information. Opinions or uncertainties have to be excluded;

4 The timescale in building a thorough and accurate flowchart has to be adequate. Time limits can mean the omission of a crucial part or operation of the process;

5 All the questions asked have to reflect accurately ownership and boundaries of the process by using a who, where, what, why, when, how much, etc, approach;

6 Flowcharts have to be drawn starting from the top of a page to the bottom, and from left to right (INPUT → CONVERSION → OUTPUT);

7 Each activity has to be carefully defined (by a verb and an objective);

8 Each activity must be accurately documented;

9 Activities have to appear in a sequential order on the flowchart;

10 No branching is allowed – 'dangling' of activities has got to be eliminated. Activities which are part of the process are inter-related. If they are not, the branching will show it and therefore they have to be discarded.

Cause and effect diagrams (Ishikawa diagram)

Cause and effect diagrams are a problem solving technique developed in 1943 by Ishikawa in Japan as a result of workers being confused by the number of factors which influence a process and thus finding it difficult to solve process-related problems. The diagram is developed after brainstorming, by identifying a problem to be solved (i.e. effect) and the likely causes.

A tree comparison was drawn up to explain the relationship between causes and effects.[24]

FOLIAGE VISIBLE → EFFECTS VISIBLE
ROOTS HIDDEN   → CAUSES HIDDEN

The foliage of a tree represents the symptoms or the effects of the problem. The roots under the ground are the causes of the problem. A typical cause and effect (C & E) diagram is represented in Fig. 5.7. It is sometimes called a 'fishbone diagram' because of its similarity to the spine of a fish.

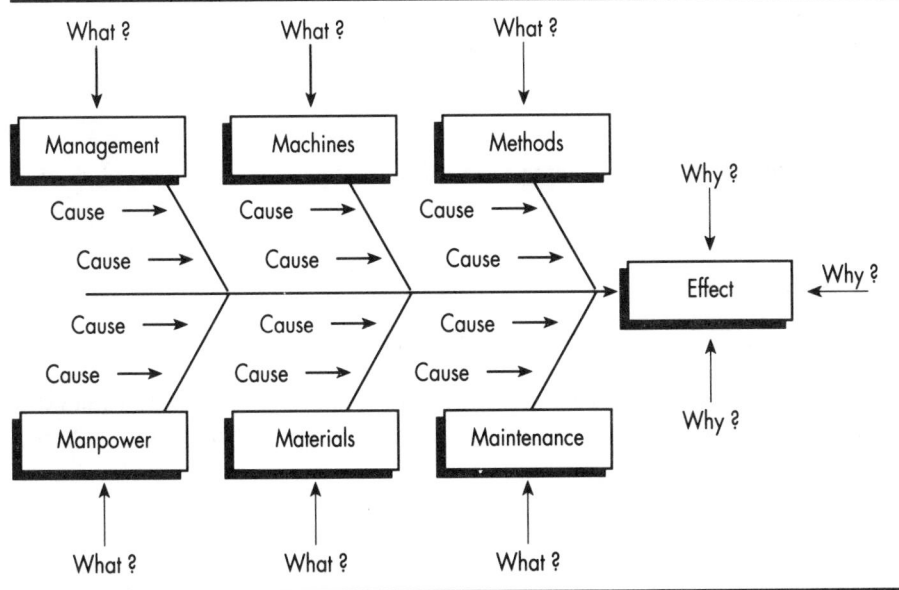

5.7 Cause and effect diagram.

There are various stages which have to be followed during the building of a C & E diagram:

1 State what the problem (effect) is: This is usually arrived at by looking at and by knowing exactly what the nature of the effect is and the major causes which have led to the effect;

2 The major causes have to be listed in categories using commonly accepted classes such as Ms (for machines, methods, manpower, etc) or Ps (people, plant, procedures, etc);

3 Potential causes should now be added to each category. This is arrived at through brainstorming. Ideas are not judged for their validity at this point;

4 Prioritising the sub-causes. All the causes are evaluated after a period of 'incubation'. The impact of each cause can be investigated by asking questions as to whether the cause is a variable or an attribute; whether it can be flowcharted; whether one can collect data on it (e.g. control charts) and what is the degree of its interaction with other causes;

5 This refinement process will lead to a shortlisting of the major causes;

6 The impact of each major cause can now be assessed by gathering data on each, through a process of asking, 'why'. This process should automatically lead to the isolation of the most likely cause.

C & E diagrams are usually used for one of the following reasons:

(i) **Root cause analysis:** This is also called cause enumeration analysis and involves in depth analysis of each cause by asking questions based on who, what, where, when, why, how. Each cause becomes treated as the effect;

(ii) **Process analysis** (also known as process classification): Each step (operation) of the process is thoroughly investigated to isolate possible causes which lead to the overall effect in the process being studied. Once all stages have been examined, the major causes can be isolated to establish their impact.

(iii) **Dispersion analysis:** A typical C & E analysis by listing all the possible causes on the same diagram.

Table 5.5 represents the advantages and disadvantages of each type of C & E analysis.[14]

Check sheets

Check sheets are used to collect data that will be used towards solving the problem selected. This TQM tool is important, as it provides the facts. There are many questions which have to be answered before data collection starts. The following need to be closely examined before the action plan for gathering information is allowed:

What do we mean by data?

Data represents the 'raw materials' or inputs which will be used to provide information that will enable the right decisions to be made. Basically the data collected is information which needs value added to it. It is the process of

Table 5.5 Advantages and disadvantages of various C & E analysis diagrams

Type of diagram	Advantages	Disadvantages
Dispersion analysis	Helps organise and relate factors	Might be difficult to facilitate if developed in true brainstorming fashion
	Provides a structure for brainstorming	Might become complex; requires dedication and patience
	Involves everyone	
	It's fun	
Process analysis	Provides a solid sequential view of the process and the factors that influence each step	It is sometimes difficult to identify or demonstrate inter-relationships
	Might help determine functional ownership for the work to be done in improvement	
Root cause	Easy to facilitate	The added step of creating an affinity diagram might add time to the process
	Provides in-depth list of all possible causes	The final diagram might be difficult to draw because of the random output of the brainstorming session

transforming information collected so that it can be used for continuous improvement.

Is there more than one type of data?

Data is principally numerical of which there are two types:

Attribute data: Go or no-go situations, binary classification, things which can be counted;

Variable data: Data which can be collected on a continuous scale. Things that can be measured.

Which type of data should be collected?

The answer to this question is the process which is under investigation. Check sheets should not be designed until the process has been properly understood and the problem clearly identified.

How do we go about designing a check sheet?

The design of the check sheet has to allow valuable information to be obtained. Whilst this is the desired outcome, it is important to keep the sheet as simple as possible so that the entire investigative effort is put towards collecting the right type of information. The sheet should also be designed so that data is collected over a certain time scale. The analysis of information will only become meaningful if enough data has been collected.

Who collects the data?

It is important that the people who understand the process best, perhaps those who are responsible for the problem, are asked to collect the information. The data collected has to be precisely attributed to the right cause so that the analysis gives accurate outcomes. Process/problem 'owners' have to be adequately trained for this task. A pre-trial exercise will make sure that the effort of data collection is as intended.

How many types of check sheets are there?

Attribute check sheet: This is a sheet designed to collect data on the number of defects in a process. The sheet can include all the possible causes and observations on defects. These are placed on the sheet systematically over a predetermined period of time, Fig. 5.8.

Switchboard monitoring incoming calls

Source of calls received	Monday 9 am- 5 pm	Tuesday 9 am- 5 pm	Wednesday 9 am- 5 pm	Thursday 9 am- 5 pm	Friday 9 am- 5 pm
Sales reps	卌 II	IIII	III	卌JII	卌 卌 I
Existing customers	III	卌 III	卌 卌J		卌 II
General enquiries	卌 卌JIII	IIII	卌 IIII	卌 卌JIIII	卌 IIII
Employee relations	IIII	II	卌 I	IIII	II
Total	27	18	28	26	29

5.8 A check sheet for attribute data.

The check sheet in Fig. 5.8 represents an investigation on the number of incoming phone calls to an organisation and the sources and frequency of calls made.

Variable check sheet: This is a sheet designed to collect data on variables through a process of measurement. The measurements follow a frequency distribution. Figure 5.9 represents an example of the fluctuations in temperature on a printing machine based on the gravure method, using plastics inks.

Defect location sheet: A pictorial representation of a product where the operator can pinpoint the location of the defect. The frequency of the crosses placed by the operator can determine which is the most likely cause.

Data collection on its own is not usually enough to provide the information required on the problem being investigated. This is usually obtained by a process of stratifying the data as discussed below.

For data collection to lead to positive outcomes, it must be conducted so that issues such as total incorporation of all the activities of the process under scrutiny are included. The process must not be changed or modified during the course of

Standard temperature: 200°C

Date / Time	Registered temperature: (°C)				
	Week 1	Week 2	Week 3	Week 4	Week 5
7.00	203	208	198	211	197
10.00	205	212	209	209	198
13.00	201	206	202	207	203
16.00	198	205	202	200	208
Daily average					
Fluctuation daily					

5.9 A variable check sheet: a study of fluctuations in temperature of rollers on an ink printing machine.

investigation, the data collected must be complete and the whole exercise must be clear of bias such as operator's opinions, measurement techniques based on estimation, etc.

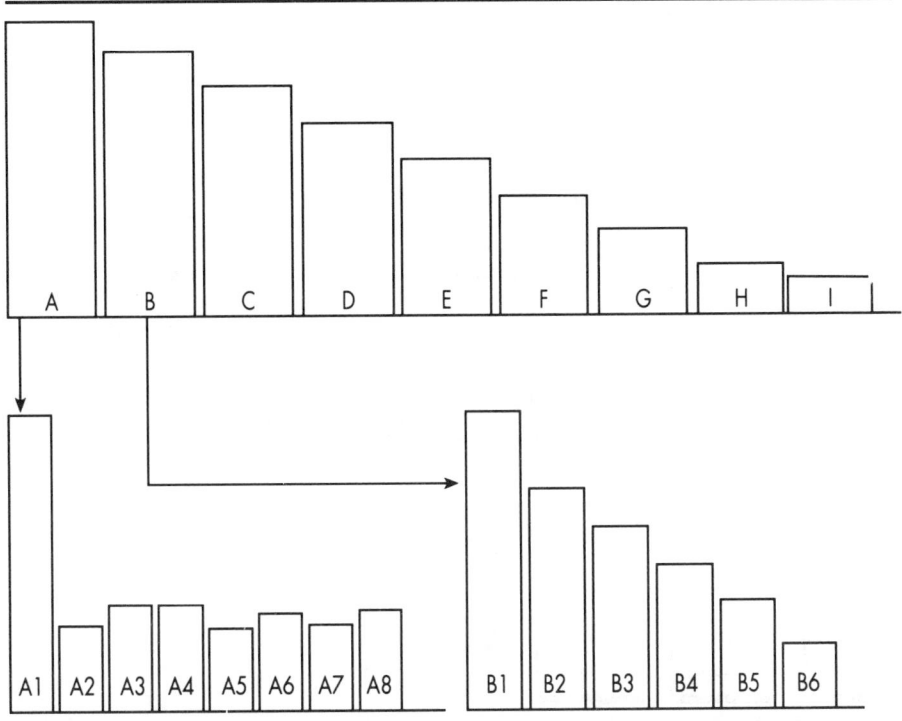

5.10 Stratification using Pareto diagram.

Data stratification

Stratification is the process of subdividing collected data in order to understand the causes better and to reach the key cause by finding what is termed the 'countermeasures' or corrective actions.

Stratification can be used with the various TQM tools and techniques. For example with Pareto diagrams, once the various observations have been represented, the key causes can be stratified to give further diagrams thus leading to the appropriate countermeasure to be adopted in order to solve the problem, Fig. 5.10.

Sometimes when Pareto diagrams show that there is little distinction between the causes (called old mountain Pareto diagram), further causes have to be added, by revisiting the process under investigation and looking for further characteristics to be studied. The newly obtained diagram (called new mountain Pareto diagram) should show that an 80:20 rule exists.

Stratification can also be used for C & E diagrams. If there are two major sub-causes for example which are thought to have equally strong influence on the effect under study, the two sub-causes can themselves be investigated under C & E analysis to find out the most effective countermeasures, Fig. 5.11.

Stratification can also be used in conjunction with Pareto and C & E diagrams combined or control charts, Pareto and C & E diagrams combined.

Stratification has to lead to the right countermeasures otherwise further problems will ensue. In addition, stratification requires enough data to eliminate the problem

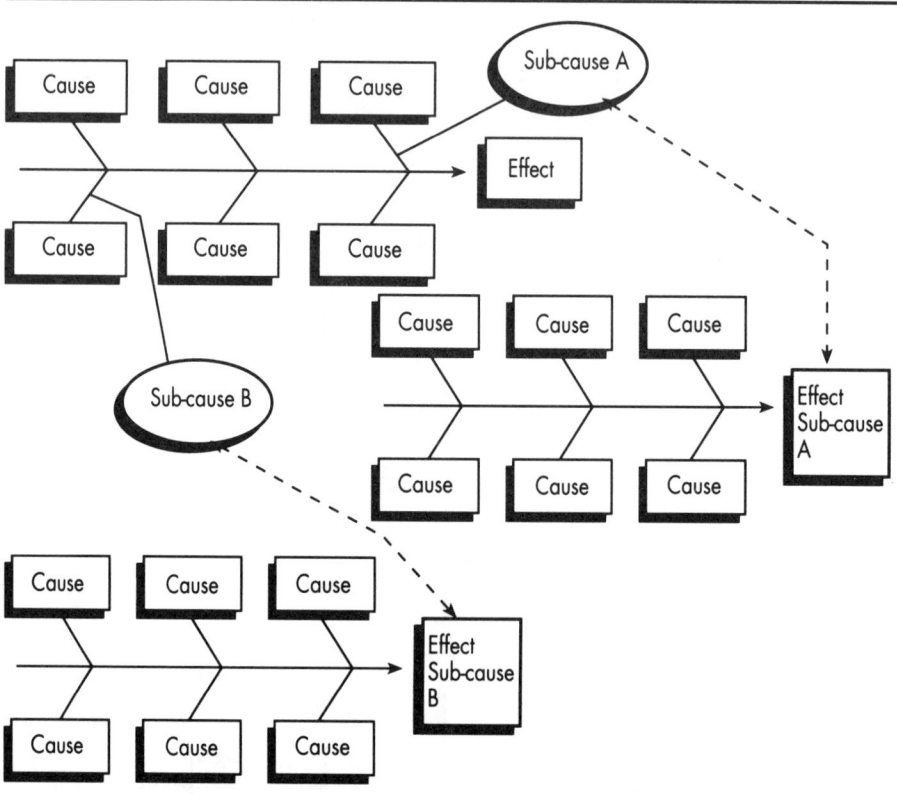

5.11 Stratification using Cause and Effect diagram.

altogether. If there are only a few data points available, stratification will lead to countermeasures only effective for the specific situation and conditions. This is called single case boring.

Pareto diagram

Pareto analysis is mainly a prioritisation tool for problem solving. Its origins are attributed to Vilfredo Pareto, an Italian economist (1848–1923). Pareto in his economic studies came to the conclusion that in every country, the vast majority of wealth is owned and controlled by a small number of people. The Pareto principle has since been widely used, for example in the area of inventory management and control. It is sometimes called the 80:20 rule or the ABC principle where a small category of materials (20%) controls 80% of the total costs.

In relation to quality, the Pareto principle was first used by Joseph Juran back in 1950 when he identified that there was a maldistribution of quality losses. He has since identified that most effects result from a small number of causes. He termed the 20% important causes 'the vital few' and the 80% less important 'the trivial many'. Figure 5.12 is a typical representation of a Pareto diagram.

Cause frequency

Type of cause	Data collected	Frequency
A	THL THL THL II	17
B	THL IIII	9
C	THL THL IIII	14
D	THL I	6
E	III	3

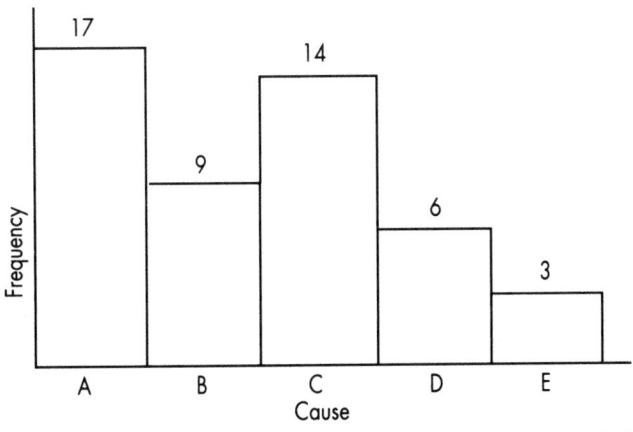

5.12 Pareto analysis: 80:20 rule.

In the example in Fig. 5.12, causes A & C are considered the vital few and B, D and E the trivial many.

Later on, Juran[15] revised the word 'trivial'. He argued that in quality all the causes are important and have to be closely considered by management. He changed the term to the 'useful many'.

To construct a Pareto diagram, the following steps have to be followed:

(i) The various causes which are thought to lead to the effect studied have to be identified;
(ii) A check sheet is designed and measurements carried out on the frequency of occurrence of each cause;
(iii) The various causes are plotted by their frequency on a bar chart (Fig. 5.12) with the highest from the left of the graph;
(iv) A cumulative line (cum line) is plotted on the Pareto diagram, Fig. 5.13;
(v) The diagram should have all the data, percentages, description of causes and titles on it;
(vi) If the causes are translated in terms of costs then a cumulative cost chart can be plotted to show the relative impact.

Cause frequency

Cause	Frequency	Relative %	Cumulative frequency	Cumulative %
A	17	35	17	35
B	9	18	26	53
C	14	29	40	82
D	6	12	46	94
E	3	6	49	100

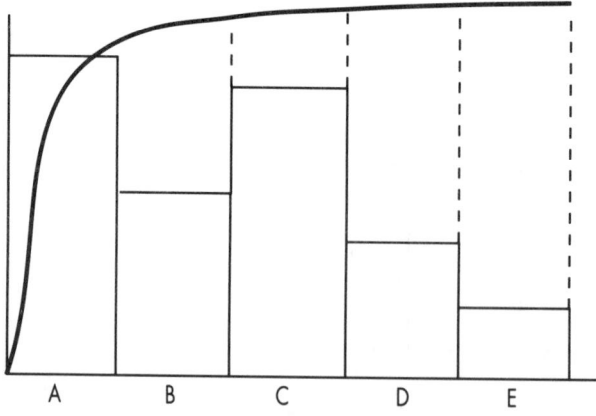

5.13 Pareto diagram based on cumulative frequency.

Pareto diagrams can be used for many purposes. For example in continuous improvement, they show the impact of improvement actions on the causes. A cumulative curve will show the extent of % reduction.

Histograms

The development of the histogram is attributed to a French statistician, A M Guerry, in 1833. A histogram represents variation in sets of data pictorially. This is useful, particularly as numerical data can sometimes be difficult to visualise and interpret.

All data is subject to variation. Different causes show different patterns of variation. A histogram demonstrates the 'distribution' in the level of variation. It is characterised by three constituents, a centre, a width and an overall shape.

There are various types of histograms reflecting different patterns of variation. Figure 5.14 illustrates the eight main types and Table 5.6 represents a short comparison between them.

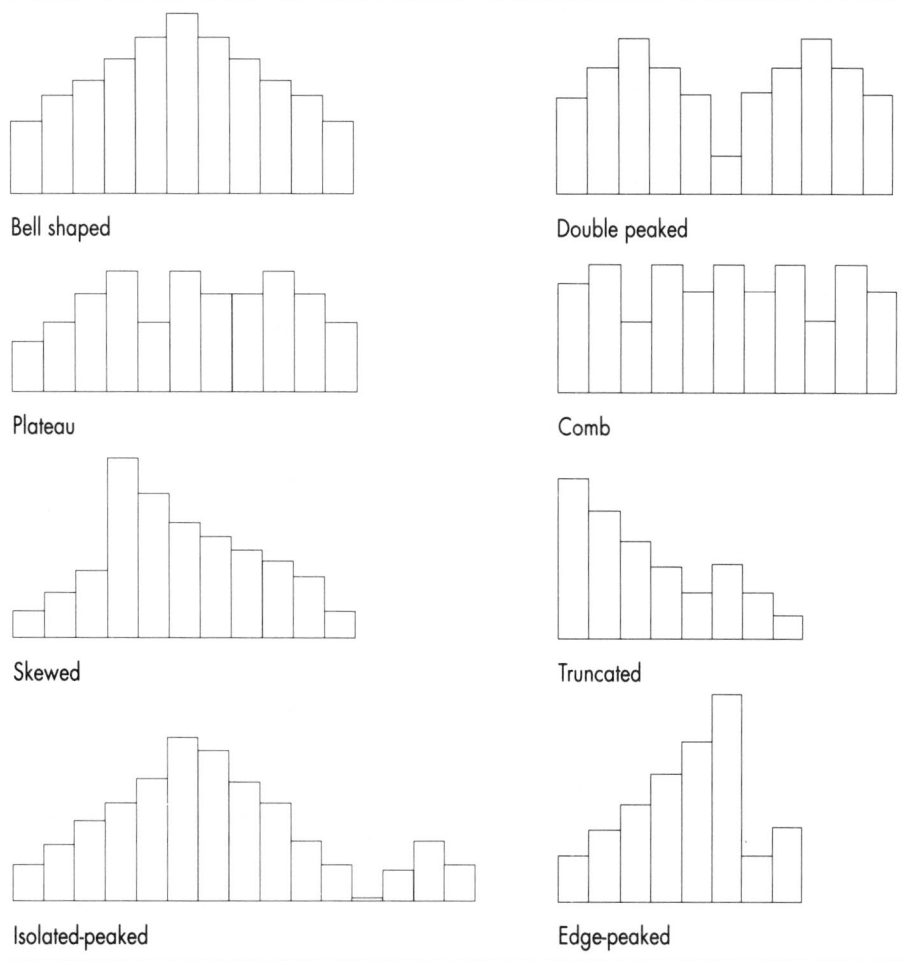

Bell shaped

Double peaked

Plateau

Comb

Skewed

Truncated

Isolated-peaked

Edge-peaked

5.14 Various types of histograms.

Table 5.6 Different types of histograms: A comparison

Name	Description
Bell-shaped distribution	Symmetrical shape with a peak in the middle, representing a normal distribution
Double-peaked distribution	Two normal distributions with two peaks in the middle indicating two processes at work
Plateau distribution	Flat top, no distinct peak and no tails – suggesting that there may be more than one distribution at work
Comb distribution	Alternative peaks, showing possible errors in data collection and analysis
Skewed distribution	An assymetrical shape – could be positively or negatively skewed – usually reflects limits in the specifications on one side (meaning less data is available on one side)
Truncated distribution	An asymmetrical shape with a peak at the end. Usually is part of a normal distribution with part of it having been removed (could be positively or negatively truncated)
Isolated peak distribution	Two normal distributions (one small and one large) suggesting two processes taking place at the same time
Edged peaked distribution	A normal distribution curve with a large peak at one end – indicates errors in data recording

Histograms are the best means by which facts are presented, particularly to the sceptics. It is however important to remember that a histogram is not by itself a conclusive way to problem solving. It merely points the direction towards further probing, observation, data recording and analysis before solutions are implemented that will solve the problem once and for all. It is vital that the histogram represents a current status and an existing behaviour of the process under scrutiny. If changes have taken place subsequently to the data collection exercise, the data collected is no longer representative of the process behaviour and a fresh set of data has to be obtained. Furthermore, to represent variation of the process accurately, enough data has to be collected. Small amounts of data are inadequate in reflecting what actually tends to take place.

Scatter diagrams

A scatter diagram, also called a 'correlation' diagram, aims to establish relationships between two variables. The scatter diagram is an investigative tool which works backward by plotting the effect against experimentally controlled changes in the causes in the process. For example there might be a correlation between employee knowledge of the process and waste production. A strong correlation would indicate that waste production is caused mainly by employee lack of training. The strength of the correlation is determined by the 'correlation coefficient' which can be calculated.

Scatter diagrams are useful when the process is complex and the causes are not obvious or appear to have similar impact on the effect. They are particularly useful for complex processes such as those in the chemical industry, where there are too many variables at work. Correlation can be represented either positively or negatively and can be strong or weak. Lack of correlation is shown by a general scatter of data, Fig. 5.15.

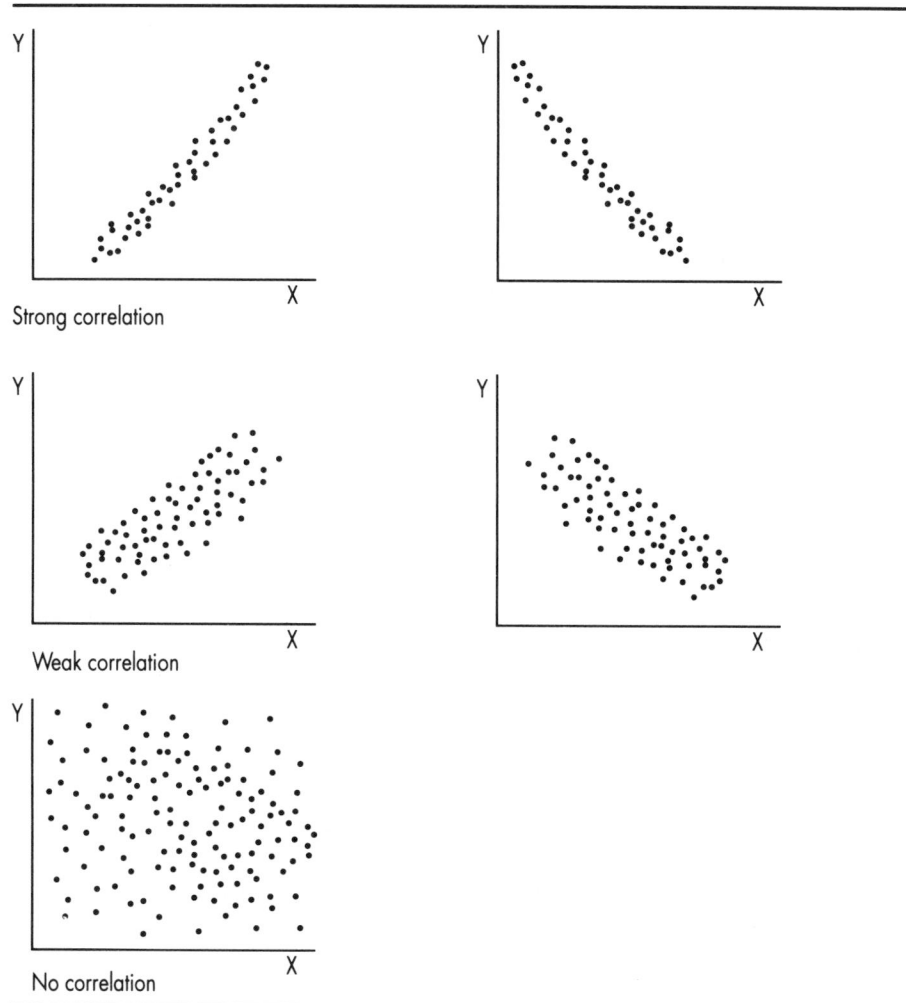

5.15 Correlation – Scatter diagram.

Drawing a scatter diagram is straightforward. The axes of the graph should represent effect (y axis) and cause (x axis). After all the points have been plotted, a line of best fit is drawn and the correlation coefficient is then calculated to indicate the degree of strength of the correlation.

It is important to remember once again that a scatter diagram is not a conclusive way of solving the problem investigated. Whether there is a strong relationship or lack of it does not necessarily mean that the investigative effort is complete. Further investigation should be carried out to make sure that the existence or lack of correlations can be confirmed.

Control charts

As it has been accepted that all processes are subject to some form of variation, the purpose of using control charts is to stabilise the process by keeping it under control and carrying out the necessary adjustments (on line). Control charts were introduced in 1926 by Walter Shewart who concluded that a distribution can be transformed into a normal shape by estimating its mean and standard deviation. A stable distribution was defined as one where variation does not exceed the set limits more than 0.26% of the time.

To arrive at a definition of a stable distribution, Shewart used the central limit theorem.[12] The theorem has three aspects which relate to control charts:

- The distribution of the averages, from individual items averages of a certain population, form a normal distribution curve (Gaussian shape);
- The distribution of the averages will have the same mean as the distribution of individual items;
- The distribution of averages will have a standard deviation much narrower than that of the distribution of individual items.

The mean and standard deviation represents a measure of accuracy and precision. Accuracy and precision have been defined as follows:[18]

Accuracy: The closeness of agreement between an observed value and an accepted reference value.

Precision: The closeness of agreement between randomly selected individual measurements or results. Thus, it is a measure of how widely spread or distributed a group of measurements is when an attempt is made to measure the same thing repeatedly and produce the same result.

The mean or average (μ) and the spread of values (σ standard deviation) are represented in Fig. 5.16. Using central limit theorem, upper and lower control limits are set at ± 3 standard deviations:

- 68.3% of the values of the variable will be within $\mu \pm \sigma$;
- 95.4% of the values of the variable will be within $\mu \pm 2$ standard deviations or probability of 5%;
- 99.7% of the values of the variable will be within $\mu \pm 3$ standard deviations or probability of 0.26%;

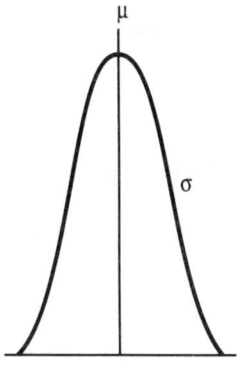

5.16 Natural distribution of a continuous variable.

Control of variables

(i) Mean charts: Periodic samples of a given sample size are taken at a pre-determined time period from the process under investigation (for example sub-groups of 25 readings from a sample size of four, every two hours). The mean from each subgroup is then calculated (mean X) and then the sample mean is calculated ($\bar{X}$). The various means and the sample mean are then recorded on a mean chart, Fig. 5.17.

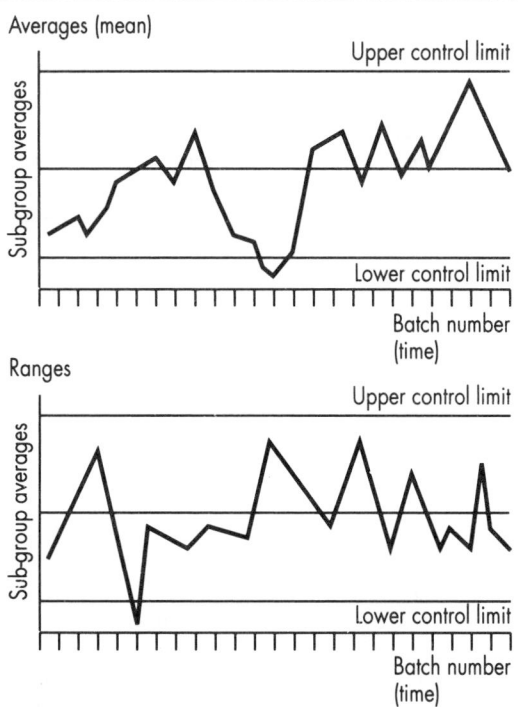

5.17 A typical mean and range chart.

Control limits for the mean chart are calculated by using the following formulae:

Upper control limit $= \bar{X} + A_2 \times \bar{R}$

Lower control limit $= \bar{X} - A_2 \times \bar{R}$

The control limits represent values which will not exceed 1 in 40 chances (warning limits) and 1 in 1,000 chances (action limits).

(ii) Range charts: This type of chart controls the spread of the process. This is important, particularly in instances when although the process mean (accuracy) is stable, process variability (precision) could be alarmingly out of control, Fig. 5.17.

Usually mean and range charts are used together. Control limits for range charts are arrived at using the following formulae:

Upper control limit = $D_4 \times \bar{R}$

Lower control limit = $D_3 \times \bar{R}$

The values for constants A_2, D_3 and D_4 vary according to the size of the sub-groups. The values can be obtained from standard tables.

Control of attributes

Attribute control is different from variables control because analysis relies on collecting the fraction of percent defective out of a sample using a process of collecting some items, checking them and plotting the fraction of defectives, for example checking colour, general finish of painted articles, etc,. The process of selection of acceptable or defective articles is called a binomial distribution. Control charts in this instance rely on the sample size (n) and proportion of defectives (p). The control chart (np) gives the number defective over a period of time. The chart looks similar to mean and range charts.

Control limits in this instance can be calculated using the mean (np) and the standard deviation $\sqrt{np\,(1-p)}$:

Action lines at $np \pm 3 \sqrt{np\,(1-p)}$

i.e. at a mean of $\pm 3\,\sigma$

Warning lines at $np \pm \sqrt{np\,(1-p)}$

i.e. at mean of $\pm 2\sigma$

If a constant sample cannot be used, a chart (p) showing a proportion of a fraction of defectives can be used. It is often difficult to inspect defectives of equal sample size because one has to wait for samples of large enough sizes so that inspection can be carried out.

A less used chart for attribute control is the C chart. This relies on counting the number of defects found on a surface of a unit. C charts are used mostly in industries such as glass, metal, plastics and paper, where product units consist of sheets. A C chart is based on Poisson statistical distribution rather than normal or binomial distribution.

The standard deviation (σ) is calculated by:

$\sigma = \sqrt{\bar{C}}$

where $\bar{C}$ = average number of defects per surface area. The control limits are calculated as follows:

Upper control limit = $\bar{C} + 3 \sqrt{\bar{C}}$

Lower control limit = $\bar{C} - 3 \sqrt{\bar{C}}$

$\bar{C}$ = sum of number of defects of a sampled surface area divided by the number of samples (usually 25).

The C chart is used for controlling processes by measuring the number of defects over a period of time with the sample size remaining constant. If however the sample size is to vary, then a different chart called the u chart can be used instead.

Cusum charts

Cumulative sum charts are useful for the detection of small changes in variables and attributes that cannot be shown clearly by other control charts. By selecting a reference value and subtracting it from every single data point, the results can be plotted, Fig. 5.18.

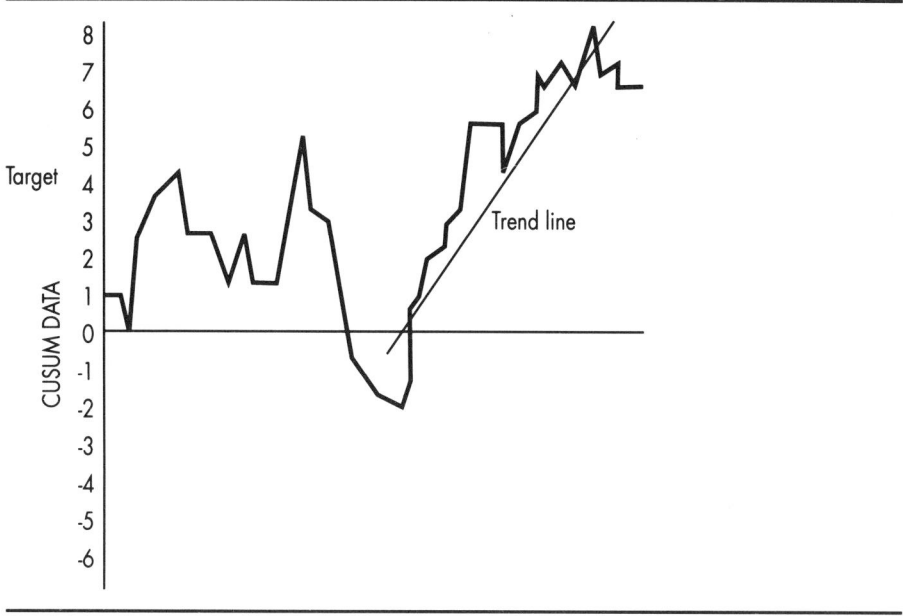

5.18 A typical cusum chart.

If the process is out of control, this can soon be detected. A horizontal line shows stability in the process, a positive or negative line shows that the process has been under or over adjusted. It is also useful to draw a dotted line to see the trend patterns that the chart depicts.

Cusum charts have to be used alongside control charts if the process is to be put in control and has to remain in control. On-line control therefore will depend on the use of control charts for attributes and variables. Cusum charts are more useful when enough data has been collected on the process to study trends. Control charts react to slight change quickly, Cusum charts look at consistency and persistence of changes over a period of time.

PROCESS CAPABILITY

Process capability (PC) is the study which needs to be undertaken to determine whether the process is stable and whether it will remain stable. It has been defined as follows:[8]

'PC is the results of which the process is capable under stable conditions; it is, in essence, a prediction developed through the application of statistical theory as to whether a process is capable of meeting the specification limits necessary to fulfill the requirements of the product design.'

Process capability therefore is the ability of the process to meet customer requirements again and again by asking the following questions:

- How stable is the process? Could we predict its performance again and again?
- Could we control its performance by changing requirements?   Process capability has to be looked at from two different angles;
- Inherent capability: the amount of variation which is existing in the process output;
- Determined capability through specifications: This is determined by selecting a standard (nominal) value and some tolerances. Process capability is usually predicted within + or − 3 standard deviations of the data from the mean representing 6σ or 99.74% of probable occurrences.

A series of indexes can be used to determine process capability amongst which are the Cp and the Cpk indexes.

The Cp index

The Cp index measures the process potential by assessing whether the natural tolerance (6σ) is within the specification limits.

$$Cp = USL - LSL/6\sigma$$

A Cp of 1 is considered as adequate and exactly the same as the total tolerance width.

If Cp < 1 the process lacks potential to meet specified requirements;

If Cp > 1 the process may have the potential to meet customer requirements.

The Cp index only looks at potential process performance by mainly concentrating on the spread of the process rather than its location. This is why another index is required.

The Cpk index

The Cpk uses the process mean to measure constantly the distance between the process mean and the upper and lower specification limits.
   The Cpk is calculated as follows:

$$Cpk = \text{Lesser value of } (USL - \bar{X}/3, \text{ or } \bar{X} - LSL/3\sigma)$$

The higher the value of the Cpk the more this is indicative of process capability.
   To highlight the difference between the Cp and the Cpk, Fig. 5.19a is acceptable because the Cpk is > 1. Figure 15.19b however, may be acceptable under the Cp index because it looks at the spread of the process under the specified limits. As the example shows this is not acceptable however, since the process settings have been changed, and the process requires new specifications.

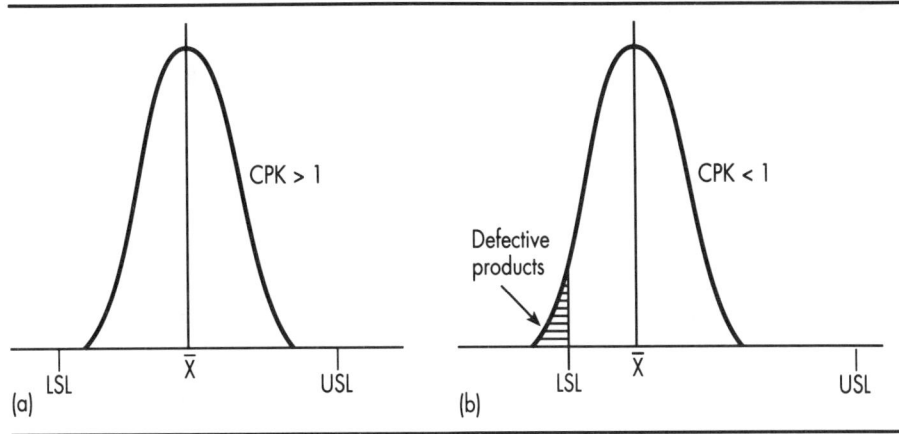

5.19 Cpk values for different process settings.

THE IMPLEMENTATION OF STATISTICAL PROCESS CONTROL

The key message from the discussions in this chapter is that variation is very much a way of life. In the context of organisational systems, all the processes which take place on an everyday basis are subject to some kind of variation at some point in time if not all the time. The purpose of TQM is to instigate a culture based on establishing Zero Defect and therefore Zero Inspection. This can only take place by prevention through the utilisation of Ishikawa techniques or Statistical Process Control (SPC) techniques.

Since the implementation of SPC is so important in establishing a culture of Zero Defect, some guidelines based on a systematic approach towards the implementation programme are provided in this section. Prior to that however, it is important to assess the problems which tend to lead to poor quality standards and problems which are generally encountered by organisations when trying to implement quality control techniques.

Tables 5.7,[42] 5.8[20] and 5.9[23] illustrate findings from different surveys which reflect problems of poor quality, difficulties in trying to implement quality control techniques and the problems encountered during the introduction of SPC techniques, respectively.

The findings of the three surveys reviewed in Tables 5.7, 5.8 and 5.9 carry the message that:

- There is a lack of training on statistical techniques;
- There is lack of management commitment and support;
- There is little awareness on the usefulness of SPC techniques in the context of quality.

The following therefore are points which can help towards positive implementation of SPC programmes:

Table 5.7 Major causes of quality problems

Factor	Reported, %
Lack of adequate training	51
Management emphasis on schedule	48
Failure to follow established practices and procedures	48
Failure to communicate changes in design, specifications, etc	38
Customer schedule requirements	34
Poor quality of vendor materials	34
Poor communication between levels of management	32
Lack of personal accountability	32
Late delivery of vendor materials	31
Company practices inconsistent with quality goals	30
Poor performers	22
Lack of clearly defined criteria for quality levels	22
Conflicting standards of quality	22
Lack of measures of quality	21
Inconsistent or unfair application of established practices	20
Unrealistic contract specifications	19
Vague/non-standardised wording on reports/instructions, etc	16
Low visibility of problems	16
Best equipment not available	16
Lack of manpower	14
Concerns about excessive cost	10
Insufficient facilities usage	6

Quality policy statement

- It is important that quality is clearly stated as part of the overall organisational mission. A quality policy statement has got to be drafted and communicated to employees at all levels within the organisation:
- Quality is initiated by management. The process of trying to make quality succeed is not through sterile statements but total commitment by senior management, the design of realistic objectives and the allocation of time and resources to implement TQM;
- Quality has therefore got to be accepted as the means by which organisational superiority can be achieved and maintained and not as a bolt on activity to inefficient and rudimentary systems.

Table 5.8 Reasons for slow implementation of QC techniques

| Problems | Estimated severity of problems (not serious 1 – most serious 4) | | | | |
	1	2	3	4	Mean score
Lack of employee mathematical skills	5	41	33	21	2.70
Lack of top management participation in QC programmes	14	32	26	28	2.68
Lack of supervisor's support	14	42	32	12	2.42
Lack of communication within the company on QC	14	51	24	11	2.32
Lack of support from design engineering	21	49	20	10	2.19
Lack of suppliers' support	21	49	23	07	2.16
Lack of production worker support	24	55	14	07	2.05
Lack of top management support	34	42	14	10	2.00
High cost of implementation	38	46	10	06	1.84

Quality procedures and systems

● Quality has to be documented at every level of the organisation. Procedures have got to specify clearly how each task is to be conducted to meet customer requirements both internally and externally;

● If prevention is the desired objective, standards have to be set based on a good understanding of process capability and the impact of variation and how to control it;

● Quality requirements change. This could lead to changes in conformance. Internal auditing is an essential activity in making sure that conformance exists all the time regardless of changes in customer requirements. Written procedures and documentation, therefore, have got to reflect the conformance.

Training on the use of SPC

● Train everyone in the organisation on the utilisation of SPC techniques;

● Convey the message that processes have to be well understood so that they can be controlled;

● Train people on the importance of data collection and its processing for providing useful information;

● Delegate process ownership to those who operate the process;

● Authorise action for ensuring process stability towards the achievement of customer requirements;

● Encourage creativity and continuous improvement through the wide spread use of statistical techniques.

Table 5.9 Main difficulties experienced in the implementation of SPC

Problem encountered	Score (N = 57)
Lack of knowledge/expertise on SPC	91
Lack of action from senior management	73
Poor understanding and awareness within the company of the purpose of SPC	63
Lack of SPC training for operators	50
General lack of encouragement	50
Lack of SPC training for senior management	46
Lack of knowledge of which parameters to measure or control	45
Negative reaction of middle management	45
Negative reaction of senior management	44
Deciding which of the various charting techniques to use	43
Negative reaction of operators	40
Lack of action from line management	37
Lack of action from middle management	33
Lack of SPC training for middle management	33
Lack of SPC training for line management	31
Deciding whether to express data in attribute or variables format	27
Negative reaction of line management	24
Poor communication between management and shopfloor	22
Negative reaction of trade unions	16
Literacy/numeracy of operators	13
Feedback of data	6
An inadequate computer system	5
Literacy/numeracy of line supervision	5
Organisational changes	5
High workload	5
Replacement of machinery	2
Insufficient data to show that SPC techniques are beneficial	2

Quality culture

- Establish customer-supplier dependability/accountability both internally and externally;
- Educate every employee that prevention is the order of the day and inspection will not be tolerated;
- Convey the message that the price of poor quality does not stop at the specific individual/process but has a far reaching effect on the whole organisation;
- Convey the message that the achievement of superior performance can only come through continuous improvement activity and that everyone's contribution is therefore valuable to the organisation.

6

TOTAL PREVENTATIVE MAINTENANCE
FOR TQM

INTRODUCTION

This chapter seeks to establish the relevance of Total Preventative Maintenance (TPM) in the TQM framework. The concept of TPM is defined and the various issues associated with it explained. It is however important, first of all, to ask a few questions such as what is the difference between the traditional concept of maintenance and TPM? Maintenance has always been an important part of manufacturing operations, so what is new? How does maintenance relate to TQM? Maintenance has always been considered as a support activity, why does it deserve special attention?

Maintenance, similarly to a large number of other activities, has been conducted in an ad-hoc manner in most manufacturing organisations. It has in the main been bolted-on to the production function to carry out 'patching' work and to minimise the number of disruptions. Output maximisation seemed to be the order of the day. The implementation of comprehensive maintenance programmes was often resisted because of the disruptions that ensue. Manufacturing organisations where maintenance policies are being operated, tended to schedule their maintenance programmes when all operations are at a halt, during weekends and holiday periods. TPM, unlike the traditional understanding of maintenance, plays an important role in TQM implementation. Its implications are numerous and so pertinent that this chapter has been specifically devoted to it. The chapter debates the relevance of TPM by raising important points such as:

(i) Total Quality Management is aimed at satisfying customer requirements. The previous chapter has debated that the former aim can only be accomplished by a good understanding of strengths and weaknesses (i.e. process capability). The tools and techniques of TQM can monitor process behaviour to detect any variation in its capability and thus bring about the required corrections and amendments. In a sense, tools and techniques are there to determine whether a process is capable or not by referring its capability to customer specifications. Total Preventative Maintenance on the other hand introduces capable processes, helps maintain their capability and implements corrections to render them more capable. One can make the analogy between instruments/knowledge and expertise used by a doctor to check the health of a patient (tools and techniques) and the patient's role in maintaining his/her own good health through healthy diet, exercise and following the doctor's advice.

Processes which are capable today may be unsuitable tomorrow. Customer requirements change frequently and a highly competitive manufacturing organisation is one which is flexible enough to accommodate new and improved customer changes in requirements.

(ii) Total Preventative Maintenance, unlike the traditional application of maintenance, uses a pro-active approach to introduce change before any chance of disruption occurs. Traditional maintenance deals with crises when they occur (fire fighting). It is about patching up at any cost and at the detriment of quality. Pro-active maintenance on the other hand is about maintaining high standards of quality and reliability so that products and services are conforming to customer requirements all the time.

(iii) Total Preventative Maintenance is a continuous improvement activity. It has already been debated previously that variation is a fact of life. Process stability is perhaps a visionary objective. It is however the role of any comprehensive TPM programme to aspire to the implementation of process stability and its maintenance. Furthermore TPM should aim at the introduction of new and creative ideas which will optimise quality standards and reduce waste and costs to the organisation concerned. With this argument in mind, isn't it right to revise the view which describes maintenance as a support activity? Would it be wrong to suggest that TPM is a value-adding activity since it aims at cost reduction and quality improvements?

(iv) Total Preventative Maintenance can have a strong strategic relevance. It contributes greatly to decision making processes related to tactical, infrastructural issues and the macrostructural issues. The choice of process equipment is a long term decision and contributions from TPM personnel can be of great value to the evaluation, selection and implementation aspects of equipment. If these decisions are made correctly, the organisation can enjoy flexibility, strength and confidence in meeting customer requirements for a long time. However, if decisions are not made correctly and there is a gap between strategic objectives and process capability, the organisation concerned will fail to achieve high competitive performance levels.

Similarly, TPM can have a great impact on the operational/infrastructural decision making processes. The planning, scheduling and control of operations depends to a large extent on process capacity and capability. The latter two conditions are provided by an efficient and effective TPM programme. Process capacity cannot be made available at the cost of quality and this decision lies with the responsibility of TPM personnel. Similarly process capability may appear to be acceptable. Information based on predictive studies may however reveal that the process has to be attended to immediately to avoid disruptions later. This, once again, is the decision of TPM personnel.

One therefore, can already see the link between TPM and TQM and the relevance of a comprehensive maintenance policy for successful TQM implementation. The following section will discuss the meaning of TPM and the various kinds of maintenance programmes which exist.

WHAT IS TPM?

In the context of manufacturing and process industries, it is perhaps useful first of all to propose the following definition which reflects what the maintenance function is:[12]

'Maintenance is the management, control, execution and quality of those activities which will ensure that **optimum levels of availability** and overall performance of plant are achieved in order to meet business objectives.'

This definition seems to indicate that optimum availability reflects the strength of the organisation in meeting existing and future customer requirements.

To provide flexible and capable processes, a sound maintenance policy should cover the following objectives:[7]

1 Ability to extend the useful life of assets (buildings, equipment, site, etc);

2 Assure the **optimum availability** of installed equipment for production (or service) and to obtain the maximum possible return on investment;

3 Ensure operational readiness at all times of all equipment required for emergency use, such as standby, firefighting and rescue units;

4 Ensure the safety of personnel using the machinery and equipment.

To achieve the above objectives, a comprehensive maintenance function has to address planned and unplanned activities, routine and long-term decisions on prevention.

● Unplanned maintenance also called 'breakdown or corrective maintenance (CM)' deals with existing crises by solving breakdowns and disruptions;

● Planned maintenance is the activity which seeks to eliminate breakdowns and disruptions and which has the role of ensuring process stability and optimum capability to meet customer requirements all the time. It interacts with all the various activities through the conduct of routine activities such as lubricating, oil changes, used parts replacement and long term activities which rely on data collection and statistical analysis to predict future performance of process equipment so that accurate decisions can be made to maintain process stability and capability.

Total Preventative Maintenance therefore is the activity which encompasses the various planned and unplanned tasks, the routine and long term decisions, through a continuous improvement approach and with meeting customer requirements as the end objective.

Principally, TPM is a distributed activity with responsibility attributed to people who operate the process, who supervise the process, who manage and control the process and who can provide technical expertise/skills to solve complex problems. The extent of ownership in TPM depends on the type of maintenance task, with the role of the operator being at the centre of a TPM drive.

The role of the operator in TPM can be made effective by thorough knowledge and understanding of the process in question. The knowledge learnt can be utilised in carrying out routine tasks and helping in the data collection exercise for the long term decisions of a TPM programme.

The role of the maintenance activity becomes one of a 'backstop'[1] helping in the technical aspects of machine diagnoses, in the performance of overhauls and in conducting audits. Severe disruptions (unplanned or corrective tasks) are also the responsibility of maintenance engineers.

To appreciate the role of TPM further, one can ask the question where does this role start and where does it finish? In the context of TQM this question can be answered by focusing on the customer-supplier chain. TPM has a much broader role than usually thought. The role extends to process equipment evaluation, selection and implementation, supplier selection and regular dealings for back up and support activity. To some extent the role of TPM should be a boardroom activity, particularly for issues such as integration of process equipment or product-market decisions for future strategic objectives. For the former, technical knowledge is particularly useful and for the latter knowledge on process capability and stability is of paramount importance.

This more comprehensive role of TPM as an integration of inter-related activities has been described as 'terotechnology'. Terotechnology covers aspects of process installation, commissioning, maintenance (engineering), replacement and removal of plant, machinery and equipment, feedback to its operation and design on its relation with other activities. Total Preventative Maintenance, in the context of terotechnology has been defined as follows:[13]

'Terotechnology is concerned with the application of managerial, financial, engineering and other skills to extend the operational life of, and increase the efficiency of, equipment and machinery.'

Figure 6.1 represents the various components of terotechnology.[13] This comprehensive view of TPM suggests that a history of process selection, implementation and performance monitoring has to be made available so that important activities such as operations and design can help meet customer requirements.satisfactorily.

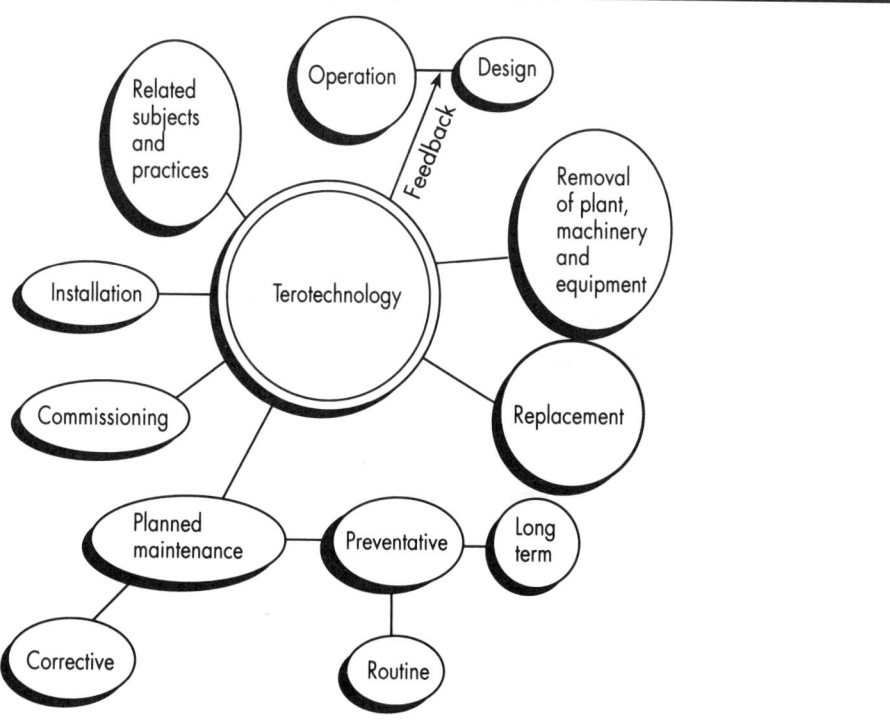

6.1 The concept of terotechnology: a model of TPM.

This model reflects the need to have wider involvement in the decision-making process on capital equipment investment and also to have knowledge workers who are responsible for the selection, implementation, operation and control of the process equipment in question.

Traditionally, manufacturing organisations tended to use one aspect of TPM only,

maintenance engineering, which deals with unplanned activities such as breakdowns and the routine aspects of a preventative programme such as servicing. Investment decisions were arrived at on an ad-hoc basis, usually based on cost criteria and made by people who are remote from the technical/operational aspects of the process.

Total Preventative Maintenance in the context of TQM has therefore got to address various aspects of process operations, not just the maintenance engineering angle. A typical TPM programme should include an aspect of Corrective Mainten-ance (CM), an aspect of Preventative Maintenance (PM) and an aspect of Improve-ment Maintenance (IM). Figure 6.2 illustrates the various aspects of a typical TPM programme. Table 6.1 describes the CM, PM, IM aspects of a TPM programme.[20]

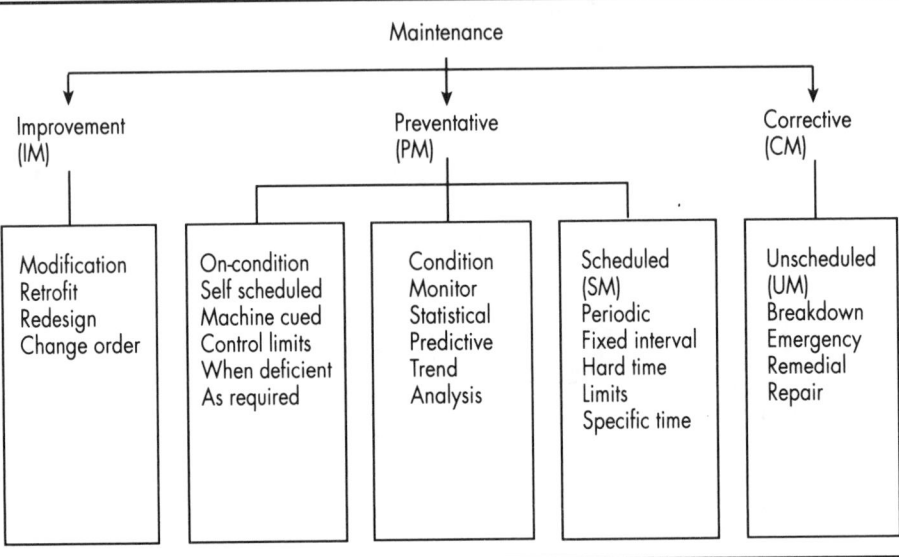

6.2 Structure of a Total Preventative Maintenance programme.

As TPM strategies are geared towards the elimination of failures in process equipment, it is important to examine the various patterns of failure in process equipment which may require different approaches.

FAILURE PATTERNS

It is generally believed that there are three main patterns of equipment/component failure.

1 Infant mortality zone: This is an area where faults can result from poor design, assembly or testing of the equipment purchased. This type of failure can be dealt with by processes of good supplier management (quality at source) or burning-in period and by allowing equipment to be operational for a predetermined period of time before shipment to the customer concerned.

2 Random failures: This is the period of normal working life of the equipment and where performance can be expected to be at an optimum. The chances of failure are

Table 6.1 A description of TPM components

Type of maintenance programme	Description
Improvement Maintenance (IM)	Efforts for the reduction or elimination of the need for maintenance
	Reliability engineering efforts need to emphasise the need for error elimination rather than maintenance
	Opportunity to preact rather than react
Corrective Maintenance (CM)	Corrective (emergency, repair, remedial, unscheduled)
	Troubleshooting and diagnostic fault detection and isolation.
Preventative Maintenance (PM) (on-condition)	Maintenance carried out when equipment needs it. Uses human thought process, electronics and sensor technology, to detect if threshold limits of established standards have been exceeded in order to take most appropriate action
Preventative Maintenance (PM) (condition monitor)	Use of statistics and probability theory for data generation and analysis to detect trends in causes of failure and therefore take appropriate measures for prevention
Preventative Maintenance (PM) (scheduled)	Has to be used only if there is an opportunity for reducing failures which cannot be detected in advance
	Different from fixed interval inspection which looks for threshold conditions

expected to be low in this period and failures which take place tend to happen randomly and are therefore unpredictable.

3 Wear out zone: This is the phase where wear and tear can lead to a high rise in the number and frequency of disruptions of the equipment. The probability of failure rises sharply and important decisions have to be made at that stage about the future of the process equipment in question.

Figure 6.3 illustrates the three patterns of equipment failure. The bath tube curve is widely used as the standard reliability failure plot. However, it is thought that most processes do not exhibit behaviour such as the one depicted.[20]

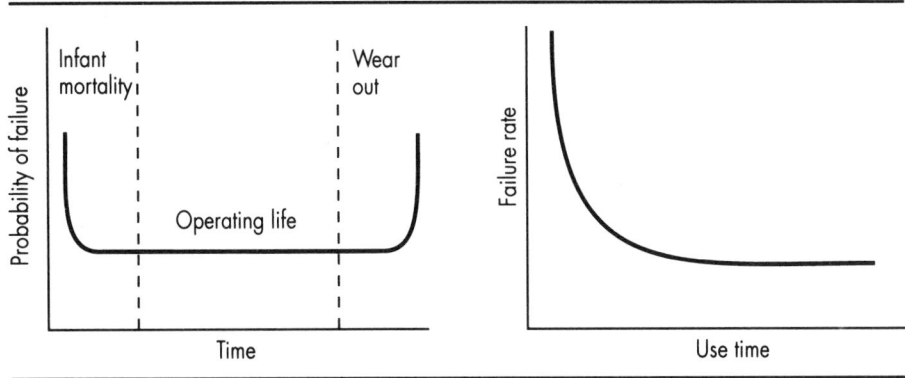

6.3 Bath tube curve: failure patterns.

6.4 Early failure pattern.

- Only 4% of equipment/components exhibit behaviour based on the bath-tube curve (infant mortality – stable period – wear out period);
- 68% of equipment follow behaviour of failure which occurs at the start of utilisation. Good supplier quality assurance and burning-in periods can usually solve this pattern of failure, Fig. 6.4.
- 14% of the equipment/components follow a flat failure pattern, Fig. 6.5. These failures are only subject to routine maintenance such as normal inspection, lubrication, etc.

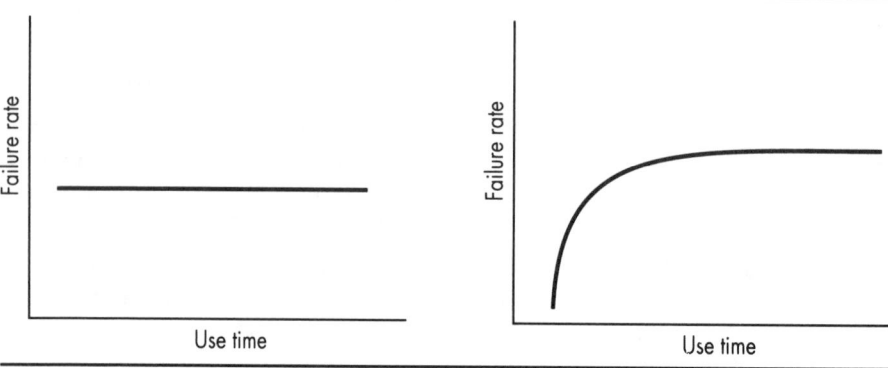

6.5 Flat failure pattern.   **6.6** Failure due to human errors.

- 7% of failures are caused by operators – human unreliability, carelessness, lack of education and poor knowledge on the process being operated. They can be minimised/eliminated by good training, supervision and motivation, Fig. 6.6.
- 5% of components exhibit failures which follow a rising pattern. A maintenance programme will therefore be ineffective and perhaps the best decision would be a replacement of the process equipment in question, Fig. 6.7.
- Only 2% of the equipment/components exhibit a pattern which shows stability over the life of utilisation until failure due to wear and tear, Fig. 6.8.

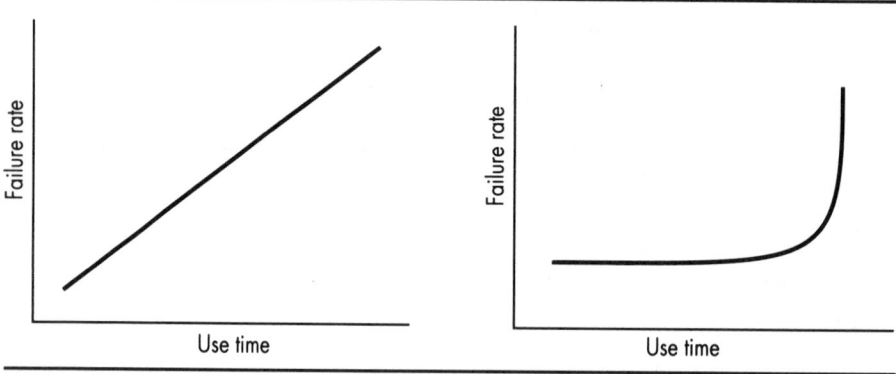

6.7 Increasing failure over life.   **6.8** Failure due to wear out.

The main objective of any comprehensive TPM programme is to have a flat pattern where there are no failures at the start of equipment utilisation and where the operational life of the equipment is extended as far as practically possible to minimise the impact of wear and tear.

The minimisation of the probability of failure can take place by implementing the following points:

1 Supplier appraisal and equipment selection: This phase is vital if infant mortality failures are to be eliminated. Suppliers have to be selected for their equipment safety, reliability, quality standards, the level of back up and support on offer, etc. The equipment has to be chosen according to degree of tests and quality inspection. Suppliers should play a major role also in the project management and implementation stages, until commissioning and start up.

2 A comprehensive TPM programme which will help achieve existing and future customer requirements, through the implementation of efficient routine and long term preventative programmes and through speedy reactions to minimise the level of disruptions when unpredictable failures take place.

3 Apply the principle of derating. Equipment should be treated with care. Longevity will be determined by the type of speeds, settings and operating conditions utilised throughout the life of the equipment.

4 The principle of continuous improvement can easily be applied to maintenance. Optimisation of equipment utilisation, the minimisation/elimination of failures and prolongation of equipment longevity is a real objective which can be pursued by organisations which seek to implement TQM philosophy successfully. Figure 6.9 illustrates how through a comprehensive TPM programme based on quality, failures can be eliminated and the operating life of equipment can be extended.

Equipment failures similarly to the production of waste or the carrying of large inventory levels mean high costs to the organisation concerned. The purpose of TPM is to achieve Zero Breakdown, similarly to the concepts of Zero Inventory and Zero Defect.

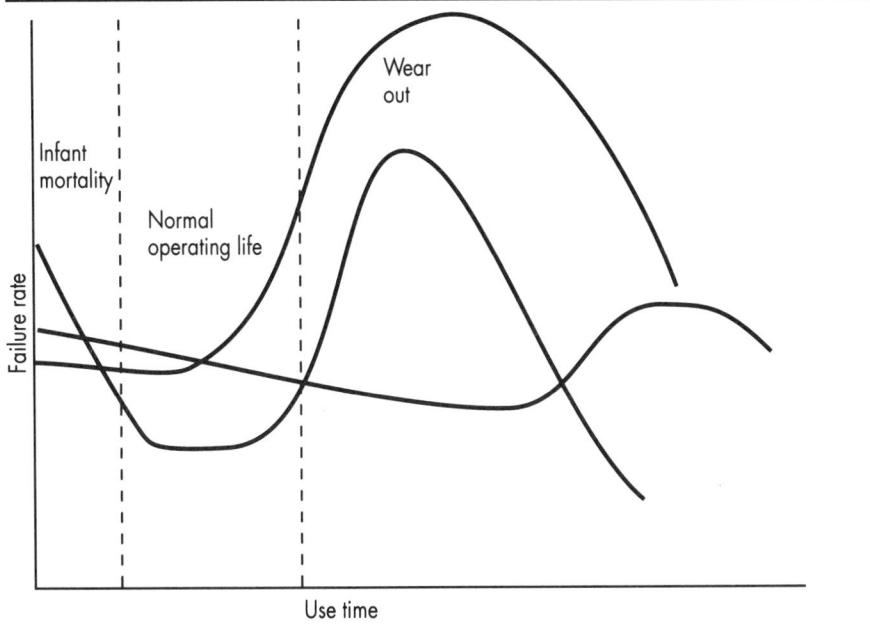

6.9 Failure reduction through continuous improvement.

COSTS AND BENEFITS OF TPM

To appreciate the benefits which could result from a good maintenance policy, it is important to understand the various costs of maintenance and their relative impact on the organisation concerned. It has been suggested that on average, 70% of maintenance time is spent on emergencies (fire fighting), 15% on non-critical repairs and only 15% on Planned Preventative Maintenance.[6] The basic question therefore is how to cost maintenance activity? Which element of the programme is considered?

A policy of firefighting for example means that a high proportion of the costs is always unavoidable. For one part, emergency repairs mean that high inventory levels have to be carried all the time, particularly on critical parts and components. Secondly, reactive maintenance means negative impact on production time. Many companies do not include process equipment which is under repair in their existing capacity. The cost of downtown however, if included in terms of possible sales/production opportunities, can be assessed much more accurately.

It appears that maintenance costing has always been conducted in a cavalier manner without real effort in trying to incorporate all costing aspects. This is in the

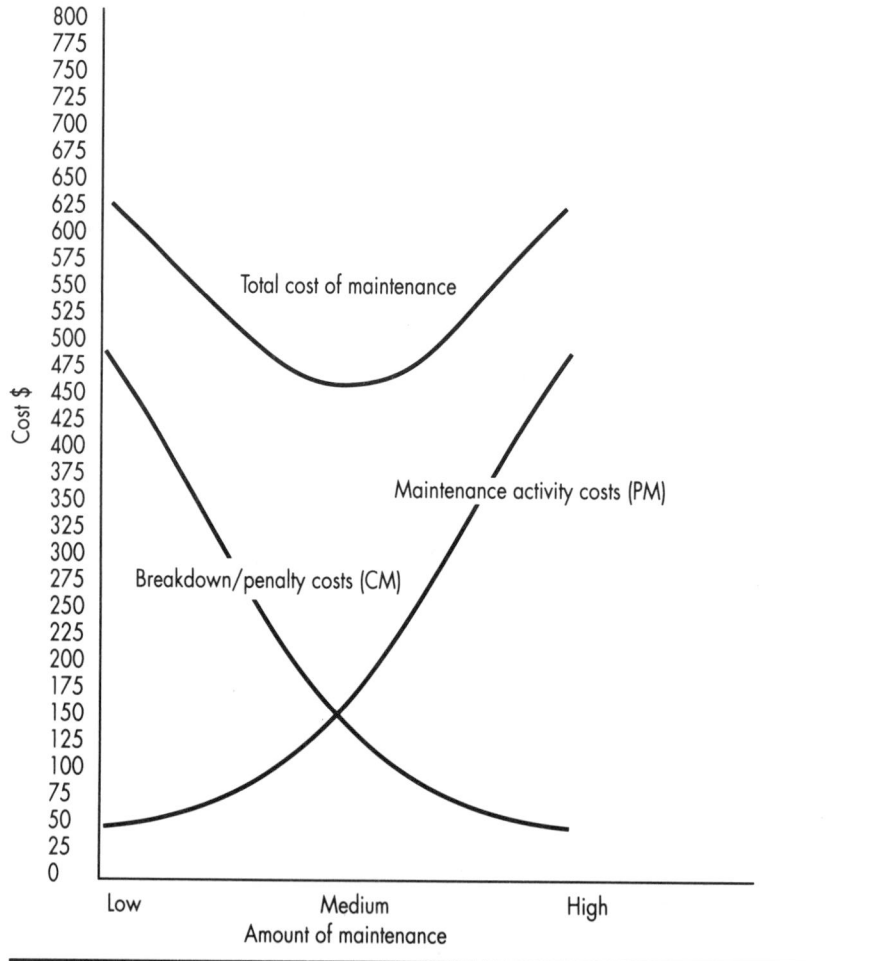

6.10 Cost trade off between CM and PM.

main due to management attitudes towards the role of maintenance in relation to business operations. A survey conducted by the Department of Trade and Industry (DTI) in the UK[12] to establish best practice in relation to maintenance, has come up with the following conclusions:

- Maintenance is not always considered at company executive level;
- Most companies seem to ignore the real cost of downtime in terms of lost sales opportunities;
- Within manufacturing industry, only 3.7% of annual sales revenue is spent on maintenance of operations equipment;
- The survey has also concluded that with good maintenance management the above costs can be drastically reduced and plant availability can be increased to lead to up to 30% increase in profitability.

The various costs of maintenance can be represented by a curve such as the one in Fig. 6.10 which illustrates the inverse relationship between costs due to Corrective Maintenance (CM) and those due to Preventative Maintenance (PM) with the resulting impact on losses in sales revenue. A change of attitude towards PM from the implementation of Routine Maintenance such as inspections, lubrication, etc, to

Table 6.2 Areas for maintenance costing

Type of maintenance programme	Areas for cost estimation/calculation
Breakdown and penalty costs	Idle capacity
	Buffer inventories
	Lost production
	Poor quality
Reactive maintenance	Manpower idle
	Desired level of service
	Number of machine breakdowns
	Level of specialisation/number of maintenance personnel used
Regularly scheduled PM	Costs derived from PM schedule
	Manpower costs based on total manpower hours required for production
	Cost of repair/parts (determined by PM schedule)
Inspection and randomly scheduled PM	Based on total number of manpower hours required for production
	Costs based on historical manpower usage data
Equipment back up	Established by depreciation schedule (fixed expense)
	Cost of maintenance (variable cost)
Equipment upgrades	Costs can either be expensed or amortised depending both on their magnitude and on the operating lifetime of the upgraded equipment

fault diagnosis and predictive studies will lead to a drastic increase in repair costs therefore minimising production downtime and losses of sales revenue, Fig. 6.11.

To obtain the optimum impact from a PM programme, it is important for maintenance/production managers to calculate or obtain estimates of the various costs involved. Table 6.2 gives an indication of areas where various costs can be calculated.[15]

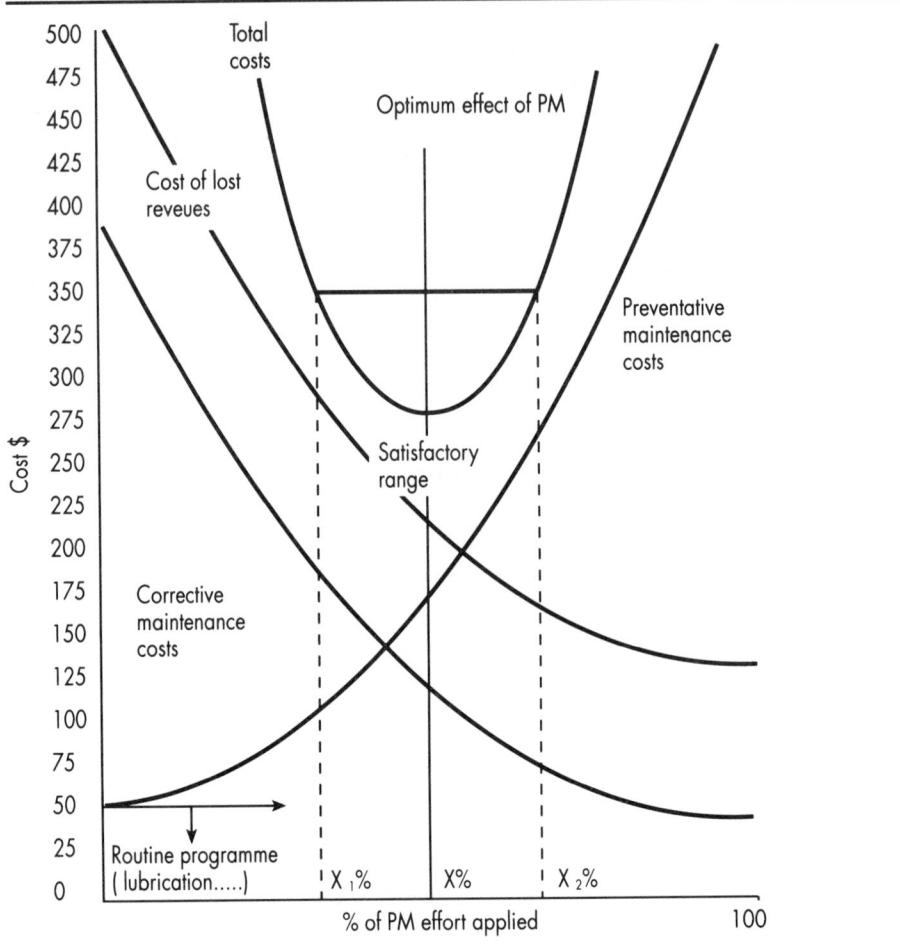

6.11 The impact of PM on cuts in revenue losses.

The impact of TPM on productivity levels can therefore only be appreciated once various costs and their impact have been well understood and calculated. Total Preventative Maintenance has a direct impact on productivity of manpower, capacity availability and utilisation and productivity of capital assets. It also has a direct impact on levels of inventory both for maintenance purposes (emergency repairs) and raw materials/components for production (by helping manufacturing companies get it right first time, inventory levels can be greatly reduced). In addition, a TPM programme which is effective can lead to the implementation of a successful TQM philosophy and therefore enable the companies concerned to meet customer requirements first time and every time.

The impact of TPM on productivity levels can therefore be classified both at a tactical/operational level and at the strategic level:

● At the tactical level, optimisation of resources/assets leads to optimum productivity levels;
● At the strategic level, the provision of a flexible, stable, efficient and reliable manufacturing facility means that market-driven demand can be met and satisfied all the time.

Superior performance of manufacturing organisations depends to some extent on performance standards of the TPM programme in operation. Table 6.3 gives an indication on how maintenance performance measures can be achieved.[12] It is not meant to be exhaustive and conclusive, but illustrates some useful areas where measurements can be calculated.

Table 6.3 Some maintenance performance measures

Overall performance
Maintenance cost, % sales value of operation
Maintenance cost, % value added
Maintenance cost per unit of output
Maintenance man hours, % total labour hours
Maintenance man hours per unit output

Downtime (by plant, area, unit and/or machine etc)
Downtime due to all causes, % of total time (absolute)
Downtime due to maintenance, % of total time (absolute)

Analysis of work load
% of maintenance hours on planned maintenance versus corrective versus emergency versus reconditioning versus tooling and repairs versus capital and installation

Analysis of material
Total annual maintenance materials spent
Spend on materials as % maintenance labour spend
Maintenance material per £1000 SVOP

Miscellaneous
Number of failures per period by category
Mean time between failures by category
Mean time to repair by category

SOME EXAMPLES OF TPM IMPLEMENTATION

Implementation of TPM is approached differently by manufacturing organisations. The following two examples offer contrasts on how different manufacturing organisations can implement TPM successfully.

Example A

One of Eastman Kodak's subsidiaries has implemented TPM successfully using the team approach.[3] Tennessee Eastman Company (TEC) has defined TPM as follows:

'A partnership between the maintenance and production organisations to improve product quality, reduce waste, reduce manufacturing cost, increase equipment availability, and improve TEC's state of maintenance. This partnership emphasises the involvement of all employees in maintaining facilities and equipment.'[3]

Total Preventative Maintenance at TEC is centred round five main objectives which are geared towards bringing together maintenance personnel and operators, broadening their skills and encouraging them to support one another. The five objectives include the following:

1 Utilisation of operators to perform specified routine maintenance tasks on their equipment;

2 Utilisation of operators to assist mechanics in the repair of equipment when it is down;

3 Utilisation of mechanics to assist operators in the shutdown and start up of equipment;

4 Utilisation of lower skilled personnel to perform routine jobs not requiring skilled craftsmen;

5 Utilisation of computerised technology to enable operators to calibrate selected instruments.

How was TPM implemented?

Study existing culture

- Understand how existing control processes operate;
- Choose a management champion;
- Get the right people on board by making sure they are committed;
- Utilise their input/influence to design and sell the TPM plan.

Designing to change the culture

- Get people to change from a way of thinking based on 'that's not my job' to a new way based on 'this is what I can do to help'.

Building commitment

- Everyone who is involved in TPM has to get first hand information on the nature of the change, how the change is to be implemented and to what extent;
- Use milestones in building commitment, such as
- All personnel trained to perform TPM tasks
- Achieving cost reduction goals
- TPM expansion goals (new tasks undertaken)
- TPM task performance goals (total task count)
- Equipment uptime;
- Recognition for achievement of milestones.

The team approach

● Conscious effort should be made to involve all levels of the organisation.

Opportunity audit

● An opportunity audit needs to be conducted to provide additional insight into areas of greatest potential;
● Start small, ensure success and build on strengths.

Implementation steps

● The approach used by TEC is illustrated in Fig. 6.12.

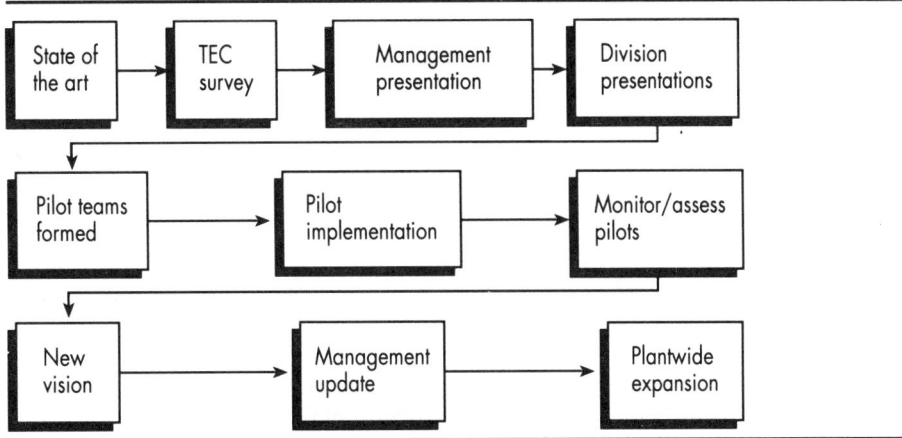

6.12 TPM implementation plan at Eastman Kodak.

Anticipating concerns/resistance

● A conscious effort has to be made to deal with concerns which may arise with positive responses.

Monitoring receptivity

● Informal feed back: use grapevine to gauge general receptivity;
● Formal surveys: to obtain input directly from everyone involved in the TPM implementation programme.

TEC has reported various successful benefits from the implementation of TPM which include the following:

● Improved product quality;
● Reduced cost;
● Improved equipment uptime;
● Improved teamwork between operators and mechanics;
● Job enrichment;
● Improved skills and flexibility of all employees;
● Reduction in emergency work.

The following list includes the major factors which have facilitated the successful implementation of TPM:

1 Management willing to commit resources;
2 A centralised, dedicated TPM manager and co-ordinators;
3 Dedicated team leaders and trainers;
4 A well defined implementation process;
5 Team approach – involvement of all employees;
6 Tasks identified at lowest level – not management dictated;
7 A flexible programme;
8 A pilot approach to tasks;
9 Emphasis placed on safety;
10 Zone concept with task analysis;
11 Tools and supplies at job site;
12 Training developed and done by area mechanics and operators;
13 Performance management plan to recognise and reinforce behaviour and results;
14 Establish vision, mission statement, key result areas, measures, and improvement plans.

Example B

This example reflects TPM implementation at Matsushita Electric Company (Washing Machine Division, Mikumi Plant) in Japan.[2] Productive maintenance was introduced because the company decided to establish a system to build in quality by producing better equipment and it was thought that conventional Preventative Maintenance alone would be inadequate in solving all the problems.

Total Preventative Maintenance was aimed at all the activities with the slogan 'maintenance for profit'. The programme was based on the participation of all employees with the following three objectives:

(i)   Improving effective operation rate of machines and equipment;
(ii) Improving reliability by the development of machines and equipment;
(iii) Enhancing manufacturing morale.

How was TPM implemented?

Organisation for promoting TPM activities

● 'Every worker is a machine keeper' was the philosophy behind the TPM activities;
● All the activities were promoted to establish a voluntary maintenance system.

Preventative Maintenance policy

● Represented in Table 6.4.[2]

Development of machines and equipment

● Consideration given to
– Development stage
– Equipment specification

Table 6.4 Mikumi Plant PM management policy

Basic policy	Major points	Equipment development
TPM activities through first-move management and human development	1) Improved effective operation rate of equipment: a) reduction in equipment breakdowns; b) reduction in defective processes 2) Improved manufacturing technology – development of human resources strong in equipment	Improved equipment which can assure quality (self-check by equipment)

- Concept designing
- Quotation, effects
- Decision and ordering
- Test operation
- Instalment
- Delivery
- Mass production;
- Special attention given to the design stage (utilisation of the designing check list, equipment manufacturing and maintenance manual);
- Test operation and introduction stage.

Maintenance system

- Routine care, regular check ups, lubrication, and other measures in accordance with the equipment control work standards;
- Voluntary maintenance based on 'every worker is a machine keeper' (using visual control and equipment plan).

Small group activities

- Plant management through the encouragement of cleaning and placing things so that equipment is used with care and the work environment is improved. This team approach is based on the 5-S activities
- Seiri (tidiness)
- Seiton (orderliness)
- Seiso (cleaning)
- Seiketsu (cleanliness)
- Shitsuke (moral training);
- S check up system.

Suggestion scheme

- Suggestion is considered to be the first step of employee involvement.

Quality circle activities

- Promoted as an embodiment of respect for people with the view of making jobs more worthwhile and the work environment more pleasant.

In house authorisation system

● Workers are encouraged to obtain authorisation of the job type related to their own work. They are also encouraged to develop a number of other job types in order to have multi-skills.

Computer-aided Quality Control system

● Use of Computer-aided Quality Control (CQC) to predict quality abnormalities and to prevent defects in advance through data analysis.

Results

● Results are plotted on charts and publicised.

The following benefits are reported to have been achieved through successful implementation of TPM:

● Reduction in inventory;
● Clean working environment;
● Improved morale;
● Reduced minor accidents;
● Improved skills and worker abilities.

Following the success achieved, managers and workers at the Mikumi plant have decided to tackle the following objectives for the future:

1 Improvement in check up techniques;
2 Building in the maintenance function when designing equipment (reduction in life cost);
3 Improvement in voluntary maintenance with the 5-S activities at the centre;
4 Increasing support for subsidiaries in their quality control;
5 Development of human resources.

The two examples illustrate that amongst the most important factors which facilitated the successful implementation of TPM, are management commitment and worker involvement. In addition, the design of a TPM policy was on the whole linked to all the other activities of the businesses concerned.

TOWARDS ZERO DEFECT: ZERO BREAKDOWN

Zero Defect aims at producing goods and services right first time and every time. This concept has mainly been people oriented involving changing worker attitudes towards the importance of waste elimination and producing goods and services to customer requirements in the context of customer-supplier chains. Total Preventative Maintenance is an opportunity for achieving the production of goods and services right first time. Indeed by determining process capability and ensuring process stability, inputs can continuously be converted into quality outputs with Zero Defects.

The link between Total Preventative Maintenance and Total Quality Control is a strong one. Table 6.5[21] illustrates the major implications of TPM on TQC.

Table 6.5 Major implications of TPM on TQC

	TPM	**TQC**
Problem	Machine breakdown	Product defects
Traditional solution	Breakdown/maintenance/replacement of broken machine parts	End-of-line inspection/sorting and rework
Improved solution	Condition-based maintenance	In-process inspection
	Preventative maintenance	Poka-Yoke (foolproof mechanism)
	Maintenance prevention	Design for quality
Information for monitoring	Machine trouble record/MTBF (mean time between failure)	Statistical Process Control/control chart
Basic approaches	Education	Education
	Employee involvement	Employee involvement
	'Maintenance is free'	'Quality is free'

It shows that TQM is much affected by attitudes towards the maintenance function. For example a reactive maintenance policy of dealing with breakdowns and disruptions as and when they occur means that the practice of end-of-line inspection will still remain inherent. A comprehensive preventative maintenance policy means that process maintenance control takes place on-line and this therefore facilitates the implementation of in-process control so that output is produced with Zero Defects. Preventative maintenance relies on the continuous recording and analysis of data to prevent process failure. This can in turn make the implementation of SPC much easier because process capability will be closely determined and the amount of variation 'stable'. Educating for maintenance means educating for quality. Employee involvement for maintenance means involvement for quality improvement.

Zero Breakdown, similarly to Zero Defects is perhaps difficult to achieve but should be aimed at as a long term objective. The principle of Zero Breakdown can be implemented by a gradual move from a culture of dealing with regular failures in

Table 6.6 A four phased approach towards the implementation of Zero Breakdown

Phase No	Type of approach	Description
1st	Forced deterioration	Lack of routine maintenance such as oiling, bolt tightening
2nd	Natural deterioration	Periodic preventative maintenance is implemented, efforts in cleaning, inspecting bolt tightening, etc
3rd	Machine redesign/improvement in restoring deterioration	Abnormal conditions are identified and solved to prevent machine deterioration
4th	Improved diagnostic technology	Machine conditions are monitored constantly so that on-line maintenance is carried out

the process to a new culture based on continuous monitoring, diagnosis and prevention of failures so that process stability is achieved. Table 6.6 represents a four-phased approach of continuous improvement in the area of TPM[21]

Table 6.6 shows the continuous effort of changing the role of the maintenance function from basic routine maintenance. Routine Maintenance only tries to preserve the utilisation of process equipment over a long period of time. The new role of maintenance is represented by a phase where efforts are made to identify weaknesses in the process design and rectifying them so that failures are eliminated completely. Perhaps the last stage is to implement maintenance as an on-line activity so that Zero Breakdown becomes a reality since faults are detected and rectification takes place before any sign of disruption. Figure 6.13[21] further illustrates the gradual move from basic routine maintenance to stages where failure is completely eliminated and maintenance is incorporated within the process using diagnostic technology.

IMPLEMENTING TPM: SOME GUIDELINES

The implementation of a comprehensive TPM programme has to be a top down approach. Unlike the traditional approach towards maintenance, TPM has to be a

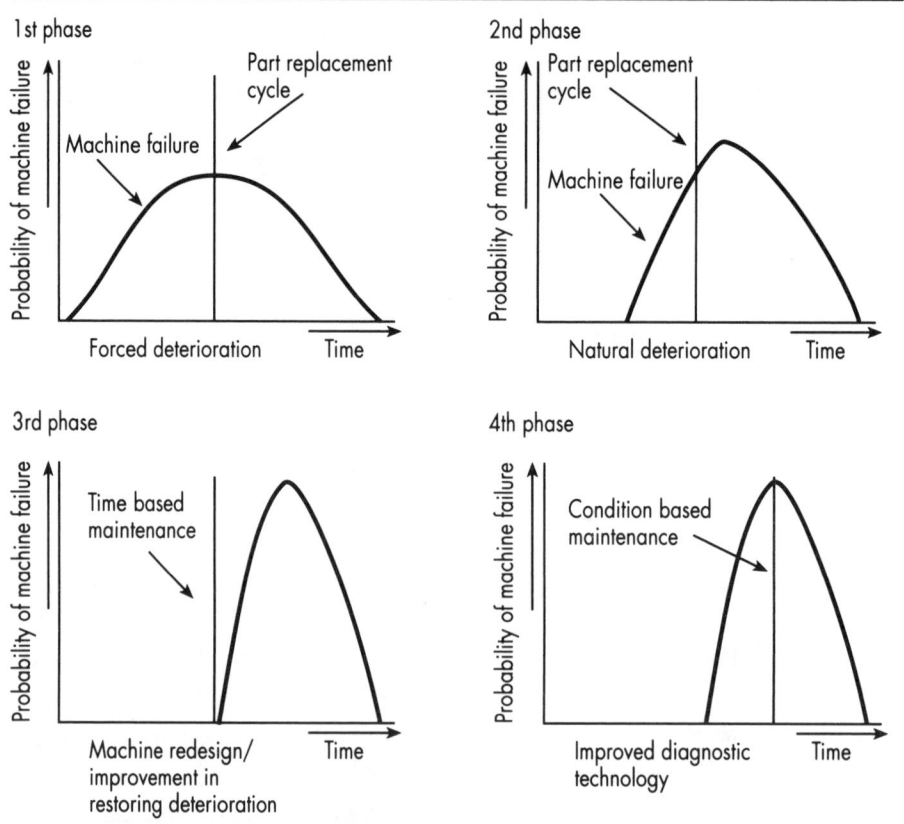

6.13 A four phased approach to TPM implementation.

boardroom activity considered for its power to add value to organisational activities by helping meet customer requirements and achieving set objectives.

Implementation needs to follow a series of stages including the following:

The corporate place

Total Preventative Maintenance has to be initiated and encouraged by top management. Its role has to be perceived not only in determining process capability but also in maintaining process stability so that customer requirements are met first time and every time. Unless true process capability is known, it will be hard for any organisation to set future objectives.

Total Preventative Maintenance interacts with key activities within the organisation, such as design (design for manufacturability through good knowledge of process capability) and operations (planning, scheduling and control are closely related to capacity availability). Its appreciation at the corporate level has, therefore, got to be followed by high levels of commitment and the allocation of adequate resources and means.

The structural consideration

One aspect of corporate management is related to the long term structural decisions on process purchasing and implementation. Total Preventative Maintenance will play a major role in facilitating the selection, implementation, maintenance and control of any new process equipment. Furthermore, TPM will ensure the integration of old and new so that operations are optimised and disruptions are eliminated.

The tactical consideration

Total Preventative Maintenance interacts strongly with other activities such as production and operations by providing vital information on process capability, capacity availability, timetables for routine and non-routine (Diagnostic Maintenance) programmes. Furthermore important decisions on equipment replacement have to rely on input from the maintenance function.

Involvement in supplier appraisal – equipment selection

Traditionally, maintenance engineers are only involved in equipment selection after the deals with suppliers have been sealed and agreed. It is of paramount importance that maintenance personnel/operators are involved at the early stages of supplier appraisal, equipment evaluation, selection and implementation. After all, if process capability has to be established and maintained, it is the people who are expected to assume the responsibility of maintaining process capability, who should be involved in decision-making.

Traditionally, capital investment decisions were the domain of senior managers who were more motivated by financial arguments than meeting customer requirements.

Decisions were on the whole driven by output optimisation and economic returns from such investments. Meeting customer requirements in a variety of ways, all the time, was hardly considered by many organisations.

TPM has to be operator centred

Operators are expected to manage process equipment and consequently manage the production of quality output with Zero Defects. It is therefore only right to design for operator requirements, by making sure that process maintainability is not beyond operator knowledge and understanding and that maintenance (routine) has to be part of operator job specification. To produce right first time and all the time, operators have to have an extremely good knowledge of the process they are responsible for everyday of their working lives. This knowledge can only be acquired through skill upgrading, continuous training and education. Operators have also got to be encouraged to work closely with maintenance specialists on complex technical problems and be closely involved in process diagnosis and data collection processes.

Use statistical techniques for TPM

Statistical techniques can be used to manage process equipment in order to make decisions on capacity availability, maintenance schedules etc. Statistical techniques can help questions such as:[18]

- Is process equipment in control? Have all the assignable (attributable) causes been eliminated?
- Are all the routine elements such as oil consumption, oil pressure drops and vibration amplitudes at the right levels within the required limits to prevent failures from happening?
- Is the previous data obtained on failures adequate enough for predictions to be accurately made?
- What parts ought to be kept in stock? What inventory levels are required?
- How can the lifetime of parts and components be determined based on previous ones which wear out?
- On what basis should routine and diagnostic maintenance programme schedules be designed?

Make Zero Breakdown a continuous improvement activity

Zero Breakdown is essential if Zero Defect is to become a realistic objective. Maintenance has to be publicised as everyone's responsibility and slogans such as 'maintenance is free' can be used to convey the message to all the employees. Improvement in maintenance can provide optimum capacity and also make sure that process capability can be extended for optimum precision and optimum accuracy.

7

TOTAL SAFETY SYSTEMS FOR TQM

THE COST OF POOR SAFETY

Building a reputation for high quality is perhaps an opportunity which does not repeat itself very often. It takes many years of commitment, effort and perseverance before a culture based on TQM, customer-supplier interactions and doing things right first time and everytime, can get established. Total Quality Management as a philosophy of competitiveness stresses the need for sustainable effort and therefore no slippage or drop in quality standards can be allowed. Organisations under the banners of TQM strive for the achievement of an image based on market respectability, business capability based on customer care and responsiveness to fulfill various needs.

Safety is perhaps one of the pillars which can support organisations so that they can enjoy a high level of respectability. Safety of course, similarly to TPM, has not on the whole been given its due in the context of competitive strategy. This is particularly the case if strategic objectives are driven by TQM implementation. It is not surprising therefore to find that many large organisations have fallen out of favour with existing and prospective customers because of safety neglect. Tarnished images are hard to reverse and competitive loss is hard to regain. This leads to some basic questions such as what is the cost of poor safety? Do safety standards need to be compromised because of economic pressures?

To answer these questions one can perhaps look at the number of organisations which have been prosecuted for safety negligence. Recent examples include the Piper Alpha explosion, the Clapham and Purley rail crashes, the Pan Am and British Midlands air crashes amongst many others.

Example A

The Zeebrugge ferry disaster is still vivid in the minds of many people. The Herald of Free Enterprise capsized resulting in the deaths of nearly 200 people. This led to public condemnation of the owner company and a public enquiry which found that the owner's management as well as members of the crew were at fault for the ship sailing with the bow doors open, which caused the disaster.[1] Although the company was subsequently acquitted of corporate manslaughter, this neglect of safety meant that its corporate image was tarnished. It will be hard to change public opinion, particularly when loss of life occurred on such a large scale.

Example B

Boeing is another company which has commanded respect for a long time by providing products with high safety, reliability and quality standards. Boeing has never suffered from a shortage in book orders worldwide. The company has been so busy that ordered planes take many years to be delivered. There has been however, growing concern that the number of problems with Boeing aircraft is increasing.

Such problems included recently the discovery of cross-wiring in a number of the 757s model; the new 747-400 a latest model is suffering from considerable delivery delays and a series of accidents have taken place recently, including:[2]

- The loss of 500 lives on a Japanese mountainside (corporate liability procedures to ascertain why there was a fault even after repairs and checks were progressing at the time of going to press);
- The bizarre peeling away of the fuselage of a Hawaian jet is still being investigated.

One is bound to ask questions such as are safety standards suffering to meet the demands of the order book.

Boeing has however admitted to being over-ambitious by taking on too many complex projects at the same time and trying to complete them in the shortest possible period. According to one of Boeing's senior executives, mistakes have taken place because of economic pressures. He concluded that:[2] .

'... we took on the job of certifying three types of engines (for the 747–400), an airframe, and a Combi (a cargo-carrying body) in four months. It was more than we could manage, hence the delivery delays ... The pressure of demand gets into our suppliers and it gets into the workforce. Once production is put out of sequence it needs to be corrected. You then get more inexperienced staff doing more overtime and therefore you are apt to make some mistakes.'

Both companies are now striving to restore quality and reliability standards to win back public confidence.

Damage of reputation and costly penalties may be caused even by minor neglect. There are examples which may not affect public confidence but worker morale and commitment to organisational objectives. Such examples include the case of a secretary working in a bank,[3] who in 1988, was awarded £45,000 because she was victim of Repetitive Strain Injury (RSI) or tenosynovitis from tapping keys on her typewriter. The bank was found to be negligent for not advising employees on risks associated with utilisation of key boards and also for not taking appropriate measures to protect its employees against the risk of RSI.

The true cost of poor safety standards can perhaps never be assessed accurately. Damages to organisations can be internal and external. They can be economically quantifiable in the short term but hard to assess in the long term, particularly if respectability and customer faith are damaged.

DEFINING TOTAL SAFETY SYSTEMS

Safety touches every aspect of organisational systems, it is not just guarding of machinery or protection of workers. Safety is not just reacting to accidents and emergencies but more importantly planning to prevent accidents from happening. Total Safety Systems (TSS) can therefore be defined as follows:

'Those procedures, guidelines and plans which would ensure the safe interaction of socio-technical systems towards the achievement of organisational competitive objectives. The main objective of Total Safety Systems is to establish a culture based on Zero Risk through continuous improvement activity.'

Total Safety Systems in the context of TQM are not just support activities but value adding ones. By ensuring that there are no risks to employees and process equipment, optimum performance can be achieved. They represent the technical and social elements of organisational systems and as such include safety of workplace design, safety of technical processes and safety of employees, Fig. 7.1. The three

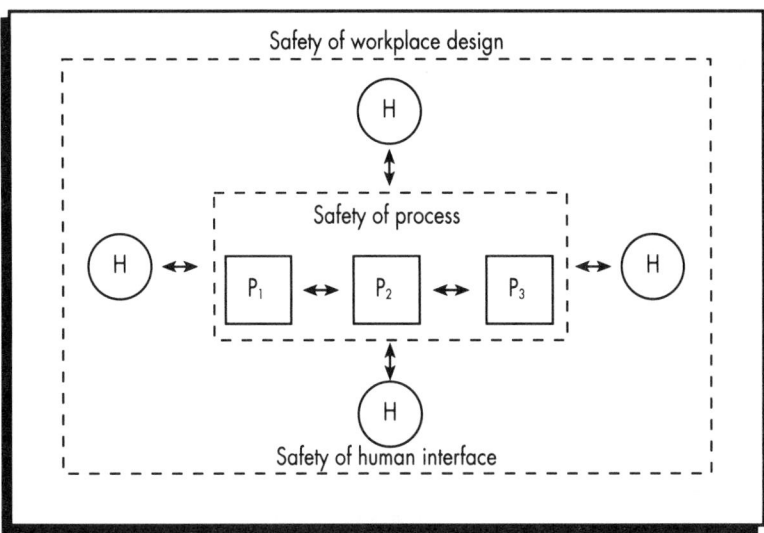

7.1 Safety system in a work environment.

components are discussed in Table 7.1 which is meant to illustrate some of the safety aspects in each category. What is most important in TSS however, is their dynamic nature in eliminating risks before accidents happen. This is different from the traditional approach towards safety where there was sole reliance on reactive plans. Table 7.2 compares the traditional with the modern approach based on TQM philosophy.

One can see from Table 7.2 that TQM does not consider safety as a 'peripheral' activity but a central one to the process of adding value to organisational performance. Total Safety Systems seek to achieve a Zero Risk objective by the implementation of a harmonious, healthy, productive, creative work environment. The systems are therefore people centred and the contribution of the worker in raising safety standards of his/her work environment through continuous improvement activities is considered to be essential. This is unlike the traditional approach towards safety where policies, plans and training programmes are decided upon away from the work environment and without any contribution from the workers themselves. Safety in the traditional context tended to follow a superimposition approach without any radical changes. On the other hand, safety under TQM,

Table 7.1 Elements of a Total Safety System

Element	Description
Safety of workplace design	Plant layout Environmental control (noise and other emissions) Emergency procedures Fire fighting arrangements First aid facilities Lighting, restroom and other facilities
Safety of processes	Physical guarding Electro-mechanical emergency stops Fail-safe systems Perimeter fencing
Safety of human resources	Safety training Personal protective equipment Supervision Medical checks

Table 7.2 A comparison between traditional and TQM-based approaches towards safety

Traditional approach	TQM based approach (TSS)
Compliance with legal requirements	Exceeding legal requirements by adopting Zero Risk approach
Reacting to identified risks only	Identifying all possible risks and striving to eliminate them
Designing safety systems for a complex workplace by a process of patching up	Designing with visibility in mind and through a continuous effort to simplify tasks
External safety measures on process guarding and emergency switches	Intrinsic safety for on-line correction and intelligent fail-safe systems
Designing for the worker	Worker involvement in safety design
Induction training as a one off experience	Training for the task with skills/task change closely monitored
Employees trained to avoid identified risks only	Employees trained to identify, help eliminate risks
Employees understand that safety is a condition for doing the job	Employees appreciate that safety contributes to the job
Standard is compliance	Standard is striving for excellence
Poor data availability (only recorded accidents)	Rich data availability (inspection, diagnosis, continuous recording and analysis)

follows an innovative approach taking incremental steps to improve, modify or change existing arrangements with task simplification, task integration for organisational objectives and with an added-value approach towards the fulfilment of organisational objectives.

Total Safety Systems introduce the concept of Zero Risk which is so essential for the pursual of Zero Defect, right first time strategies. The incorporation of preventative safety within socio-technical elements of organisational systems, comprises the contribution of Total Preventative Systems which provide the Zero Breakdown principle and Human Development Systems which intend to educate and train workers for the application of right first time principles. Figure 7.2 illustrates the impact of Zero Risk on the implementation of TQM.

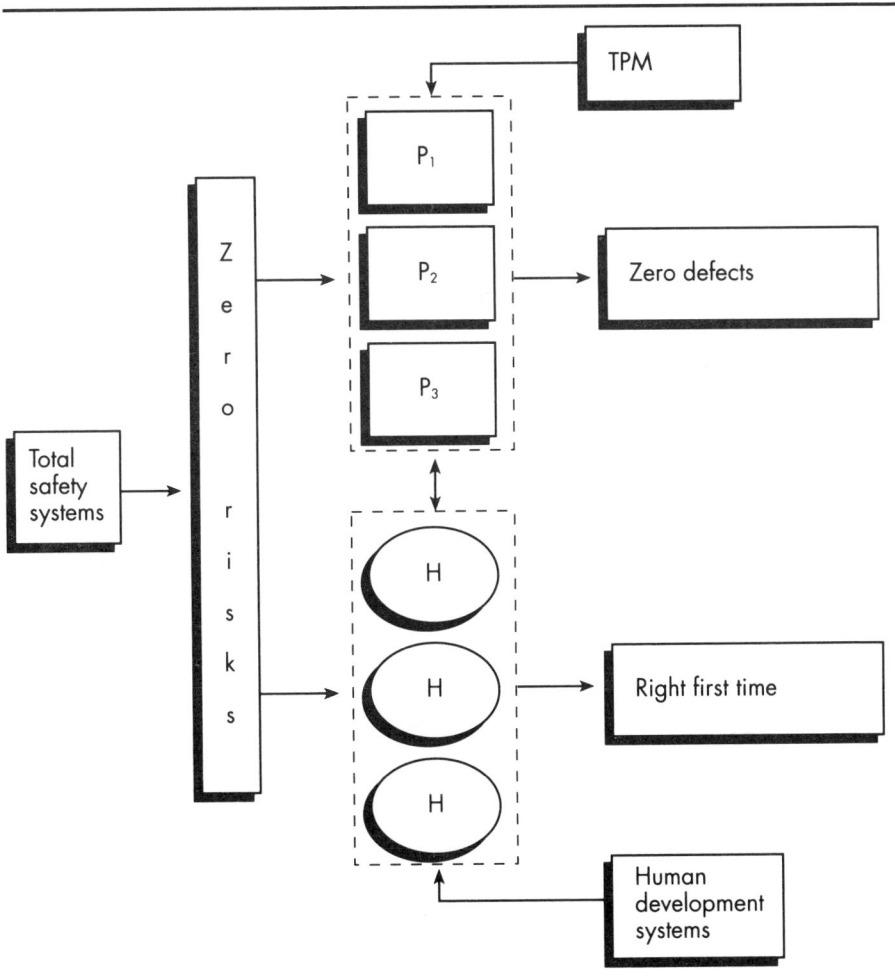

7.2 The concepts of Zero Risk in relation to TQM.

One can see from the figure that Zero Defect cannot be obtained in isolation. It has to depend on the contribution of other principles which traditionally have not been considered as value adding activities, such as TPM and TSS.

THE ECONOMIC VALUE OF SAFETY STANDARDS

If one accepts the notion that risks of any nature are disruptive, costly and damaging to organisational business performance, then their minimisation or total elimination would mean that organisational competitive objectives can be achieved. A safety strategy for TQM success would however place emphasis on risk elimination (Zero Risk) rather than risk minimisation. Figure 7.3 illustrates the relationship between expenditure on risk elimination efforts and the degree of success in identifying and eliminating risks.

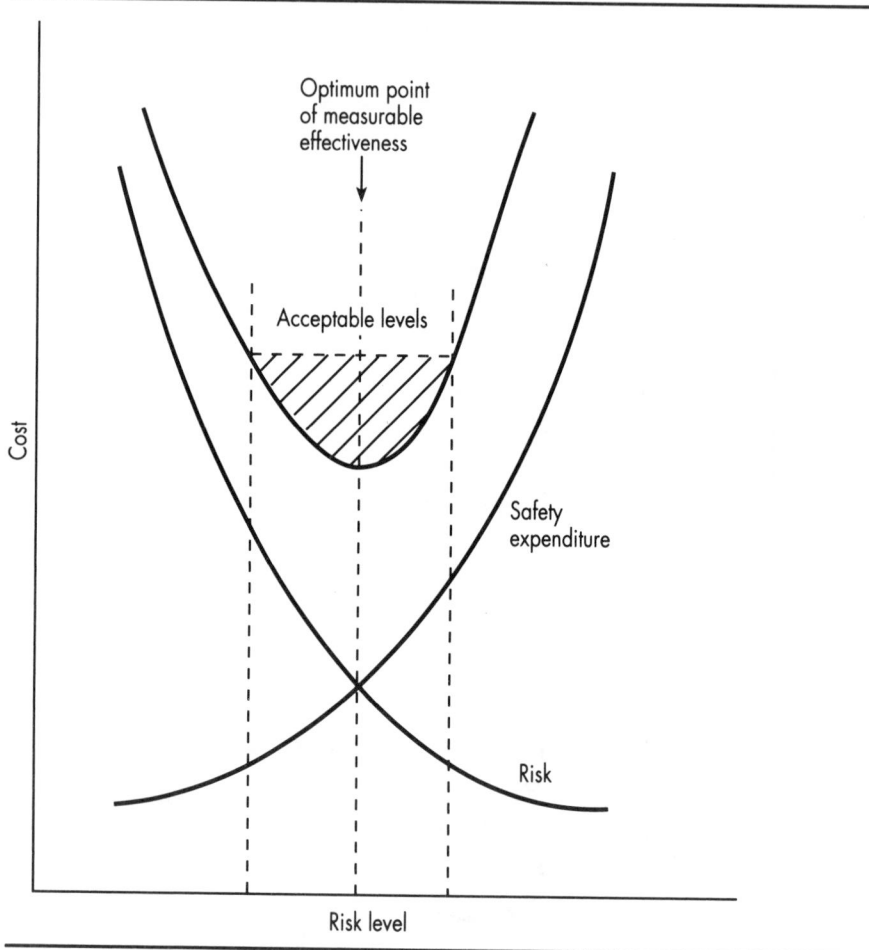

7.3 Safety effectiveness and risk reduction.

It is quite feasible that some of the risks will never be eliminated or would require a long term effort before they are completely removed. It is therefore more feasible to adopt a strategy of containment/improvement for certain risks. There is a similar analogy to process capability and the impact of random variables.

One would therefore find that there will be an optimum point where expenditure on safety would be most effective after which, other factors have to be considered before further improvements can take place. Generally speaking there will be a broad range where any level of expenditure would be effective and acceptable. Whilst it may be difficult or it would require longer to raise high safety standards to a higher level (because of economic viability, business/operational or structural constraints), lower standards are easily identifiable because at that point risks are at an optimum level. Any slippage results in disastrous consequences for the organisations concerned.

The relationship between expenditure on safety (i.e. the establishment of safety standards) and economic gains via optimisation of business operations is better explained by the matrix in Fig. 7.4. There are four quadrants representing a degree of dependency between increasing operational activities from the point of view of achieving maximum economic and competitive gains on the one hand, and the impact of a high or low safety standard on the former objective.

	Optimisation of business operations	Normalisation of business operations
Low safety standards	High economic/ competitive gains (short term) Very high risk of failure (long term)	Economic/ competitive gains (short term) Possible disruptions/ failures
High safety standards	Very high economic/ competitive gains Commanding position in market place Superior competitive performance	Economic + competitive gains Sustainable competitiveness based on strength

7.4 Business economics and safety standards.

Quadrant 1: A low consideration of safety standards at the detriment of maximising short term economic gains means high and persisting levels of risk.

Quadrant 2: Even if the intention is to run business operations under normal conditions without seeking to optimise output, low safety consideration still means that there are risks of failure.

Quadrant 3: There is a strong correlation between the establishment of high safety standards/optimisation of operations and the level of competitiveness. If companies strive for excellence in every aspect, superior performance can be achieved by the development of Zero Risk, Zero Defect strategy.

Quadrant 4: This is perhaps a more realistic option where on the one hand optimisation of operations is closely determined by process capability and safety standards are improved upon through a continuous improvement programme. It is likely that the highest percentage of organisations would most realistically be able to achieve a sustainable competitive advantage whilst aspiring to be the best by having a commanding position in the market place (quadrant 3).

THE IMPLEMENTATION OF TOTAL SAFETY SYSTEMS: A MANAGEMENT RESPONSIBILITY

Traditionally, safety was considered as one of those activities which organisations are required by law to conduct to ensure the safety, health and welfare of their employees. All the activities were conducted as a legal must rather than a moral duty or a general belief that safety is important towards the fulfilment of organisational objectives. This leads to another argument related to the legal requirements themselves. Safety legislation has always been vague and words such as 'reasonably practicable' have meant that standards of safety are never set and organisations are not encouraged to raise their standards more than legally required. This begs the next question – whose responsibility are safety activities? How is the effectiveness of safety management measured? What is the role of senior managers in the implementation of safety programmes?

Measurement of safety performance

Many researchers have come to the conclusion that measurement of safety performance has so far been using criteria which are unreliable such as accident reports. This is because the data collection methods comprise the collection and analysis of statistics related to accidents and injuries which have actually taken place. Most of the companies are only legally required to collect statistics on the type of incidents reportable under the Reporting of Injuries, Diseases and Dangerous Occurrences Regulations 1985. This regulation refers to the collection of statistics on fatalities, certain types of major injury and dangerous occurrences and accidents leading to worker absence for three or more consecutive days.

The statistics collected were traditionally used to determine safety performance by using the following accident rates:

- Accident incidence rate = No of reportable accidents/No of persons at risk per thousand
- Accident frequency rate = Lost-time accidents/Hours worked per hundred thousand
- Accident severity rate = Hours lost through accidents/Hours worked per hundred thousand

This approach to managing safety performance only measures failure and improvements on failure rates of previous years. As such it is a reactive and partial measure since for every serious accident there are a large number of near misses and some minor injuries. Various studies have been conducted to establish the ratio between major to minor accidents.[5] There are three major accident ratio studies represented in Table 7.3.

The various studies seem to suggest that there is a knock on effect between near

Table 7.3 Accident ratios based on three major studies

Year	Name of study	Ratios
1931	Heinrich accident ratio study	1 – serious 29 – minor 300 – near misses
1969	Bird accident ratio study	1 – serious or disabling 10 – minor injuries 30 – property damage 600 – accident with no visible injury or damage
1974/75	Tye accident ratio study	1 – serious 3 – minor 50 – first aid 80 – damage only 400 – near misses

misses and accidents. The general consensus suggests that if near misses are eliminated, subsequent accidents, injuries and damages can also be eliminated. This is one of the reasons why the concept of Zero Risk is a valid one. The ignorance and neglect of near misses by management for such a long time seems to indicate their failure to appreciate the importance of improving safety standards. It reflects that they often considered their role in complying with safety legislation by recording only the 'necessary statistics' which are failure statistics with limited usefulness for the implementation of safety continuous improvement programmes.

Under the concept of Zero Risk, safety performance needs to become more of a preventative effort by identifying possible hazards and eliminating them before they develop into major disasters, Fig. 7.5.

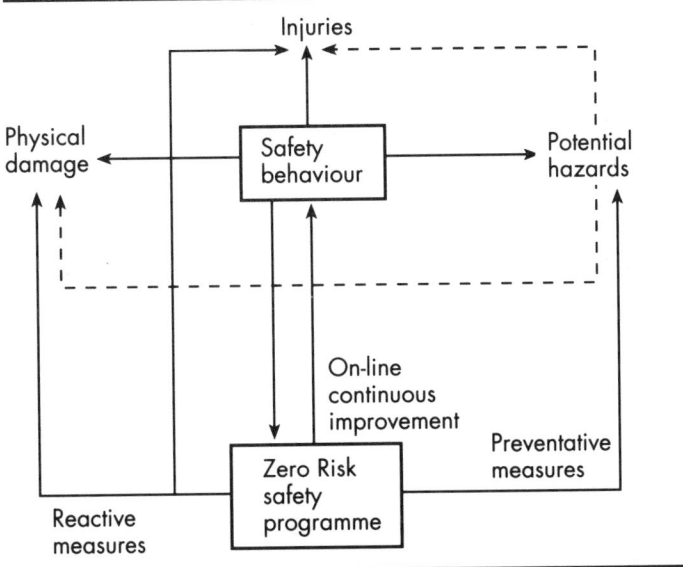

7.5 The study of safety behaviour through a Zero Risk safety programme.

Management responsibility in the implementation of safety policy

Besides the negative approach in measuring safety performance, another issue in the implementation of TSS is the responsibility of management. Many reports have drawn attention to the superficial role senior managers play in the implementation, monitoring and control of safety programmes in their organisations. Inquiry reports on some recent disasters[10] seem to indicate that there is confusion among supervisory and management personnel about role clarification, inadequate systems for monitoring breakdowns in safety standards and importantly that the system used for appraising investment decisions tended to provide 'organisational disincentive' to safety. Other research has come to the conclusion that a significant proportion of managers believe that it is not their responsibility to maintain the standards of health and safety within their organisations.[14]

Table 7.4 demonstrates that only a small proportion of senior managers perceive the responsibility of evaluating the effectiveness of safety training of their own staff to be their direct responsibility.[14] The study has also revealed that only a small

Table 7.4 Management responsibility for safety matters

Summary of rankings of managerial perceptions of responsibility for evaluating the effectiveness of health and training of their own staff	N = 60
Respondents seeing it as 'their job most'	33.3
Respondents seeing it as the 'safety officer's job most'	36.7
Respondents seeing it as the 'safety representative's job most'	6.7
Respondents seeing it as mostly job of one or more elements of safety machinery before a line management job	53.3
Respondents seeing it as mostly job of personnel/training department before a line management job	3.3
Respondents seeing it as mostly job of safety representative before their own job	13.3

Summary of rankings of perceived responsibility for the management of health and safety matters concerning subordinates	N = 60
Respondents seeing it as 'their job most'	28.3
Respondents seeing it as the 'safety officer's job most'	18.3
Respondents seeing it as the 'safety representative's job most'	11.7
Respondents seeing it as mostly job of one or more elements of safety machinery before a line management job	58.3
Respondents seeing it as mostly job of safety committee chairman	15.0
Respondents seeing it as 'health and safety committee's job most'	16.7
Respondents seeing it as mostly job of safety representative before their own job	40.0
Respondents uncertain whose job it was most	5.0

proportion consider the management of health and safety matters to be their own responsibility.

A further survey which looked at what kind of human-errors are most common, what causal factors are responsible for those errors and what actions are being taken to deal with them, has revealed that there is wide neglect in management's responsibility.[16] Table 7.5 is a summary of the key findings of the survey.

Tables 7.4 and 7.5 convey a series of messages which reflect serious neglect in the

Table 7.5 Most common safety human errors, their causes and the resulting actions

Most common errors	Misunderstanding of spoken and written instruction/information
	Mistake in performing a simple, familiar task
	Failure to notice something wrong
	Forgetting completely or missing a step in a task
	Mis-estimation of quantity of work and time required to do it
	Taking inappropriate action
	Mistake in performing complex/unfamiliar tasks
	Failure to comprehend the full implications of decisions
	Mistakes involving passing information from one person to another
	Difficult and unfamiliar tasks are less reported to give rise to error
Causal factors	Workload too high
	Boredom
	Emotional pressure (from boss, colleagues and outsiders)
	Time pressure
	Interruptions
	Environmental pressures (noise, temperature, etc)
	Feeling tired/unwell
	Use of (faulty) informal/unapproved procedures
	Faulty job and system designs that lead to mistakes
	Objectives/instructions unclear
	Absence of plan to deal with contingencies
Action currently taken	Post-accident investigation carried out by people who may be poorly trained thus leading to the possibility of ignoring/overlooking key clues
	Management response through inflicting 'punishment'
	Re-writing instructions, introducing additional instructions
	Conducting training programmes related to the new/additional instructions
	Consideration of automation/computerisation as a substitute

implementation of safety programmes. The following conclusions can therefore be drawn from the various reported findings:

● Managers do not always consider safety to be their direct responsibility. They tend to rely on the input of safety specialists and perceive their role only in declaring the organisation's intention to comply with the legal requirements in order to ensure the safety, health and welfare of all employees;
● Managers do not consider safety to be a value adding activity. As such they confine its role to the bare minimum for compliance with legal requirements. Statistics which are collected measure failure rates than preventative measures;
● Poor interest in safety matters is also characterised by the lack of proper procedures, emergency plans, adequate investment on safety and proper training strategies;
● Workplace and job designs are not developed with safety in mind. Workers are constantly pressurised to meet economic requirements without being properly prepared for changes in workload, task variation or process modification. In addition, economic motives often mean that investment on better design of work environment is discarded because it cannot be justified, since this is not directly linked to output.

One can elaborate on deficiencies in the role of senior managers in the implementation of safety to date. It is sufficient however to say that TQM is an ideal opportunity for many organisations to take stock and re-assess their approach to safety. The principles of Zero Risk and considering safety as a productive function are essential if superior performance is to ensue from the implementation of any TQM programme. Zero Risk also means that the measurement of safety performance depends on a TSS which involves continuous effort in identifying potential hazards and eliminating them, with less reliance on reactive safety.

The implementation of a TSS has therefore got to be a corporate effort where commitment has to come from the most senior level and where the philosophy of working safely is practiced by everyone within the organisation. It is suggested that the following approach be adopted:

● Safety corporate policy has to be considered within the framework of overall competitive strategy. Perhaps safety standards/expenditure levels should be linked with the desired competitive objectives, Fig. 7.4;
● Safety implementation, monitoring and control has to involve senior managers constantly. A safety steering committee including senior managers from the various business activities should be established;
● Safety representatives should be allowed to influence policy and the implementation of change which can affect the safety, health and welfare of employees. In addition safety representative committees can brief the steering committee on progress, suggestions and recommendations resulting from continuous improvement activity in the area of safety;
● Safety has to be widely practiced at the grass root level. All employees have to be fully trained, fully aware and conscious of the risks to their health and that of their colleagues. Employees should be encouraged to design their jobs with safety in mind and to be in charge of their immediate work environment so that high safety standards can be achieved;
● Incentives can be used to encourage the practice of good safety standards, such as the use of posters and slogans such as 'safety is free', 'safety = health', 'think

of others', 'your neighbour is grateful for your concern over safety'. Other incentives can be used such as suggestion schemes, rewards for clean, tidy work environment and good safety statistical record;

● The role of the safety adviser is crucial to the implementation of TSS. The adviser may or may not have a seat in the boardroom but does influence a great deal the design of a safety strategy in the context of corporate strategy. The safety professional can also advise senior managers on 'best practice' and changes which need to be brought about as a result of what he/she learns from dealing with external agencies. The safety advisor works very closely with the steering committee, employee representatives and oversees the practice of safety at the grass root level. It is important however to realise that this role is purely and simply of an advisory capacity and that safety is everyone's responsibility, Fig. 7.6.

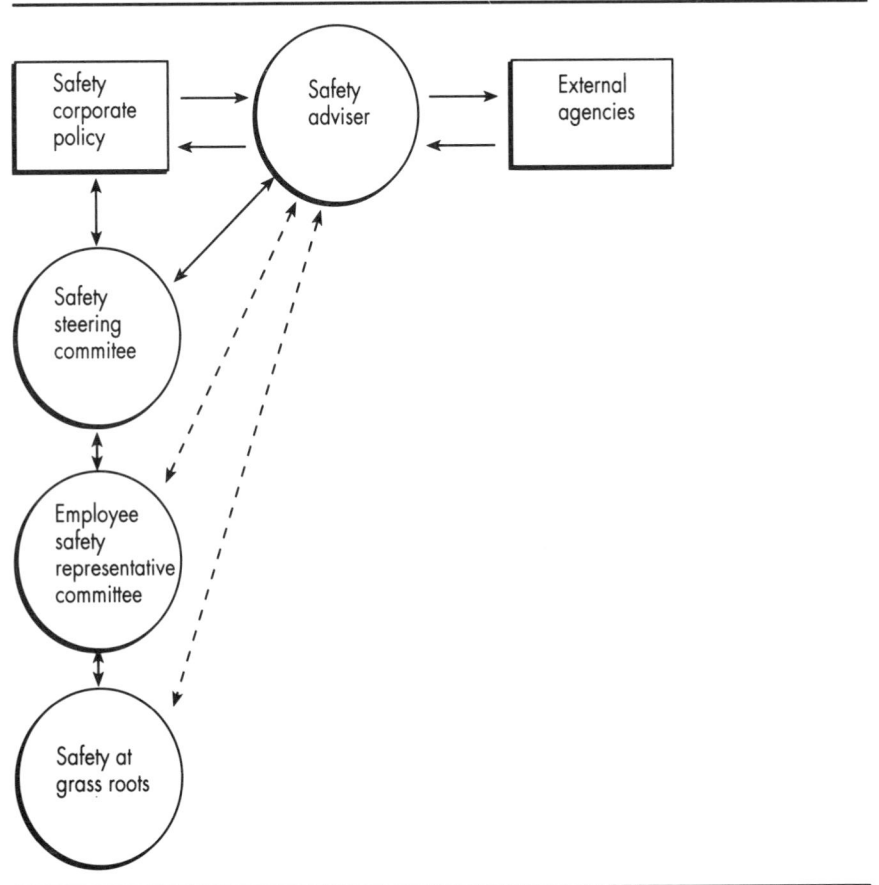

7.6 Implementing Total Safety Systems.

TOOLS AND TECHNIQUES FOR THE ACHIEVEMENT OF ZERO RISK

It has already been debated that the use of statistical techniques based on frequency rates is inappropriate in the context of TQM. Frequency rates are descriptive statistics and as such they have no power in determining performance improvements. Figure 7.7 illustrates a typical accident frequency rate chart which can be obtained by plotting frequency rates of monthly recordings.

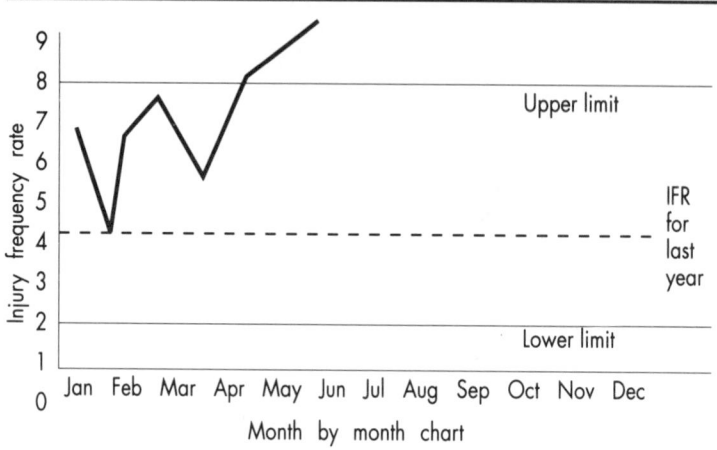

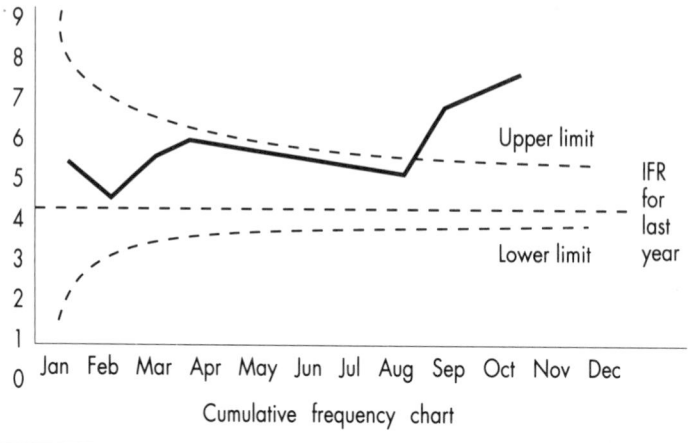

7.7 Accident frequency rate charts.

The dotted line represents the mean frequency rate of the previous year. A CUSUM chart can be obtained to reflect true trends of accident frequency rates overall.

There are three major statistical techniques used for the purpose of measuring failure rate. These include the following:[14]

● Frequency rate = The number of disabling injuries per million employee hours.

$$FR = \frac{\text{No of disabling injuries per million}}{\text{No employee hours worked}}$$

● Incident rate = No of recordable injuries and illnesses for every 200,000 hours that are worked by employees.

$$IR = \frac{\text{No of disabling injuries per two hundred thousand}}{\text{No of employee hours worked}}$$

158

● Severity rate = Number of days charged for lost-time injuries per million employee hours worked.

$$SR = \frac{\text{Total days charged per million}}{\text{No of employee hours worked}}$$

These statistics may be useful in specifically analysing failure frequency. They do however suffer from a large number of shortcomings which include the following:

● They are unable to measure performance since they are only descriptive in nature by providing comparative figures from year to year;
● Frequency rates do not reflect the overall safety performance standard company wide;
● FR provide overall statistics of accidents without pinpointing level of impact and degree of harm both short term and long term;
● FR are open to subjective interpretation since they do not provide an insight into the processes of hazard development which subsequently led to failures taking place;
● The standard used (mean of previous year's FR) can be misleading if it is interpreted as the standard to achieve;
● FR do not reflect true cost resulting from various losses. They measure cost of days lost but not opportunity costs, human costs in terms of poor morale, negative attitudes, etc;
● FR are absolute measures and do not look at failure in terms of the complex processes which lead to accidents. They do not identify the near misses, the minor injuries which do not have to be recorded legally and do not take into account unreported incidents.

In the context of TQM therefore, FR are unacceptable since they focus on failure. Zero Risk as a principle seeks to eliminate failure all together. As illustrated in Fig. 7.5, a continuous improvement programme with Zero Risk as the ultimate objective seeks to identify and eliminate hazards before they develop into major failures or lead to serious injuries. The use of SPC techniques is required for this purpose. The following approach needs to be adopted:

1 Process understanding to identify possible hazards (use flowcharting);
2 Hazard identification and selection for study (use tally sheets for data collection);
3 Use Pareto analysis, data stratification, cause-effect analysis and scatter diagrams to identify causes and eliminate the hazard.
4 Use of control charts. There may be some random causes which mean that hazards cannot be completely eliminated and therefore the use of control charts would mean that the hazards are confined and contained so that they will never develop into major disasters.
The two types of control charts used in safety are the attribute charts P and C.[4]

(i) **Behaviour Outcome Control Chart (P):** Based on binomial probability. Refers to large populations (safe, unsafe) criteria.
(ii) **Accident Control Chart (C):** Follows Poisson distribution which refers to limited number of observations over units of time. C chart is used for determining when accident frequency is out of control or when unstable accident frequency patterns are present. Through continuous analysis of trends in their positive/

negative developments, one can predict future possible outcomes and take appropriate measures to eliminate severe incidents.

The use of Safety Control Charts has many benefits, amongst which are the following:

1 Control charts provide a true measure of safety performance for each individual process and can be used to establish and improve overall safety standards within organisations;
2 They seek to establish stable processes in terms of risk presence/development;
3 Their main objective is to minimise and ultimately eliminate persisting risks so that Zero Risk becomes a realisable objective;
4 They consider safety as a productive function by linking objectives of Zero Defect, Zero Breakdown and Zero Risk for the achievement of the common objective of meeting customer requirements;
5 They encourage shared responsibility for raising safety standards by allocating process ownership to operators and people who are directly involved in performing the tasks;
6 They provide the best motivational method since process improvement is carried out by and standards are set by the workers themselves;
7 The availability of on-line data on hazard identification, monitoring and control can enable the safety adviser and safety steering committee to assess existing standards accurately and to devise realistic improvement targets;
8 More accurate measures of costs can be obtained since safety is accepted as an intrinsic part of process performance and therefore its productive output can be measured;
9 They facilitate the implementation of TQM by having an impact on corporate culture change, since TSS encourage improvements in workplace design, job design and worker involvement;
10 They have a major impact on corporate image and company respectability in the market place.
11 Savings from accident reduction, risk elimination and reductions in employee absence due to injuries, mean that money can be re-allocated to better the working environment;
12 Total Safety Systems mean that compliance with legislative requirements is not a measure of safety performance. Performance targets are set internally by seeking to establish a Zero Risk environment and externally by identifying and introducing best safety practice.

One of the typical reactions of management to dealing with safety hazards is the consideration of automation and computerisation as a cure to all the ills. Particularly, automation is considered to be capable of eliminating all accidents which are caused by human error. This raises two main questions:

● Are safety problems a behavioural question?
● Is new technology a cure to safety problems?

The two questions will be considered in the following two sections, starting by an assessment of the safety-effectiveness of new technology.

DOES NEW TECHNOLOGY LEAD TO EFFECTIVE SAFETY PRACTICES?

The author, in a joint project[18] has looked at the degree of safety of automated and computer-based systems. This work has led to some interesting findings in that new technological equipment such as robots, which is mainly introduced as a direct substitute for humans, tends to introduce new risks. The wide application of computerised systems has also raised many questions on safety.

Safety of robots

There are four main types of risks associated with the utilisation of robots:

Risks associated with the hardware: Some robots are susceptible to environmental changes and malfunction or more erratically in response to changes in radio frequency, voltage and temperature variations, dust and humidity or presence of chemicals and vibration;

Risks associated with the software: Imperfections in the program sometimes cause the robot to behave in an unexpected manner;

Risks associated with poor level of maintenance: Robots are sophisticated and complex systems which require frequent and adequate maintenance, especially of hydraulics and electric systems. Infrequent or poor quality maintenance increases risks to human beings;

Risks of collision: Robots can harm humans or damage machinery or can cause injury through emissions which cause burns, electrocutions, radiation and shock. Faults in the balance or grip can cause serious injury if the load is shed.

There is limited data available on accidents involving robots since their application is not wide spread as yet. The limited statistics however seem to indicate that robots are dangerous and can cause serious injuries. Tables 7.6 and 7.7 illustrate the number of accidents involving robots in Sweden 1979–83[20] and the frequency of accidents in relation to occupational status.[21]

Table 7.6 Number of accidents involving robots in Sweden, 1979–83

Activity	Contact with moving machine part, material	Other events	Total number of accidents
Adjustment in course of operation	14	–	14
Movement against robot	1	1	2
Repair, programming, putting robot in order	13	2	15
Miscellaneous	–	–	–

Table 7.7 Frequency of robot accidents by occupation

Groups at risk	% Frequency
Programmer/fitter	57
Staff for clearing stoppages	26
Maintenance, repair staff	4
Operating personnel	13

Risks associated with computers

Computers are mainly applied in the office environment. Their wide spread utilisation has led to concerns over risks associated with Visual Display Units (VDUs). The following is a list of the areas where risks to health have been reported:

- Deterioration in vision, development of cataracts, eye diseases and epilepsy, eye strain;
- Risks due to emission of radiation;
- Skin rashes;
- Miscarriages and birth defects;
- Stress related problems, Table 7.8;[22]
- Repetitive Strain Injury (RSI) causing tenosynovitis;
- Uncomfortable work environment, Table 7.9.[23]

Table 7.8 Stress in VDU and non-VDU clerical users

Stressor	VDU, %	Non-VDU, %
Bored with work	48	23
Unable to choose own work	96	82
Dislike of workload	45	21
Behind in work at least a week	27	8
Dissatisfied with pace	41	18
Worried about reprimands	24	8

There are two major outcomes from the introduction of new technology for the purpose of maximising economic benefits and eliminating health risks.

- That technological innovation such as robotics can cause high physical damage and major injuries, through erratic movement. What is alarming in this is that robots are susceptible to environmental conditions such as humidity, heat, dust, etc. This leads us to conclude that the risk will always be inherent and complete human isolation is the only answer;
- The use of VDUs does in the long run lead to some health conditions. Although the statistics collected so far are not conclusive, the reported cases seem to

Table 7.9 Work environment design and the use of VDUs

Problems	Responses	%
Glare from nearby windows/lights	144	63
Room too hot, cold or stuffy	114	50
Desks too low, awkward or no foot rest	66	29
Chair uncomfortable and/or difficult to adjust	64	28
Noise level too high (e.g. from printer)	60	26
Difficulty in reading text on VDU screen	50	22
No regular breaks from keying	39	17

suggest that more ergonomic design and equipment design may minimise some of the risks. One has to be alarmed at the variety of health conditions which may result from continuous interaction with computer systems.

An important outcome which has emerged from the discussion in this section is that TQM or rather Zero Risk cannot be achieved by replacing people with automated, computerised systems. The introduction of new technological innovation may have clear economic/business benefits and some technical features which contribute towards the implementation of TQM, such as reliability, ease of maintainability, quality of design, etc, but will also have with it some potential risk/hazards which may be a new breed and require a different approach towards identification and elimination.

IS SAFETY A BEHAVIOURAL QUESTION?

The above analysis has revealed that safety of technical elements within organisational systems can be managed through better design, better understanding of the limitations of operational characteristics of process equipment and better procedures and guidelines on utilisation, maintenance and management of technical processes. A joint project[18] involving the author, has made the following recommendation, in relation to technological processes:

'If health and safety, in relation to new technology, is to follow the tremendous pace of technological innovation, systematic data collected consistently over time is a prerequisite to any evaluation of risks. Such statistics are all the more important as their analysis can lead to the diminution, if not eradication, of certain types of injuries by suggesting changes either in working practices or machine design. The dialogue between the legislator, the designer, the supplier and the customer must be an informed dialogue and hard data on the incidence, frequency and severity of injuries per type of production process and types of accidents must be given a prominent place within their decision making process.'

This suggests that a determined effort to eliminate hazards by close control of processes can be achieved. This does not however mean the complete eradication of all types of risks. Organisations are socio-technical systems. What is therefore important is the safe management of the interface between technical systems and people systems. This is the challenge of TSS. The question therefore as to whether safety is a behavioural question is a valid one.

The answer lies in not only carrying out semantic and symbolic changes but a committed effort in behaviour modification through continually educating, training, involving and rewarding people for their contribution on an everyday basis in meeting organisational objectives. This is to some extent the ethos of TQM philosophy which seeks to implement quality in a 'cultural context' as a voluntary desire to achieve high standards of excellence rather than through the 'carrot and stick' principle. Behaviour modification is at the heart of making principles such as Zero Defect, Zero Breakdown and Zero Risk realisable. Behaviour modification will gradually lead to changes in corporate culture which many organisations find to be an important challenge for the implementation of TQM, but, which often they cannot easily define.

There are various concepts which can be applied for behaviour modification.[4] Table 7.10 describes some of the ideas which can be applied to modify behaviour.

Table 7.10 Some concepts of behaviour modification for TSS

Type of concept	Description
Reinforcement	The purpose is to increase the frequency of a desired behaviour for acting safely; positive reinforcement (complimentary recognition); negative reinforcement (removing unpleasant aspects)
Punishment	Two types: positive punishment (forcing something unpleasant); negative punishment (taking away something pleasant)
Reward	A positive reinforcer. Helps guide behaviour to what is acceptable and what is expected
Token economics	Symbolic reward for a positive act/behaviour (e.g. badges)
Premark principle	Changing specific behavioural responses. Rewarding acceptance so that rejection can be minimised and therefore behaviour can be modified

Behaviour modification for TSS can be part of an integrated effort in modifying the behaviour of workers so that quality, efficiency, creativity and safety are optimised. In fact it is more appropriate to educate workers that Zero Defects can only result by looking after processes for capability (Zero Breakdown) and by making sure that there are no potential risks which will lead to physical damage or harmful injuries (Zero Risk).

TOWARDS A POSITIVE IMPLEMENTATION OF TOTAL SAFETY SYSTEMS

The previous sections have discussed different aspects of TSS and their degree of importance towards the attainment of Zero Risk. The following points can serve as guidelines for the implementation of TSS in the context of TQM.

The strategic relevance of TSS

Safety has to be appreciated at the corporate level for its productive contribution and not just as a support function whose role should just be confined to meeting legal requirements. With this in mind, the implications of poor safety standards have got to be fully weighed and the right balance of safety standards and economic competitiveness has to be implemented.

The development and implementation of a safety policy

It is important that a safety policy has to be comprehensive, with its short term and long term objectives in relation to overall organisational objectives. The safety policy has to be developed by senior managers using the advice and guidance of the safety adviser. Its implementation should be steered by a committee of managers at the senior level, with employee representation and involvement in tactical/operational aspects. Finally safety has to be widely applied at the grass roots level with employees determining their own standards in conjunction with the wider objectives of achieving Zero Defects.

Utilisation of statistical tools and techniques

A breakaway from the traditional approach to measuring safety performance is essential. A TSS strategy should be geared towards the identification and elimination of hazards before they develop into major disasters. The use of SPC techniques and safety control charts is compulsory in the form of managing behavioural aspects and technical aspects of processes.

Ensuring positive interface between social-technical processes

Safety control systems have to eliminate risks from technical processes, protect humans against identifiable/known risks but more importantly develop positive interaction between people and technical systems through behaviour modification.

Aim for a Zero Risk goal

Close involvement of people, the encouragement of continuous improvement programmes and team work should be oriented towards the achievement of standards of excellence. An integrated approach therefore with working safely, reliably and carefully towards producing what the customer wants, has to be instigated in people's minds.

8

ESSENTIALS OF TQM: LEADERSHIP

LEADERS, WHO ARE THEY?

Successful implementation of TQM is often reported to be due largely to the actions of a champion, the commitment of senior managers, the vision of people at the top, good strategists and strong leadership. So what is really meant by leadership? Does it refer to a rare breed of people with unique skills? Can leadership be taught and learnt? Furthermore, why is it that strong leadership is more easily identified with organisations which have just gone through a period of crisis.

Leadership can take many styles and is based on both situational and transformational factors. It may well be that leaders can emerge because they happen to be the right people, in the right place and at the right time. Leaders tend to adapt styles according to changes surrounding them. For example it is argued that a style adopted during a time of crisis is different from times of stability:[43]

'The kind of leadership needed in times of crisis or great peril is very different from what is needed in times of stability, peace and prosperity.'

Leadership is about wanting things to happen. Senior managers tend to think about how to create effective organisational processes capable of responding to various concerns and capable of achieving desired goals. As Kotter[51] suggests, general managers are concerned with developing and maintaining an extensive interpersonal network, and formulating an agenda. Organisational processes are only the arena, and interpersonal processes represent the actors. Leaders need to identify what the priorities and agendas are for each actor, and have to bring the various people together so that the act is complete.

Leadership is certainly not about 'getting your own way through other people'. This, it has been suggested, is manipulation.[43] Drucker[27] in relation to this point, writes:

'The leader who basically focuses on himself or herself is going to mislead. The three most charismatic leaders in this century inflicted more suffering on the human race than almost any trio in history: Hitler, Stalin, and Mao. What matters is not the leader's charisma. What matters is the leader's mission. Therefore, the first job of the leader is to think through and define the mission of the institution.'

Leadership therefore is making sure that the tasks are distributed and that goals are achieved by involving everyone in the organisation. The task therefore for any leader, is to create an environment where not only individual genius can flourish but more importantly, an environment in which the collective capacities of other people in the organisation is the end objective.[22] This is also recognised by a leader who transformed his organisation from what he calls 'authoritarian control to authoritarian abdication'.[23] Ralph Stayer writes:

> 'No one had asked for more responsibility; I forced it down their throats. They were good soldiers, and they did their best, but I had trained them to expect me to solve their problems. I had nurtured their inability by expecting them to be incapable; now they met my expectations with an inability to make decisions unless they knew which decisions I wanted them to make.'

Stayer believed that his role was to create the agenda and then motivate people to carry it out. He makes the analogy of his style of leadership to the buffalo. He adds:

> 'In fact, I expected my people to follow me the way buffalo follow their leader – blindly. Unfortunately, that kind of leadership model almost led to the buffalo's extinction. Buffalo hunters used to slaughter the herd by finding and killing the leader. Once the leader was dead, the rest of the herd stood around waiting for instructions that never came, and the hunters could exterminate them one by one.'

This is typical of many leadership styles which, in the short run achieve a great deal of success, particularly financial. The centralised control, the biased interest in only financial criteria, the lack of delegation means that success can lead to the 'land of make believe' because people are used only as tools and their manipulation is expected to lead to higher and higher performance levels. This of course, is not the style of leadership which TQM implementation requires. Total Quality Management to a large extent is a bottom-up, led and supported activity. Authoritarian styles would certainly pose a major obstacle to success in the implementation of TQM.

Leadership has to be about representation of a general consensus rather than dictation of terms and direction for the achievement of superior performance. It is through people and by different levels of contributions representing knowledge and creativity input, skills and discipline, that organisational objectives can be met. Stayer[23] compares this to what he calls 'a flock of geese on the wing'. He adds:

> 'I didn't want an organizational chart with traditional lines and boxes, but a "V" of individuals who knew the common goal, took turns leading, and adjusted their structure to the task at hand. Geese fly in a wedge, for instance, but land in waves. Most important, each individual bird is responsible for its own performance.'

It has already been mentioned that strong leadership is often associated with solving crises. Drucker[27] argues that the task is not to avert crises but to anticipate and to be ahead of them by creating the 'battle-ready' organisation which knows how to behave, trusts itself and where people trust each other and can work with each other. This is contrary of course to the traditional styles of leadership where emphasis has always been on the positive and where failure was always considered unacceptable. This style has often led to people shielding problems from their bosses because the latter cannot take bad news. This culture is in deep conflict with TQM, which encourages visibility, problem-solving, admitting weaknesses and combatting waste without punishment or reprimands but rather encouragement to improve continuously.

Leaders therefore have to be all over the organisation. They have to be seen through the way activities are conducted, through people's discipline and commitment, through the creative effort, care, attention and pride for individual tasks and the belief that safety is assured and destinations will be reached, with full confidence, because the 'captain of the ship' (the leader) is trusted and widely respected for his/her ability. Peters and Austin[1] provide a broad definition of leadership which is suitable to TQM implementation:

'Leadership means vision, cheerleading, enthusiasm, love, trust, verve, passion, obsession, consistency, the use of symbols, paying attention as illustrated by the content of one's calendar, out-and-out drama (and the management thereof), creating heroes at all levels, coaching, effectively wandering around, and numerous other things.'

Some of the essential elements of strong leadership which are often reported are described in Table 8.1.

Table 8.1 Elements which make up strong leadership

Vision	Ability to conceptualise and execute through effective communication
Experience	Ability to grow with experience and learn from previous mistakes
Making things happen	Ability to bring the best out of others and make them improve their standards all the time
Intuition	Ability to sense that a problem exists, to react to them in the right way, to make experience work, use data analysis effectively
Problem management	Ability to manage series of problems in an orderly and *most* effective manner
Leading by example	Making others feel wanted and important, helping them fulfill their goals and expectations, facilitating climate of individual growth and development

Whilst the table does not include the whole list of criteria which make up good and strong leadership, it illustrates some important points which any leader should have if the organisational transformation to facilitate the implementation of TQM can take place.

Strong leadership is much affected by various processes which can facilitate or inhibit what managers desire to achieve. The strength of leadership therefore is to react to the various processes to make things happen. Figure 8.1 represents the various stages involved in the achievement of organisational transformation which is crucial for TQM implementation.

The criteria described in Table 8.1 are all reflected in Fig. 8.1. Strong leadership relies on intuition and experience to deal with the various dynamic processes. It is also heavily dependent on wanting things to happen and having a clear vision. It is also reflected by the ability to lead by example in shaping the right organisational climate fit for strong competitiveness and in making others feel wanted and important, so that they can contribute efficiently and effectively in making objectives realisable.

It is argued here that corporate culture cannot be modified easily until all the other aspects of organisational systems have been set right. Corporate culture is reflected everywhere within organisations and tends to reflect the sum total of what is good or bad about organisations. It is also argued that in the context of TQM, the major focal point is the type of leadership which is inherent, since things can only happen if people at the top dearly wish them to do so.

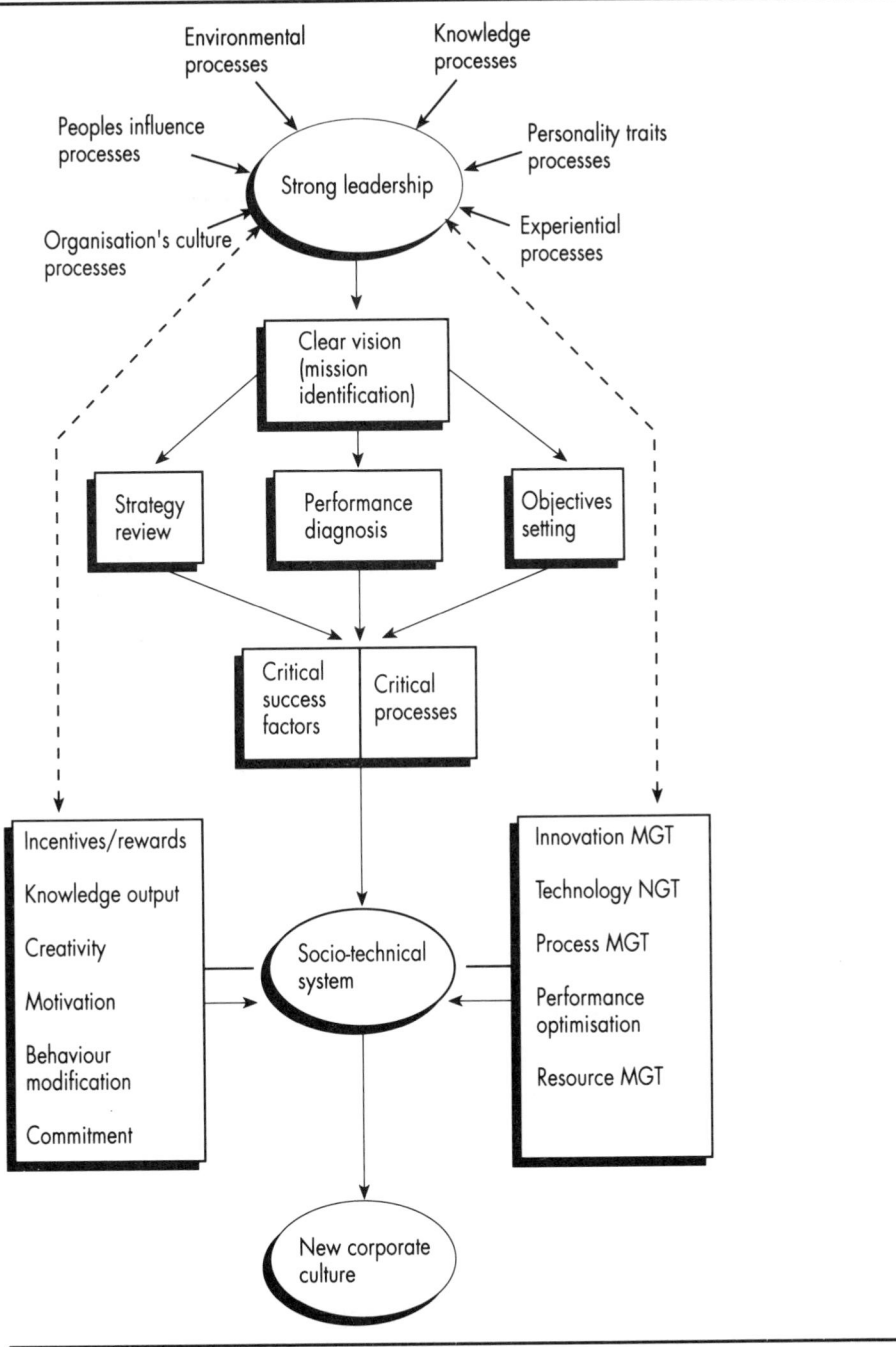

8.1 The impact of leadership on corporate culture change.

MANAGEMENT OR LEADERSHIP – WHAT IS THE DIFFERENCE?

It is often considered that leadership and management are the same. This is not the case. Management and leadership tend to complement one another. Strong leadership with weak management is no better than strong management with weak leadership. For organisations to deal with the various complexities and frequent changes, there has to be strong leadership to direct the organisation forward and strong management to pull the strings together. Kotter[14] writes:

'Leadership is different from management, but not for reasons most people think. Leadership isn't mystical or mysterious. It has nothing to do with having "charisma" or other exotic personality traits. It is not the province of

Table 8.2 Most common management styles

Style	Description
The godfather	Demands complete control of their organisations and total loyalty from employees;
	Subordinates are given freedom in their routine duties, however their goals are not decided by them;
	Groups led by godfathers are normally goal oriented and known for getting things done.
The ostrich	Like to stick their heads in the sand rather than face unpleasantness of any kind, always wish for problems to go away;
	Prefer non-confrontational approaches to problem-solving – avoid big debates;
	Often very capable and knowledgeable in their areas of expertise. Would be better suited as assistants rather than managers;
	Value more their superior's opinion on their own performance rather than developing their subordinates.
The do-it-yourselfer	Desire to control everything especially more challenging projects – delegate only trivial projects or ones which require special skills;
	Capable individuals, workaholics.
The detailer	Want to know everything that subordinates do;
	Consider their task to be wiser and know more than their subordinates.
The politician	Good at saying what people want to hear;
	Tend to stratify employees and management (tend to look for the winning side).
The arbitrator	Very successful in dealing with large groups because of their good understanding of people;
	Believe in team work and team decision;
	However cannot be competitive leaders.
The eager beaver	Create ever greater workloads to the point of interrupting the smooth functioning of their organisations;
	Measure their worth by the number of letters and reports they generate and by how hard their subordinates work.

a chosen few. Nor is leadership necessarily better than management or a replacement of it. Rather, leadership and management are two distinctive and complementary systems of action.'

In most instances people do not manage and lead at the same time. It is also quite possible that some brilliant managers do not wish or aspire to become leaders. Brilliant leaders may not desire to become managers because they may lack the patience or sense of detail which is required when managing complex operations.

Similarly to leadership, there are various management styles which can be adopted by organisations, most of them can be effective in some respects and perhaps reflect weaknesses in other areas. Seven styles which are thought to be the most common are described in Table 8.2.[12]

These seven styles have all got strengths and weaknesses and certainly in the context of TQM implementation, if individual styles are adopted, these will have some shortcomings. It is very desirable to adopt a style which blends the various positive attributes. Ninomya[12] argues that effective management is comparable to the 'wagon masters of the Westward movement in the last century'. He writes:

'A wagon master had two jobs. He had to keep the wagons moving toward their destination day after day despite all obstacles. He also had to maintain harmony and a spirit of teamwork among the members of his party and to resolve daily problems before they become divisive. A wagon master's worth was measured by his ability to reach the destination safely and to keep spirits high along the way. He had to do both in order to do either.'

It is perhaps not unreasonable to consider both management and leadership under the same umbrella. This is particularly important since TQM requires people with vision, and who have a strong desire to want and make things happen, as illustrated in Fig. 8.1. Effective management (strong leadership + strong management), has been described in many different ways, for example effective managers have been referred to as requiring ten different characteristics including being: available, humble, inclusive, objective, humorous, fair, tough, effective, decisive, and patient.[52] Table 8.3 illustrates some of the key characteristics that effective managers (leaders) require.

The three examples discussed in the table are ideal for the implementation of TQM which requires resoluteness and the urge to see things happen, big transformations using people as the powerful means. Figure 8.2 represents a model where the continued effort to delight customers has to be matched by the constant need to innovate, using people as the best means. The whole effect is instigated, managed,

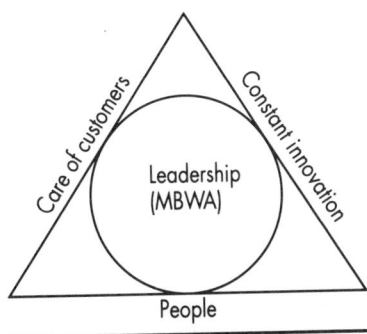

8.2 A leadership model: management by walkabout (MBWA).

Table 8.3 Effective management styles suitable for TQM

Reference	Characteristic	Description
12	Decision maker	Most important tool for effective management
	Listener and communicator	Must learn how to sense group dynamics and be sensitive to moods and attitudes. This is important for fulfilling employees' needs for recognition and appreciation
	Teacher	Training everyone with potential to become a manager
	Peacemaker	Knowing how to minimise conflict
	Visionary	Setting goals which are firm and meaningful
	Self-critic	Ability to admit own mistakes and learning how not to repeat them
	Team captain	Consensus decision making
	Leader	Must have drive and determination
		Must have qualities such as trust, modesty, politeness, patience, and sensitivity
		Appreciate people, do not just manipulate or command but lead
1	Managing by walkabout (MBWA)	Surviving organisation is the adaptive organisation. Four variables: two external (customers and innovation) and two novel (people and leadership). Leadership is about focusing on sensing change and adapting to it with people involvement, Fig. 8.2
		MBWA is about listening, empathising, staying in touch
47	Challenging the process	Searching for opportunities
		Experiment and take risks
	Inspiring a shared vision	Envision the future
		Enlist others
	Enabling others to act	Foster collaboration
		Strengthen others
	Modelling the way	Set the example
		Plan small wins
	Encouraging the heart	Recognise individual contribution
		Celebrate accomplishments

co-ordinated and controlled by a leadership style which is informal and values the human creative potential. In all the examples emphasis has been placed on vision and team work and achieving results through human potential. This therefore seems to indicate that having a vision and fostering human achievements are prerequisites for a sound leadership style which can be applied in the context of TQM.

Effective management therefore is the best approach to combine management with leadership. Managers have to be encouraged to take an outward focus and bring about change. Leaders on the other hand have to be encouraged to take an inward interest in the detailed operations of their organisations. In the context of TQM, continuous improvement should encompass the establishment of an effective management style strong in management and strong in leadership. Table 8.4 contrasts the key aspects of management and leadership roles.[14] The ability to combine both roles effectively will undoubtedly lead to strong TQM leadership.

Table 8.4 A comparison of management and leadership roles

Management	Leadership
Coping with complexity	Coping with change
Involves deciding what needs to be done, creating networks of people and relationships that can accomplish an agenda	Involves deciding what needs to be done, creating networks of people and relationships that can accomplish an agenda
Manage complexity first by *planning and budgeting* – setting targets or goals for the future – establishing steps for achieving those targets – allocating resources to accomplish those plans	Leading an organisation to constructive change begins by *setting a direction* – developing a vision of the future along with strategies for producing the changes needed to achieve the vision
Achieve plans by *organising and staffing* – creating an organisational structure and tasks, staffing the jobs with able people, communicating all plans, delegating responsibility and devising systems to monitor the implementation of various plans	Achieve plans by *aligning people* communicating the new direction to people who understand the vision and are committed to its achievement
Ensures plan accomplishment by *controlling and problem-solving* monitoring results compared with set plans – identifying deviations and solving problems	Achieving a mission requires *motivating and inspiring* – keeping people in the right direction by appealing to basic human potential often untapped

One can see from the table that there is a high degree of compatibility between the role of management and leadership. Organisations which are striving for excellence and superior performance have to narrow the gap between the roles of managers and leaders and make sure that they are the same. After all being an effective leader requires internal operations to be managed efficiently. It is the interface between internal efficiency which would ultimately lead to fulfilling a vision most effectively. If the people who have the vision and want things to happen are the same people who have good understanding of their organisations' strengths and weaknesses, then objectives are realistic and achievable.

LEADING THE LEADERS: THE ROLE OF THE BOARDROOM

Leaders can only flourish and achieve success if they are supported by other leaders both as subordinates and bosses. A leader is only as good as the chairman/board of the organisation they represent. Company chairmen have often been criticised for not fulfilling their roles properly by depriving management of an opportunity to implement change which would lead to success;[20] not fulfilling their obligations set by law and expected of it by owners of the business, shareholders and the public in general[49] and by adopting the 'let's not rock the boat approach'.[21]

Leadership is a distributed process and has to be defined according to the environment individuals operate in, the scope of their expected contribution, the degree of flexibility they have and most importantly the type of individuals there are. The strength of leadership in an organisation however will be indicated by the strength and commitment of its chairman/board of directors. The effort for TQM implementation has to be spear headed from the boardroom, otherwise it can be doomed to fail.

It is difficult to describe exactly what is expected of the board in terms of leadership. Some suggest that the planning role of the board needs to include the following:[50]

● The definition of corporate objectives and strategy;
● Establishing how planning is to be done;
● Examining and questioning subsidiary company plans;
● Forming an overall corporate plan;
● Communicating decisions;
● Motivating management to perform;
● Monitoring performance and acting where there is failure to achieve objectives.

Others have suggested that the primary role of a boardroom leader has to include the following:[37]

● Strong basic convictions;
● Clear strategic vision;
● Intellectual capacity;
● Management experience;
● Political skills.

These various roles may on the whole reflect what boardroom leaders tend to do. There is however one important point to be raised, which refers to the 'management role'. Although the second list mentions management experience, it may well be that this experience has been acquired in a different organisation or may be outdated for today's business environment. A leader essentially is an instigator of change, catering for tomorrow's requirements. This is why leadership has to be a distributed role otherwise effectiveness cannot be maintained if there is a point of overloading leaders with work, problems and information, Fig. 8.3.

Boardroom leaders have to set the path, create tomorrow's companies today and then let other leaders formulate strategies and objectives. Drucker[53] on this point, writes:

> The boards of directors cannot work out a company's strategy ... but it is the duty of the board to make sure that a company ... has adequate strategies ...'

Leadership therefore as has been suggested,[37] is composed of two complementary roles:

(i) **Corporate governance and direction:** The function of the chairman and the board;
(ii) **Strategy development and implementation:** The function of the chief executive and the management team.

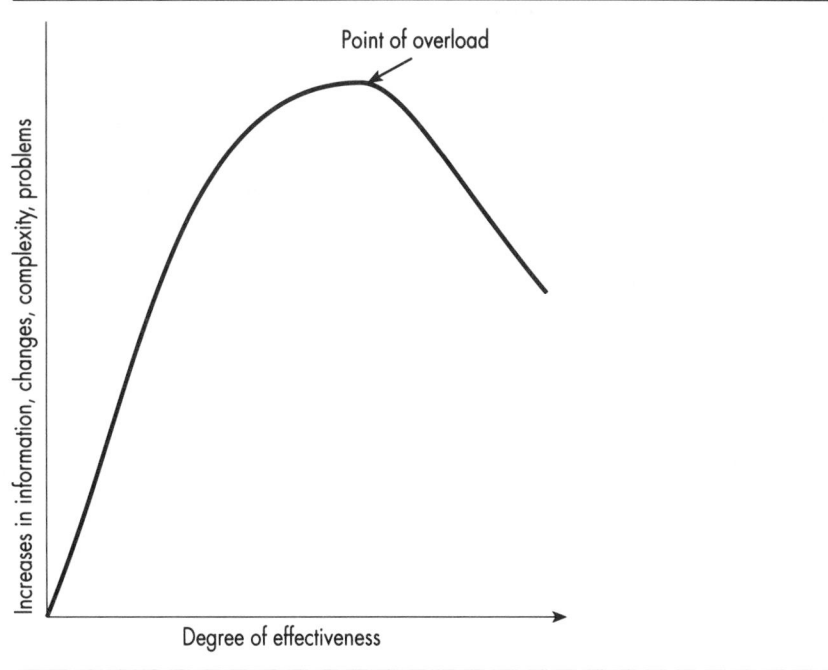

Point of overload

Increases in information, changes, complexity, problems

Degree of effectiveness

8.3 Effectiveness of leadership in decision making.

It is the degree of effectiveness between the two roles which is going to determine how successful organisations can achieve the transformation required for the implementation of TQM. Whilst it is easy to focus on one aspect of leadership, this may not be enough to carry out all the changes necessary for instigating 'a corporate culture' change so essential for modern competitiveness and for making TQM the means by which future competitiveness has to be driven.

Table 8.5[37] describes the process of transforming today's organisation into tomorrow's strong competitor and how the process of transformation is managed by the dual leadership role, both at the governance level and the strategic level.

THE FIRST TASK OF A LEADER: SETTING THE CORPORATE IDENTITY

The role of leaders in any organisation is to form a corporate identity which will enable the company to compete and be recognised. Corporate identity has been defined as follows:[9]

'The controlled and explicit management of the ways in which an organisation's activities are perceived.'

Corporate identity is usually defined by a mission statement, which sets any business apart from rivals and main competitors. Through implicit aims and explicit intentions, the statement reflects the mission of the organisation in fulfilling its clearly defined role, having identified products, markets, technologies and skills which can effectively be used to translate demand into goods and services for customer

Table 8.5 Transforming organisations towards successful competitiveness: The dual leadership roles

Governance and direction: chairman/board

Today's company May have the following characteristics	Role	Tomorrow's company Should have the following characteristics
Bottom-up 'operations push' strategy or no clear strategy at all	Formulate a clear vision and strategy	Clear top-down 'vision-driven' strategy
Ineffectual 'custodial' board	Compose and lead an effective board	Strong board capable of helping the chairman to 'set the drumbeat' for the company
Unclear basic policies and weak 'cultural value' signals	Set a new 'drumbeat' of basic values, policies and priorities	Cultural values are visibly and constantly enacted by the chairman and all board members
Benchmarks and standards are internally set and aim for incremental improvement	Appoint an MD with a clear mandate to develop new business strategies and operating plans with demanding targets and standards	Benchmarks capture the best external practice and aim for order-magnitude improvement

Strategy and implementation: MD/management

Organisation structure is out of date, not matched to tomorrow's business structure	Restructure the business portfolio and the management organisation. Redefine the strategies and operating plans for each business, setting demanding targets and standards	Market-based organisation structure
Control is by systems		Control is through people
Recruitment and development are seen as staff jobs	Establish a new cultural climate in which the quality and motivation of people are given the highest value and priority	The managing director is the chief recruiter and development is a priority for managers at ALL levels
People are protected		People are respected
Uncompetitive performance, poor financial results, a vulnerable P/E ratio	Monitor the operating and financial results against new targets and standards and insist on their achievement	Winning performance and a strong P/E ratio

consumption. It has been suggested that a mission statement should include the following five key elements:[9]

- The organisation's history, its ethics, its philosophy, its culture and its policies;
- The current preferences of the owners and management;
- Environmental considerations;

● The organisation's resources;
● The organisation's distinctive competencies – aiming to do that which it can do best.

Campbell[31] who wrote a book on 'a sense of mission' argues that a mission statement needs to reflect purpose, strategy, values and behaviour standards. He concludes that:

'Writing a mission statement is no easy task. It requires commitment, energy, vision and, above all, endless patience. A management team that seriously wants to create a meaningful and powerful statement will be forced to ask itself some searching questions.'

An example of a corporate mission is that of Nissan's.[48] The corporate philosophy was printed on a card and distributed to all its employees. It contained the following:

'Our first commitment is to customer satisfaction. Through diligent efforts to develop new customers and expand our customer base we are contributing to the on-going progress and enrichment of society.'

Nissan's corporate principles

1 To create attractive products by capitalising on the company's innovative and highly reliable technologies, staying in constant touch with the needs of the global market;
2 To be sensitive to customers' needs and offer them maximum satisfaction based on steadfast sincerity and ceaseless efforts to meet their requirements;
3 To focus on global trends, making the world the stage for the company's activities, and to nurture a strong company that will grow with the times;
4 To foster the development of an active and vital group of people who are ready and willing at all times to take on the challenge of achieving new goals.

These corporate objectives once known by everyone employed in the organisation, can be easily implemented since the objective is common to all. The mission statement has to be followed by another task that leaders have to undertake, that of identifying the Critical Success Factors (CSFs) and the Critical Processes (CPs) which have to be analysed and controlled so that CSFs can be achieved. Critical Success Factors were defined in 1961 by Daniel.[54] He referred to them as follows:

'The limited number of areas in which results, if they are satisfactory, will ensure successful competitive performance for the organisation. They are the few key areas where "things must go right" for the business to flourish. If results in these areas are not adequate, the organisation's efforts for the period will be less than desired.'

Essentially CSFs are performance indicators, which are important to TQM as they reflect the strengths and weaknesses of processes and give management better control mechanisms for the optimisation of operations and therefore for achieving superior performance.

The achievement of all the corporate objectives and making CSFs a reality is dependent on the effectiveness of leaders in managing people and generating commitment.

THE SECOND TASK OF A LEADER: GENERATING COMMITMENT

'Low commitment or not enough commitment' is a common expression. It is important to ask what is meant by commitment. Managers, in particular, have always accused subordinates of not showing as much commitment as they are. Others have only played lip-service to this essential element of the quality transformation. Expressions such as 'quality is our business', 'excellence is our next stop' are highly publicised but unfortunately tend not to be backed up by action and determination. It seems that managers consider their role to make policy statements and for others to realise the vague, ill-understood, poorly resourced goals. A dichotomous situation prevails. Managers would like optimised throughput, cost reduction and short term focus. On the other hand they desire continuous improvement to be introduced with Zero Defect as the ultimate objective. Are the two compatible? Can mediocrity be superimposed on excellence?

Commitment, according to most writers is managing knowledge workers, liberating the mind so that it becomes creative and fostering a positive climate fit for human development, human existence and human potential exploitation. Gilbert[24] on the issue of commitment, writes:

> The commitment required to empower, rather than eviscerate, improvement efforts is no less than vigorous and informed management involvement from the very beginning and the view that quality issues are inseparable from general strategic planning. Well-intentioned but uninformed efforts will not suffice.'

Five factors can be specified which should make the generation of high commitment a more plausible goal as follows:[55]

(i)   An awareness of the overriding importance of company mission or goals;
(ii) A major increase in the disclosure of information;
(iii) The devolving of responsibility for quality to the shop floor;
(iv) Reassertion by management of its basic right to manage;
(v)   Elimination of status differentials – a move away from a 'them and us' culture.

These five major changes result from placing more and more faith in people, and communicating more information to the workforce to make them realise what the organisational objectives are and why their individual contributions are valued. In addition management assertion comes from competence rather than authority. These five changes on their own would not lead to the generation of high commitment. They are however important for realising the human potential and gaining a mutual understanding between management and workers. What is required from leaders however is transforming the established positive environment into a creative and productive one. This is what commitment is all about.

It is suggested that there are three pillars essential for the generation of high levels of commitment. Firstly, creating a sense of belonging in contrast to alienation caused by the previous eras of mass production. Secondly, making workers feel excited about their work and proud of their achievement so that they start to realise that they are trustworthy which will also lead to them accepting accountability more readily. The third pillar is inherent within the leaders themselves, creating confidence in management leadership and leading by example. Table 8.6[6] illustrates ways which can help leaders generate high commitment, using the three pillars discussed.

Two challenges in particular need to be closely considered by leaders during the generation of commitment for TQM. One is related to fear and the other is related to conflicts.

Table 8.6 The three pillars of generation commitment

Pillar	Method of implementation
How to produce a sense of belonging to the organisation	Inform people by: – team briefing – open disclosure – simple language and examples Involve people by: – single status conditions – consultation – visits and company celebrations Share success with: – share option schemes – productivity gain sharing – local lump sum bonuses
How to produce a sense of excitement in the job	Create pride by: – responsibility for quality – direct identification with output – comparison with competitors Create trust by: – abolition of piecework – peer group control – removal of demarcation Create accountability for results by: – pushing decision-making down the line – challenging assignments – quality circles
How to produce confidence in management leadership	Exert authority by: – no abdication to shop stewards – willingness to discipline – maintenance of standards and objectives Show dedication by: – reduction of management overhead – seeking productivity through people – attention to commitment Display competence by: – establishing mission and objectives – new management initiatives – professional standards

(i) **Driving out fear:** Fear is the enemy of TQM. Fear means the destruction of a harmonious working climate, the absence of team work, divisions between workers and management and the burial of human potential. In the dictionary, it is defined as follows:

'An unpleasant, often strong emotion caused by anticipation or awareness of danger, discomfort, pain, or loss.'

Taylorism has instigated fear by the introduction of the notion which is based on 'telling people what to do and how they should do it'. Fear has robbed organisations for so long of so much human potential. TQM is an ideal opportunity for giving organisations the incentive to drive out fear and tap the unlimited human potential within organisations. It has been suggested that there are various sorts of fear.[35] These include fear of reprisal, fear of failure, fear of providing information, fear of not knowing, fear of giving up control and fear of change. The model discussed in Table 8.6 is perhaps one of the best ways of driving out fear. If TQM implementation considers that people are the pillars of any organisation, and that performance is reflected by the human effort, then this will make leaders more determined to eliminate fear all together.

(ii) **Resolving conflicts:** Managing human nature is the most difficult challenge for any leader. Indeed, people's emotions, attitudes, feelings and beliefs change all the time. It is only by good understanding of each individual that conflicts can be eliminated. Furthermore, conflicts can be eliminated if there is a climate of trust and total honesty. What is challenging for a leader is that a conflict has to be resolved not by pinpointing who is right and who is wrong, but dissipating the conflict by finding the solution without looking for the causes. Conflicts can also be solved by 'association' rather than 'dissociation'. In other words, managers have to show a positive attitude so that people feel motivated enough to resolve the conflict themselves. The solutions of conflicts have to take into account human vulnerability and fragility, so therefore leaders have to ensure that there is no right or wrong. Finally, leaders have to eliminate the source of the conflict and not just tackle the symptoms. A harmonious working climate is a lasting one. A harmonious work environment should be the norm rather than the exception.

THE THIRD TASK OF LEADERSHIP: MANAGING POWER PROCESSES

The previous section relates to employee integrity, which is vital for the implementation of TQM. Power however is another important task that leaders have to be able to manage and control. Power has been defined by Price[16] as follows:

'... the force which gets things done. Without it all the foregoing is nothing more than potential and its actualisation cannot happen without the exercise of power ... power could be defined as the imposition of the will of one individual upon the actions of others.'

Power affects individuals differently. It is almost impossible to predict how different leaders will behave under the influence of power. Power however, if used to good effect, can serve as a facilitating tool for instigating a harmonious climate rather than seeking to achieve one's goals and desires. Power differences tend to affect interpersonal relationships. In the context of establishing customer-supplier chains, power is the crucial point since the relationships between bosses and their subordinates is going to determine the type of climate for TQM implementation.

Power has a dual effect. Most managers in organisations are both 'masters and servants'.[13] Most managers have subordinates who report to them and in turn, they have to report to their own superiors. Managers who worry about offending their superiors are quite unlikely to be protective over their subordinates. A study was commissioned to look at the dual expectations of power (masters and servants) on 105 executives of major companies.[13] The various respondents were asked to identify what they expect from their subordinates and what they expect from their superiors.

Table 8.7 Power expectations in the context of leadership

Question	Desired traits	% of managers who mentioned this trait (multiple choice allowed)
What managers expect from subordinates	Good task performance	78
	Loyalty and obedience	60
	Honesty	53
	Initiative	31
	Other skills	26
What managers expect from superiors	Good communication	64
	Leadership	60
	Encouragement and support	50
	Delegation and autonomy	37
	Professional competence	21
	Information	17

Table 8.7 shows the paradoxical approach to power distribution. On the one hand, managers as subordinates appear to accept that they have little power to change their bosses and therefore only expect to be briefed on what the tasks are, how they have to be done and encouraged to do them. They feel that they are in no position to influence their bosses' behaviour as they do not consider that delegation or communication is important. Ironically, as masters of power, managers who consider that communication, encouragement and support are vital to them performing well, do not give them to their subordinates. They consider that their subordinates should perform well and be loyal, obedient and honest. Is this because they wish to have more power and control over their subordinates? This is reinforced by the fact that they do not welcome initiatives from their subordinates very often (only 31%) and they do not want them to exhibit other skills which may help them achieve more.

This study, although not conclusive, does reflect the implications of unfairly shared power. In the context of TQM and particularly during the drive to establish customer-supplier chains, power has to be considered at both the 'servant and master' levels. Each manager has to prepare a check list for the dual role they assume.

As a master of power

- Is what I expect from my subordinates reasonable?
- Should I ask them what they think?
- Is it what I expect from my own superiors?

- Should I tell my subordinates what the task is, what my opinion of its achievement is and invite them to suggest alternatives?
- Do I provide them with enough information?
- Do I communicate with them effectively?
- Do I clearly indicate to them that they have my total support and encouragement?

As a subordinate of power

- Should I just do what my boss expects from me?
- If I consider that a request for a task is unreasonable or could be done in a different way, should I tell my boss that it is so?
- Should I be honest with my boss and tell him/her what my strengths and weaknesses are?
- To gain my boss's full support and encouragement, do I have to display discipline, honesty and loyalty?
- If I know that I can help my boss perform his/her task better, should I offer my help or wait until I am asked?

One can go on asking more and more questions. What is vital however is the importance of weighing up each question both from the point of view of the leader as a subordinate and as a master of power. In this way power processes can be managed effectively to lead to strong customer-supplier chains which are essential for successful implementation of TQM.

THE FOURTH TASK OF LEADERSHIP: MANAGING THE CULTURE TRANSFORMATION

Is culture real or is it a fad? In recent years more and more attention has been given to corporate culture. Once again one is bound to ask questions such as what is corporate culture? How do you measure it? Can it be changed? Why is it important in the context of TQM?

First of all, culture is not a fad. Fads are 'flavour of the month', quick fixes to complex problems. Corporate culture however is at the heart of any organisational system. It has history, a past and a present, and is affected by management systems, people, structures, processes and externally by society and the wider environment. The importance of culture has been described by R H Kilmann.[46] He argued that:

'Success in business is not determined by an executive's skills alone; nor by the visible features – the strategy, structure and reward system – of the organisation. Rather the organisation itself has an invisible quality – a certain style, a character, a way of doing things – that may be more powerful than the dictates of any one person or any formal system. Culture provides meaning, direction and mobilisation, a social energy that moves the corporation into either productive action or destruction.'

The term 'social energy' seems to be at the heart of corporate culture. This is picked up again by Kilmann et al,[10] who conclude that:

'Culture is the social energy that drives – or fails to drive – the organisation. To ignore culture and move on to something else is to assume once again, that formal documents, strategies, structures, and reward systems are enough to guide human behaviour in an organisation – that people believe and commit to what they read or are told to do. On the contrary, most of what goes on in an organisation is guided by the cultural qualities of shared meaning, hidden assumptions, and unwritten rules.'

The impact of culture on any organisation is measured by its thickness (i.e. level of penetration), extent of sharing, clarity of ordering[41] or by its direction of impact (where is it leading the organisation to?), its pervasiveness (how widely spread and shared amongst members?) and the strength of its impact (the pressure culture exerts).[10] A combination of the various factors cited will lead to an overall positive or negative impact. One can refer to the above various factors as the *roots*. The more deep seated they are, the stronger the organisation is going to be. Looking after the foliage, branches and leaves (strategies, reward systems, plans, policies and people training) can only be an effective task if the roots are healthy and holding the organisation tightly together.

Various definitions have been given to describe corporate culture. Some have been grouped together in Table 8.8.

This selection of definitions of corporate culture reflects how vague it is and how difficult it would be to transform. The best way to understand the complexity of corporate culture is to refer to the Burke-Litwin Model developed in 1987.[34] The model refers to interrelationships between organisational variables and the degree

Table 8.8 Some definitions of corporate culture

Reference	Definition
39	... a pattern of basic assumptions – invented, discovered or developed by a given group as it learns to cope with its problems of external adaptation or internal integration – that has worked well enough to be considered valid and, therefore, to be taught to new members as the correct way to perceive, think and feel in relation to those problems.
J Elliott (1951) in 34	The customary or traditional ways of thinking and doing things, which are shared to a greater or lesser extent by all members of the organisation, and which new members must learn and at least partially accept, in order to be accepted into the service of the firm.
34	Set of norms and values to which people conform and covers values, rewards, career development, loyalty, power, participation, leadership, communication and innovation.
32	Culture is the sum total of the intellectual, constitutional and creative values produced by a firm's people, as well as its knowledge and skills, behaviour patterns, customs, and value judgements, procedures and departments which, in their structural inter-association and organisation, represent the work content of its people in a certain period of time or era.
2	The amalgam of shared values, behaviour patterns, mores, symbols, attitudes and normative ways of conducting business that, more than its products or services, differentiate it from other companies. Cultural uniqueness is a primary and cherished feature of organisation, a critical asset that is nurtured in the internal value system.

of change which results from certain dynamic behaviours. There are two categories of cultures or modes of behaviour, according to the Burke-Litwin model.

(i) Transformational dynamics: These represent areas which are mostly influenced by environmental factors (mission, strategy, leadership). These variables shape the corporate culture of the organisation.

(ii) Transactional dynamics: These represent the short term organisational changes. They include variables such as structure, management practices and systems (policies and procedures).[34]

The best way to distinguish between transactional and transformational cultures is the unit of time. Transactional change happens all the time, and is really a transitional type of culture. These changes can happen overnight and can last for as long as it is necessary or desired by management. Transformational change however is much more difficult and reflects corporate culture. Usually it is a long term objective and can take between 3–15 years.

There are various ways of achieving complete corporate culture transformation. Prior to discussing the different alternatives, the first important task for leaders is to make the culture of their organisations explicit through a 'cultural audit'. This task needs to be considered by senior managers who are directing their organisations to identify the shared beliefs and how they are practiced. Once this task is carried out everything about corporate culture becomes visible and leaders can then choose to retain the valid beliefs and discard those which are no longer valid. Culture audit can include areas such as beliefs about goals, distinctive competences, product-market guidelines, management employees, etc.[5]

Together with a strategic review process, a cultural audit can serve the basis for conducting incremental and radical transformation. It is vital that long range planning is considered in parallel to corporate culture. It has been argued that long range planning affects the changing of corporate culture by a process of unfreezing (disclosing problems and thus creating a sense of crisis); change (the planning process is an ongoing exercise and as such forces management to consider constantly the various organisational factors which affect performance); refreeze (long range planning is a formal, authorised plan which has to be implemented as agreed. Thus no changes can be carried out apart from what has been authorised).[36]

Culture transformation has to lead to a dynamic process which can adapt to different environmental conditions and where a high degree of flexibility can allow organisations to modify and change their strategic plans. Long range planning can only become effective if the corporate culture state dynamically evolves to encompass the necessary requirements for strategic plans to succeed.

There are various scenarios which can be considered.[36] Rather than ask the question 'which comes first the chicken or the egg?', the cultural audit and strategic review exercises determine which approach needs to be adopted for achieving the necessary changes. Figure 8.4 represents four different approaches to achieving cultural transformation.

(i) Dynamic corporate culture – dynamic strategic planning: This is a ready state situation, where culture and strategic planning are interconnected and constantly being adapted to different situations. This perhaps, is the ideal situation for most organisations to achieve. Control over cultural elements leads to tight control over strategic objectives;

(ii) Culture – strategic planning: partial dependency (not fully dynamic: In this situation culture and long range planning are not closely interconnected, but the existing corporate culture complements the long range plan. This gives employees the initiative to take innovative action that leads to revitalising corporate culture and making sure that it is dynamic and does not just complement strategic plans but is closely associated with the process of long range planning;

(iii) Stagnant corporate culture – dynamic long range planning (incremental changes): This is a top down approach whereby the strategic planning pushes and forces changes in corporate culture. This very much depends on the type of leadership approach and also employee responsiveness. It could be very slow and leads to incremental changes;

(iv) Corporate culture spearheading changes in long range planning: This is the

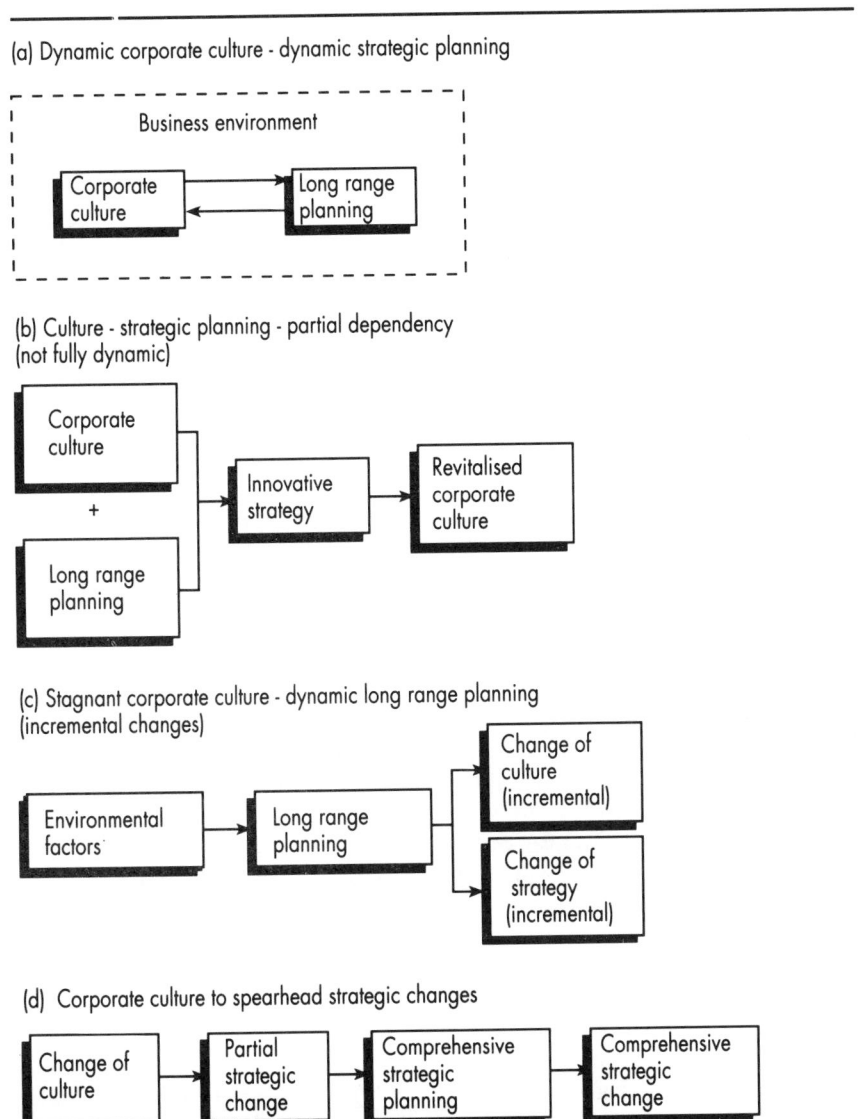

(a) Dynamic corporate culture - dynamic strategic planning

(b) Culture - strategic planning - partial dependency (not fully dynamic)

(c) Stagnant corporate culture - dynamic long range planning (incremental changes)

(d) Corporate culture to spearhead strategic changes

8.4 Culture transformation and strategic planning.

most radical approach, where bottom up initiatives are adopted through strong and dynamic corporate culture to influence changes in strategic thinking, firstly, by establishing incremental strategic changes to comprehensive processes for long range planning.

The corporate culture change therefore can take any of the above forms. It will depend on the status of the organisation concerned, its history, values, beliefs, systems and type of leadership. The transformation approach to be adopted is thought to be dependent on four different factors including information approach (can change people's attitudes); symbolic product-market strategy (experiences lead to new behavioural patterns); sanction system (changes in structure and management systems leads to responsibility, control, rewards, etc); top management (leadership).[36]

THE FIFTH TASK OF LEADERSHIP: AVOIDING BEING A VISIONARY LEADER

Just as having a clear vision is the main distinguishing factor between managers and leaders, vision can lead to a state of illusion if it is not based on organisational objectives. Vision could be the leader's own personal obsession, and as such leads to his/her behaviour changing so much that vision has to be achieved at any cost. The blindness to assess organisational strengths and weaknesses and identifying clearly what the external opportunities and threats are leads to 'failed vision'. Failed vision has been reported to be caused by a variety of factors[29] including the following:

- The vision reflects the internal needs of leaders rather than those of the market or constituents;
- The resources needed to achieve the vision have been seriously miscalculated;
- An unrealistic assessment or distorted perception of market and constituent needs hold sway;
- A failure to recognise environmental changes prevents redirection of the vision.

If a leader ignores all the above sources in pursuit of a personal goal, the latter has been termed 'a pyrrhic victory'[29] costing all the organisational resources so vital for the future. Leaders with visionary missions tend to use the CONVINCING and PERSUADING approach rather than invite input to the shaping up of the vision. These leaders therefore manipulate others by using their communications and impression management skills.[29] For example to have their own way, this category of leaders will surround themselves with people who would not challenge their ideas and who do not pose a threat to them. People who take the 'I go along approach' obviously help bury the realities of situations and make the world of 'make believe', the leader's dream, a reality. Some of the tactics used by leaders to have their own way, include the following:[29]

- Exaggerated self-descriptions;
- Exaggerated claims for the vision;
- A technique of fulfilling stereotypes and images of uniqueness to manipulate audiences;
- A habit of gaining commitment by restricting negative information and maximising positive information;

- Use of anecdotes to distract attention away from negative statistical information;
- Creation of an illusion of control through affirming information and attributing negative outcomes to external causes.

A strong leader will however be aware of all the various factors which can render a vision not applicable to the organisation they represent. Leaders during the implementation of TQM have to be fully committed to the success of their organisations and strongly believe that the vision supported by everyone else can be channeled by utilising to the optimum level possible all the organisation's resources. A strong leader is not a vulnerable leader and therefore welcomes feedback and criticism, so that what is put on track all the time is the organisational objective which everyone supports and would like to achieve. Strong organisations are those which plant the seeds today so that the harvest tomorrow will be better. If the organisation's resources have been totally depleted, this will leave it vulnerable in the future.

IS CHARISMA ENOUGH FOR STRONG TQM LEADERSHIP?

Charisma has been described in a variety of ways. Some descriptions reported in Adamson[40] refer to charismatic leaders as those who tend to generate organisational excitement by developing a common vision for the organisation; creating value-related opportunities within a large framework of the organisation's goals; enabling employees to feel more in control of their individual and collective destinies. Others refer to charismatic leaders as the 'maximum man' because of the glow of confidence their inner light gives them. People are drawn to them by their power of conviction and visions of reality. An in-depth study of charismatic leaders[56] has revealed that they tend to have the following common traits:

- Vision;
- Captivating and inspiring oratory skills;
- Ability to excite;
- Countercultural and/or unconventional behaviour and practices;
- High energy and dynamism;
- Brilliance in terms of strategic insights and knowledge;
- Active campaigning for organisational goals.

Charisma however is not just good speaking and public popularity, with a strong personality. Charismatic leadership is a style of leadership in its own right. Research has indicated that charismatic leadership includes the following factors:[19]

- Envisioning: – Articulating a compelling vision
- Setting high expectations
- Modelling consistent behaviours;
- Energising: – Demonstrating personal excitement
- Expressing personal confidence
- Seeking, finding and using success;
- Enabling: – Expressing personal support
- Empathising
- Expressing confidence in people.

This style of leadership is certainly suitable at the early stages of spreading the benefits of TQM and trying to get people on board. It is often said that people have been inspired by gurus and quality experts who talk about the great benefits of quality with passion, enthusiasm, belief and excitement. This style although positive has got some limitations as all the action centres around one individual. Some of the reported limitations include 'unrealistic expectations', 'dependency and counterdependency', 'reluctance to disagree with the leader', 'need for continuing magic', 'limitation of range of the individual leader' amongst others.[19]

These criticisms of the charismatic leadership style are shared elsewhere. Senge[30] writes that:

> 'Leadership in learning organisations centres on subtler and ultimately more important work. In a learning organisation, leaders' roles differ dramatically from that of the charismatic decision maker. Leaders are designers, teachers and stewards. These roles require new skills: the ability to build shared vision, to bring to the surface and challenge prevailing mental models, and to foster more systemic patterns of thinking. In short, leaders in learning organisations are responsible for building organisations where people are continually expanding their capabilities to shape their future – that is, leaders are responsible for learning.'

Senge argues that leadership in the context of the learning organisation consists of the 'principle of creative tension'. He argues that vision has to be matched by a true and accurate picture of current reality. The division between the two is the effort to be made. Charismatic leaders may have problems matching vision with an accurate picture of reality since they may have problems achieving control, rely too much on positive feedback and may be too reluctant to break bad news and deliver unpleasant messages.

Charismatic leadership has to be backed up by another style, called 'instrumental leadership' which includes three main elements:

- Structuring (building teams and creating structures for expected behaviours in the organisation);
- Controlling (creating systems and processes to measure, monitor and assess behaviour and results so that corrective action can take place);
- Rewarding (rewarding or punishing according to the degree of consistency to the requirements).[19]

Instrumental leadership is useful in that it ensures that people behave in a consistent manner to the set goals and any deviation from those, will have to be followed by appropriate action.

Both types of leadership are necessary for the implementation of TQM. They are however dichotomous and furthermore, in both styles there is heavy emphasis on one individual doing everything.

The need for transformational leadership

Transformational leadership means that besides the important task of making others achieve organisational goals, leaders have to share their vision, thoughts, knowledge, skills and power with all the people around them. They have to instigate a process of inspiration for others to aspire to becoming leaders. In a way they have to 'coach' leadership experiments in their organisations and create what one may refer to as the leadership process. One remembers the saying:

'Individuals make up organisations, but organisations are not individuals.'

Nadler and Tushman[19] who argued the limitations of both the charismatic and instrumental types of leadership, propose a more global model which encompasses elements of charismatic and instrumental types. This model which has been termed 'institutionalising the leadership of change' includes three leverage points:

(i) **Leveraging the senior team:** The development of an effective, visible and dynamic senior team to complement the limitations of the individual leader;

(ii) **Broadening senior management:** Move beyond the senior team and include a broader range of individuals (even from the junior management level);

(iii) **Developing leadership in the organisation:** Use organisational structures, systems and a process of leadership development to encourage those with ability, and skills to aspire for a leadership role.

Total Quality Management at the present time is not fully incorporated as a means of doing business in most organisational systems. It is still at the infancy stage in trying to modify people's attitudes and get them on board so that quality becomes a way of life. In these frequent instances therefore, it is expected that a charismatic style of leadership would be most appropriate. Leaders have to reach out for support, commitment, trust and at the same time support, encourage and motivate people. None of the other styles of leadership can do this task better than the charismatic leader.

It is expected that once TQM has penetrated certain levels of organisational systems, some measurement and control has to be instigated. Instrumental leadership therefore has to introduce the kind of discipline which is required to make sure that organisations are on course for achieving the desired competitive objectives. The third type, where leadership becomes a distributed function within organisations has to be a long term objective albeit important. It is vital for organisations to make sure that the momentum of competing under the banners of TQM has to be an ongoing process, and not dependent on individual people's contributions. Team leadership reflects commitment, strength, high consensus, confidence and progressive thinking.

The model which was discussed in Fig. 8.1 started with the issue of leadership and concluded with the cultural transformation. To achieve a TQM based competitive organisation, the issue of leadership has to be at the heart of any drive, desire or determination to compete on quality criteria.

9

ESSENTIALS OF TQM: CUSTOMER-SUPPLIER CHAINS

INTRODUCTION

Customer-supplier chains are probably the most central issue for TQM. Indeed, without forging links internally and externally between people and functions, the principle of Zero Defect and Right First Time will remain elusive objectives. For example managing supply chains has changed from being a mere logistical problem at an operational level, to a strategic issue which involves senior managers.[27] There is growing realisation that the business cycle does not stop within the confined boundaries of organisations. The business cycle represents three sets of processes including supplier processes, manufacturer processes and customer processes, Fig. 9.1.

Customer-supplier chain formation therefore is the process of establishing the necessary links so that the ultimate goal of enlightening the customer can become realisable. The business cycle therefore under TQM is extended beyond the boundaries of traditionally structured organisations where control of quality is very much localised. The extended business cycle model however cannot be achieved overnight. It seems that customer-supplier interactions are culturally based rather than being propagated by specific factors such as technological innovation for example.

Some research work which looked at the evolution in customer-supplier chains in the automobile industry[36] has led to the conclusion that there are various stages of evolution in establishing strong relationships between suppliers and customers which include FRICTION, TOLERANCE, COMMON UNDERSTANDING, COMPLETE PARTNERSHIP. It has been concluded that for the relationships to remain strong there has to be an effort reflecting not only contacts at the engineering or the purchasing levels but also at the strategic and policy making level. This positive evolution was characterised by four models which include:[36] the traditional model, the stress model, the resolved model and the Japanese model. The main facilitator in this transition was found to be common understanding and the ability to compromise.

Similar research in the context of technological innovation has led to similar conclusions.[37] A comparison of user-supplier interactions in the UK and West Germany established that poor relationships between UK based suppliers and their customers is due to lack of customer involvement. In contrast, the German suppliers tended to involve their customers closely at each stage of the product development

(a) Traditional model of business cycle

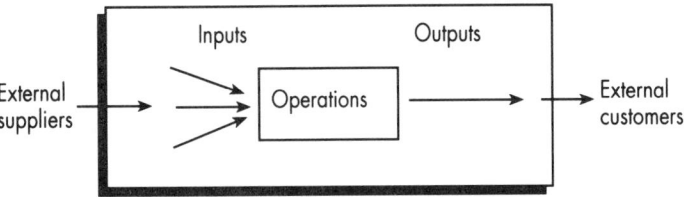

(b) TQM - based business cycle

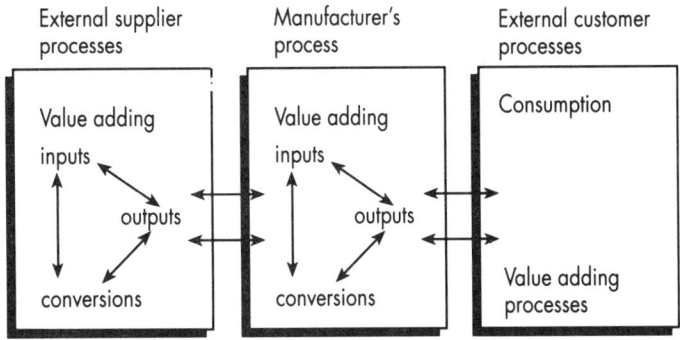

9.1 Traditional versus TQM based business cycle.

process from idea generation to the evaluation of alternative design concepts and to evaluation of prototypes.

It is therefore important to understand how customer-supplier chains are developed, what criteria tends to facilitate successful co-operation and interaction and what the key inhibitive criteria are. Without strong customer-supplier links both internally and externally, TQM efforts are doomed to fail.

INTERNAL CUSTOMER-SUPPLIER CHAINS

Every employee in any organisation is expected to play a dual role as a provider of goods/services and as a customer. This is the first challenge of forming a customer-supplier chain. Senior managers seeking to implement TQM have to consider the following points:

● Re-define customer/supplier relationships – change people's attitudes from adversaries/competitors to collaborators;

The following questions have to be considered and answered:

● In order for me to carry out my job efficiently, would I need to rely on anybody's help and contribution?
● For others to carry out their jobs efficiently, do they need to rely on my help and contribution?

These two broad questions can be followed by more specific questions such as:

● How can I help you? What do you require from me?
● What happens to my output after you get it? Who takes ownership?
● How well have I satisfied your requirements? What is missing?
● How can I find out if all your requirements have been fully satisfied?

The line of questioning which is supposed to take place is a reflection on how value adding effort is propagated throughout the organisation. Other issues which must be addressed by senior managers considering the implementation of TQM include the following:

● Make goals and objectives common to everyone in the organisation through proper communication means;
● For team work to succeed, the mission statement has to be effectively communicated and explained to all concerned;
● Goals and objectives are determined by a close participation and involvement effort;
● Senior managers must champion the effort of establishing customer-supplier chains and team effort;
● A concerted effort has to be conducted to change organisational culture so as to encourage communication and employee participation.

The process of establishing internal customer-supplier chains which can work effectively in a TQM environment can be suggested to include the following stages: CUSTOMER EXPECTATIONS, EXPECTATIONS FULFILMENT, BEHAVIOUR MODIFICATION, MOTIVATION. Customer expectation has been defined as follows:[12]

'The sum total of anticipations a customer(s) or potential customer(s) may have regarding a product or service.'

Expectations management is the process by which expectations can be satisfied or exceeded. The outcome of expectations management leads to enhanced consideration of quality (behaviour modification) and if this process is repeated, quality becomes a self-motivation outcome. Amongst the various internal customer expectations are the following:[25] comparative value; adequate resources; responsiveness; reliability; flexibility; clear and adequate communication; accountability; empathy and understanding; interpersonal skills; etc.

DEFINING EXTERNAL CUSTOMER-SUPPLIER CHAINS

Webster[38] writes:

'... buying and selling are the same process, two sides of the same coin.'

This once again leads us to argue that similar questions such as those raised in the internal customer-supplier chains, will be applicable in the context of the external customer-supplier chain. The external customer-supplier chain therefore can be considered from the supply angle and from the customer angle.

The supply chain has evolved from an era where manufacturing organisations were most concerned with controlling the flow of materials/components from their suppliers, to an era where supply chain management started to become concerned with supplier management, material management, information flow, customer service and long term relationships. Under Just In Time (JIT), customer-supplier chains are encouraged to move away from the adversarial approach to a collaborative approach with mutual benefits for suppliers and customers.[8, 15, 16]

It is lack of trust in the past which leads customers to spread the risk through multiple sources and playing suppliers off one against the other to get low prices. Various research has led to the conclusion that, under JIT, customer-supplier chains can be successful and based on long term partnerships. It was also found that the long lasting relationships are established regardless of how easily materials/components can be resourced.[11]

Since under TQM any organisation competes with the banners of QUALITY, DELIVERY and PRICE, JIT is considered to be the best method for achieving the objectives. Just In Time tackles waste, lead time and unnecessary complexities so that planning and control become easier to carry out. To work effectively, JIT requires certain components to be present. Table 9.1 represents the various components of JIT and the potential benefits.[16]

Table 9.1 The use of JIT in customer-supplier chains

JIT component	Potential benefit
Kanban	Better quality
Reduced set up time	Less scrap
Smaller lot size	Less raw material
Production smoothing	Less work-in-progress
Standardisation	Fewer finished goods
Uniform and invariable output rate	Increased teamwork
Multifunction workers	Higher worker motivation
Streamlined process design	Increased worker and equipment efficiency
Flexibility and versatility	Saved space
	Increased productivity

All the potential benefits which can be derived from the utilisation of JIT can help the establishment of Zero Defect as a realisable objective. Just In Time is the best approach towards managing suppliers since the objective from its introduction is the obtainment and sustainment of superior performance. It therefore addresses supplier management issues at the strategic, tactical and operational levels.

The other side of the coin in external customer-supplier chains refers to the management of customer processes. The purpose of TQM is customer enlightenment and long term partnerships. Customer Expectation Management is therefore an essential activity if strong, long and lasting relationships are to be established. It is argued in various literature that for suppliers to ensure long term commitments from their customers, the former have to do a number of different things right and consistently over time to meet both short term and long term customer requirements.

Two models which examine customer behaviour from a different perspective are considered in the next section. This is followed by a suggested role for sales representatives in helping manage customer processes.

Model 1

This model assumes that customer behaviour can be looked at in terms of two different dimensions: net price realised and cost to serve.[10] There are four possible categories of customers:

(i) Carriage trade customers cost a great deal to serve but are willing to pay top price;
(ii) Bargain basement customers are sensitive to price and relatively insensitive to service and quality. They can be served more cheaply than the carriage trade customers;
(iii) Passive customers cost less to serve and are willing to accept high prices;
(iv) Aggressive customers demand the highest product quality, the best service and low prices.

In today's cut-throat market customers are thought to be of the 'aggressive' type. This further highlights the importance of being able to provide customers with a mix based on high quality, excellent service and low price.

Model 2

This model assumes that customer behaviour is based on one of the following models:[29]

(i) Always-a-share model: Customer can easily switch from one supplier to another, because of low switching costs. Suppliers assume that as long as they provide products with good quality, quick delivery and low price, they have a good chance of winning an order. This model reflects behaviour which is based on short term commitment;
(ii) Lost-for-good model: This is the opposite to (i) in that it reflects customer commitment to one supplier and the existence of long term relationships. This is because the switching costs are high. The relationship in this instance is considered on a long term basis and supplier capability is likely to be assessed from the point of view of its future development rather than its short term readiness.
(iii) Intermediate types: It is expected that most customer-supplier relationships are hybrids of (i) and (ii). This is because customers are always prospecting and would not tolerate slippage as far as the level of services, quality and price their current suppliers are offering. In fact other research seems to confirm that customer-supplier relationships are always subject to market threats and opportunities. A study which looked at the impact of JIT on customer-supplier relationships concluded that:[11]

'Despite the appearance of an apparently trustworthy buyer/seller relationship, it could be inferred that there is a tendency for one or either of the parties in the relationship to indulge in opportunistic behaviour transactions.'

Understanding customer behaviour is therefore vital if long term customer-supplier relationships are to be established. The lesson which can be derived from the two model examples is that customer sophistication should be expected to increase and to be reflected by a more and more aggressive style expecting optimum levels of quality, service and low price. Secondly, a long term partnership is subjected to scrutiny all the time and has to be dynamically managed so that Customer Expectations Management (CEM) is always positively accomplished.

Sales representatives can play a crucial role in helping manage customer processes. Sales representatives can be assumed to play the following three roles:

(i) **Contacts developers:** Usually sales representatives are the first contact between supplier and customer organisations. In a sense they forge the first link in the customer-supplier chain;

(ii) **Relationship controllers:** Maintaining regular contacts and monitoring changes in customer behaviour is an important aspect of the sales representative role;

(iii) **Crises diffusers:** This is a very important role in ensuring Zero Defects and soothing customer discontent. Sales representatives, by assuming this role, have to ensure that no slippage takes place from their organisation, so that customers will not be driven to consider switching.

The management of customer-supplier chains therefore has to consider two important aspects:

● Making sure that customer satisfaction (short term) is transformed into the commitment (long term) objective;
● Making sure that supplier management is for a win-win situation.

FROM CUSTOMER SATISFACTION TO CUSTOMER COMMITMENT

There is a difference between a company's ability to achieve customer satisfaction and its ability to secure their long term commitment. What is the difference between the two? Table 9.2 briefly contrasts customer satisfaction and their commitment:[5]

Table 9.2 Customer satisfaction versus customer commitment

Customer satisfaction	Customer commitment
Short term	Long term
Assessing and meeting needs	Many heroic acts which create loyalty and devotion
Customers feel good as long as their needs are fulfilled	Customers look beyond short term pleasures
Customers are pleased, humoured and fulfilled	Customers are dedicated and faithful
Customers remain independent	Customers are interdependent
Customers can be satisfied without being committed	Implies intense, long term loyalty and dedication

There are two major requirements for establishing full commitment: information and behaviour.[5] It is suggested that the more information is disclosed to customers, the more committed they become. Commitment could take place at two levels; at the strategic level, where there is a clear indication that the customer organisation has decided to adopt specific products and services, and commitment at the organisational level where customers are committed not only to products and services but also participate in the design, production and delivery of products/services. It has been suggested that most customer commitment takes place at the strategic level, where decisions are made based on the information received. Ulrich[5] argues however, that total customer commitment occurs when information is followed by behaviour in the form of customer involvement and participation in organisational activities.

Commitment usually is followed by collaboration which leads to the establishment of a partnership. Collaboration has been defined as follows:[22]

'Collaboration is a bilateral mode of managing exchange in which the exchange partners adopt a high level of purposeful co-operation to maintain the trading relationship over time.'

Full collaboration is futuristic in nature, it evolves with time and does not require full sets of preconditions. In addition collaboration means that both parties represented share the power to dictate changes equally. Collaboration leads to full partnerships where performance can be improved through joint efforts on a sustained and regular basis. A model of full partnership is illustrated in Table 9.3.[7] This model defines total partnership in terms of factors which make it work on an everyday basis and factors which encourage its sustainment over time.

Table 9.3 A model of total partnership

Partnership style	Description	Determinants
Partnership in context (PIC)	Dimension which looks at key factors that establish participants' belief in the longevity, stability, and inter-dependence	Mutual benefits Commitment Predisposition (trust, attitudes)
Partnership in action (PIA)	Dimension which looks at the key factors that create the day-to-day working relationship	Shared knowledge Distinctive competency and resources Organisational linkage

Through the six determinants, it highlights total commitment to have a shared destiny. In reality however, the commitment can be described in terms of a 'transactional style of relationship' where the expectations from partnerships are clearly identified and quantifiable. The above model of total partnership can perhaps be arrived at through a learning period of conducting a series of transactional partnerships successfully, to the point where total trust has been established and where attitudes have been changed in favour of a common destiny.

FROM A WIN-LOSE TO A WIN-WIN SITUATION

There has been too much emphasis on 'supplier ratings' in recent years. Whilst they are important in measuring supplier performance from the point of view of quality, delivery and price, they do not really reflect relationship management. To some extent one could argue that supplier ratings are no different from the adversarial mode which persisted in the past thus presenting a win-lose situation.

Performance management, in contrast to performance measurement, is thought to be a better approach to a win-win situation or an equal partnership. Performance management, it is argued[18] is future oriented and considers problems as opportunities to improve the relationship, 'not as clubs to beat the vendor with at negotiation time'.

A win-win situation can only be achieved by drastic changes which take into account the needs, strengths and weaknesses of each party. It seems that trust is a prerequisite[32, 35] together with a climate of openness in communication and disclosure of information and a high commitment to see the other party succeed. For a win-win situation, it is not in the interest of the customer to weaken the returns of suppliers, since this will kill off the partnership after a short term.

Xerox and GM have for instance rationalised their dealings with suppliers and introduced a programme of continuous supplier involvement and feedback.[20] In the case of Xerox, they involved suppliers in the design of new products, in many cases substituting performance specifications for blueprint so that suppliers can design final parts themselves. GM on the other hand use team reviews for both GM's operations and suppliers' operations so that they can help each other.

A win-win situation is a transformational process where benefits are maximised gradually and disadvantages eliminated. A typical list of advantages and disadvantages for both customers and suppliers is shown in Table 9.4.[2]

The table shows that partnerships are still transitional and not focusing on long term objectives, since there are many hurdles to cross and differences to sort out. Nevertheless it reflects that a win-lose model is no longer valid and suppliers may benefit as much as customers in partnership styles of relationships. Under TQM, both suppliers and customers are realising the persistent need to establish strong partnerships. The common understanding for such strong customer-supplier chains to succeed is reflected in Table 9.5.[28] Indeed it is as a result of certain changes that partnerships can be established.

TOWARDS SINGLE SOURCING CUSTOMER-SUPPLIER CHAINS

Multiple sourcing has been traditionally seen as the more viable option for many reasons. Amongst them are the following:[24]

● Reasons for protection such as prevention of disasters, fear of price increases, supplier unpredictability in delivery and supplier shortages in inventory;
● Fluctuations in volume demand may not be easily met by specific suppliers;
● Some suppliers may not be able to respond to tight specifications and may not have the necessary knowledge and know-how.

Multiple sourcing has however always been recognised as inadequate for reasons such as costs of administration, travelling, inventory costs due to the carrying of

Table 9.4 Customer-supplier chains: Advantages/disadvantages

Customers

Advantages	Disadvantages
Reduced manufacturing and labour costs	Increased dependence on supplier
Improved quality	New negotiating style
Reduced complexity and cost of assembly and buying	Less supplier competition
Supply assurance	Increased managerial skills
Co-operative relationships with suppliers	Reduced personnel mobility
Contract predictability	Increased communication and co-ordination costs
Fair pricing assurance (open book)	Increased support for supplier
Negotiated price reductions during contract life	New reward structures
	Loss of direct contacts

Suppliers

Advantages	Disadvantages
Contract predictability	Cost information shared (loss of proprietary information)
Workforce and production more stable	
Increased R & D effectiveness	Pressures to assume burden of all phases from design to warranty while improving quality and reducing costs
Customer allies supporting firm's status	
Buyer resistance	Decreased autonomy
Influence on customer's future decision making	Increased communication and co-ordination costs
Insider information on buying decisions	Reduced personnel mobility
Firm becomes gatekeeper for competitor's innovations	Potential pendulum reversal
Information about competition	

various items, difficulties in controlling levels of variation in incoming materials/ components because of the variety of sources, etc.

This raises the question as to whether single sourcing is a much better alternative? What happens if only 65% of the components/materials can be supplied by one firm for example? The answer to this question can perhaps be viewed by considering the extended control of customer-supplier chains (primary, secondary and tertiary layers of suppliers).

The Japanese Zaibatsu model

The Japanese Zaibatsu model assumes that there is a strong relationship between a customer (Original Equipment Manufacturer) and a supplier company (first tier). The latter manage their own relationships with their suppliers with whom they have

Table 9.5 The transition in customer-supplier dealings for a TQM environment

Old practice	New practice
Price is dominant	Price is still important
Check product quality	Control process with supplier
Long delivery time	Short delivery times
Batching (big) lot/sizes	Small lot/sizes
Infrequent deliveries (week, month resolution)	Very frequent deliveries (day, hourly resolution)
Malperformance: change supplier	Prevent malperformance by offering (preventative) help
Re-negotiate all the time	Build firm relation
Relation at arm's length	Relation is asset, comakership
WIN-LOSE relation	WIN-WIN relation

established long term partnerships (second tier) and so on. It is anticipated under this arrangement that no changes at all take place at the first tier level where the ties are strong. Any changes that take place occur at the second or third tiers. The customer (Original Equipment Manufacturer) may have direct dealings with second tier suppliers. The Zaibatsu model is represented in Fig. 9.2.[17]

A study which compared the Japanese approach towards customer-supplier chains based on the Zaibatsu model and the American approach of establishing customer-supplier chains has concluded that there are nine main criteria which facilitate the creation of strong customer-supplier chains based on single sourcing.[17] These include the following:

- Well defined mandates, goals and objectives: The responding companies seemed to have clear ideas of what they were expected to do;
- Focused customers: Optimised outsourcing to reduce fixed costs and to enable better communications, co-ordination and compatibility of JIT philosophies;
- Supplier aggressiveness: Tight profit margins mean that suppliers have to optimise production efficiency and economies of scale so that prices are reduced further;
- User/producer interface: Co-operation and involvement at various stages of the product development process. Use joint task forces to tackle problems together so suppliers get a good understanding of customer's production processes;
- Selection of suppliers based on equipment compatibility: Sychronisation of production processes between suppliers and customers. Supplier equipment capability and compatibility is often the issue rather than price;
- Zero Defect policy: High commitment to producing Zero Defect products;
- Just In Time delivery: as part of a wider JIT philosophy which links suppliers and customers together;
- Encouragement of innovative thinking: Evidenced by team work, inter-organisational activities for development of new designs/products, successful implementation of quality circles;
- Culture, people, and attitude: Performance of customer/supplier chains is viewed from a macro level, from a societal perspective rather than measured in too specific terms.

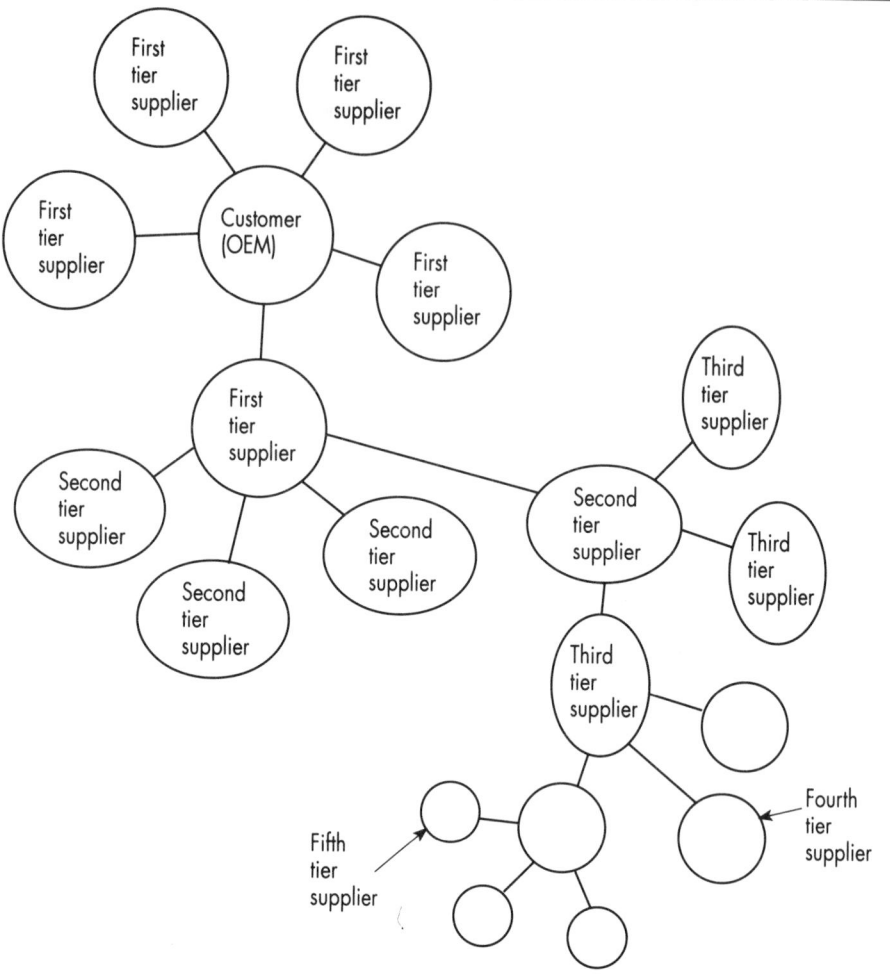

9.2 The Zaibatsu approach to managing customer – supplier chains.

The comparative study has also concluded that there are six main factors which distinguish the American approach from the Japanese one. These include the following:

● Independence of suppliers from customers (OEM): Lack of synchronisation, desire to remain independent;
● Selection of suppliers based on price quotation: Price is still the deciding factor and therefore multiple sourcing is an easier alternative;
● Less user/producer interface: Limited to the order at hand rather than long term R&D relationship and co-ordination of common efforts. Less emphasis on team work and exchanges;
● Zero Defect policy: Emphasis on quality control rather than 'built in quality';
● A forced Just In Time Delivery: Half hearted effort, carried out because of pressures rather than a firm belief in its possible outcomes;

● Less emphasis on innovation: Less abundant innovative thinking because of limited exchanges.

This study clearly highlights that single sourcing can be rendered possible if some of the nine key criteria in the Zaibatsu model are applied in the West. One can also suggest that societal expectations may have rendered this approach possible. Is therefore a cultural transformation necessary for implementing customer-supplier chains based on single sourcing?

The starting point in successfully establishing customer-supplier chains based on single sourcing, seems to be the choice of a small number of first tier suppliers. Many companies in the West have managed to achieve it such as Xerox, who have reduced their suppliers by 50% and started to involve the remaining suppliers much more closely in the product-design process and started to share longer term information with them. Xerox has demanded a high commitment to quality, innovation, and continued effort to reduce costs from its suppliers. The screening of first tier suppliers besides conventional tests of compliance to quality, delivery and price criteria, must include questions such as the following:[14]

● How has the supplier signalled commitment?
● How early into the design stage is the supplier willing or able to participate?
● Does the supplier understand the level of commitment required to help achieve long-term quality gains?
● As the company grows and becomes more expert, is the supplier able to grow with it?
● Does the supplier have adequate technical support?
● Does the supplier present a team solution to purchasing, manufacturing, or quality problems?
● Is the supplier's senior management committed to the processes inherent in strategic partnerships?
● How much future planning is the supplier willing to share?
● How well does the supplier know the company's business?
● What does the supplier demand?

These are the questions which need to be addressed when considering first tier suppliers and the various processes need to be properly managed for partnerships to prosper. This creates what has been referred to as customer bonding.[13] Customer bonding has been defined as follows:

'The process of tying a customer to a particular firm's product or service.'

Customer bonding means that the commitment is shifted from providing 'customer service' to 'service to the customer', which may mean that a dynamic approach to responding to customer requirements is implemented rather than mechanical response by providing customers with the same things again and again. Service to the customer means a willingness to help customers solve problems. Customer-supplier chains based on single sourcing have to some extent reflect more similarities than differences. The level of closeness should show a mirror-image, common approach towards competitiveness, Fig. 9.3.

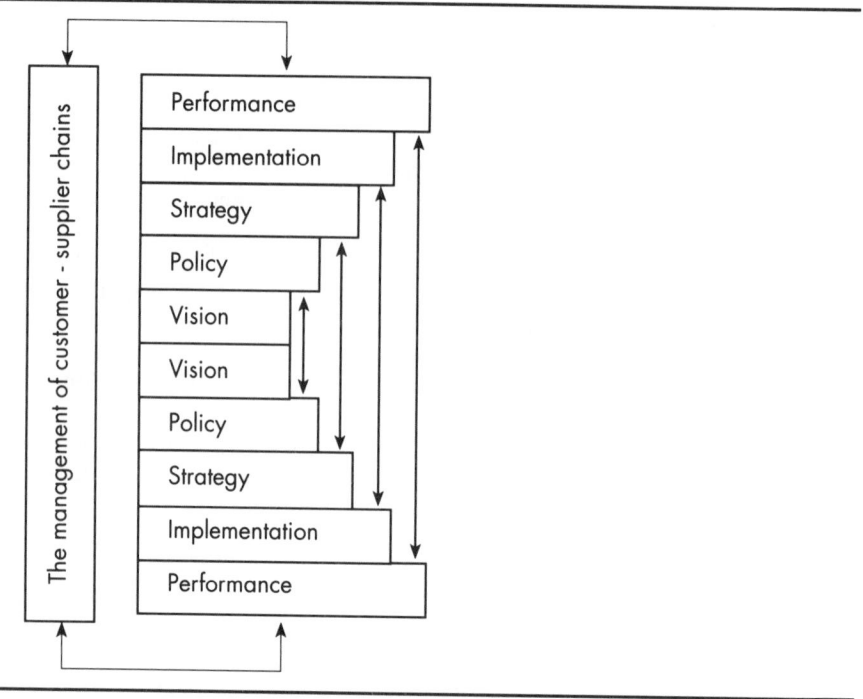

9.3 Shared aspirations: A common destiny.

THE POWER OF COMMUNICATIONS IN CUSTOMER-SUPPLIER CHAINS

Communication can be characterised by suppliers' breadth of knowledge and their level of understanding of customer requirements. This is usually a two stream process, as good communications generally mean that a large amount of useful and beneficial information is fed back to the supplier. Customers' contributions in the communications process can be significant. Various transactions and trade relations take place.[39, 40] Technical interdependence between suppliers and customers is common in the joint development of products and manufacturing capability.[41] Good communication processes between customers and suppliers were also found to be the key factor in the successful implementation of technological innovation in the US automobile industry.[42, 43] Good communication processes were also found to be the ultimate key to industrial marketing success.

Communication processes can be simplistic or complex. An example of a complex communication process is illustrated in Fig. 9.4. This model resulted from a research project conducted by the author, on the implementation of Advanced Manufacturing Technology (AMT). The communication systems box depends on a variety of inputs coming from the customer, the relationship itself and the various people who represent the personal contacts (the link) between suppliers and customers. The level of complexity of the communication process is closely determined by the degree of customer/supplier involvement and the level of sharing of information, resources and knowledge.

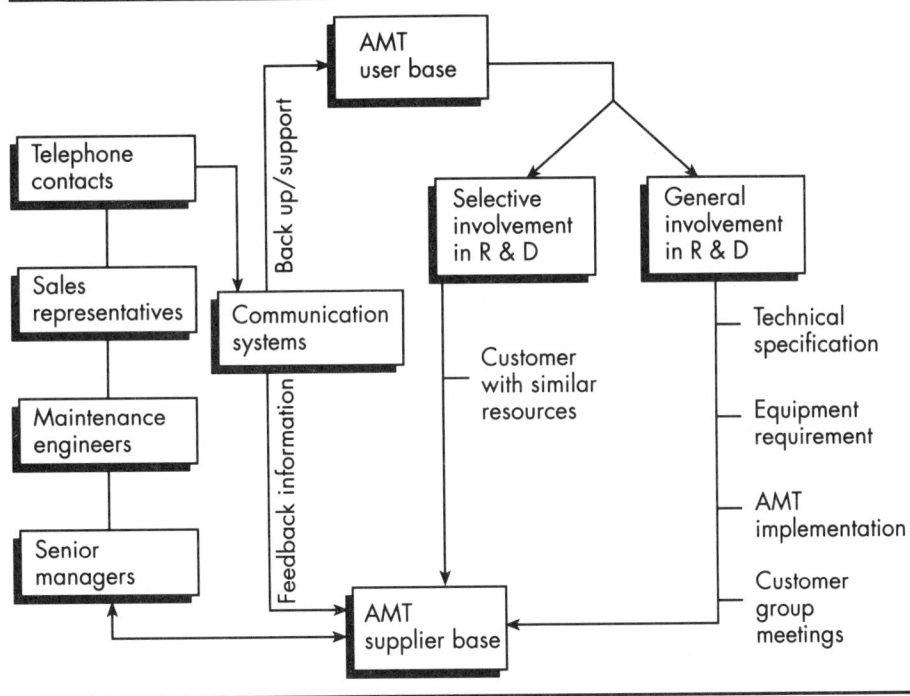

9.4 An explanatory model on suppliers' communication strategy for existing customers.

This research project has established that personal contacts are a key determinant in establishing strong communication processes.[46] Personal contacts were found by other research to play a major role in bringing organisations closer together and in channeling information from and to their organisations. Most of the information and facts can be relayed back by personal contacts. It is not surprising therefore that although there are various means of communication such as telephone, telex and mail which are cheaper, companies prefer to send representatives.[47, 48] In their model on supplier-customer interaction,[49] the International Marketing and Purchasing (IMP) group concluded that individuals representing both the customers and suppliers determine both the short term involvement between organisations and the long term relationships. The importance of personal contacts in establishing strong customer-supplier chains has been referred to as the 'lifeblood' of customer-supplier chains.[45] Cunningham and Homse[45] concluded that:

> 'personal contacts ... are the vehicle of communication, not only of factual information but ideas, impressions, attitudes, commitment, integrity, and sometimes of commercial or technical information provided only to the trusted and privileged.'

Cunningham and Homse suggest that there are nine distinct roles assumed by personal contacts. These are surveillance, communication of resources, demonstration of commitment, information gathering, distance reduction, problem-solving, crisis insurance, negotiation and social bonding.

CUSTOMER-SUPPLIER CHAINS IN A TECHNOLOGICAL CONTEXT

Customer-supplier chains based on the JIT philosophy and the regularity of supplies of components and materials is well documented. Customer-supplier chains based on technological innovation is less well documented however. In the past few years technological equipment started to play a major role in conducting business operations for the achievement of superior performance. More and more technological sophistication is being introduced and issues of compatibility, integration, optimisation, flexibility and maintenance are constantly being raised. The strength of the bond between customers and suppliers in the context of technological innovation is dependent on a variety of factors such as level of complexity of the innovation, the existence/absence of supplier R&D/manufacturing base, the level of customer involvement, etc. Research carried out by the author[46] has established that there are six possible types of customer-supplier chains based on AMT innovation. The six patterns represented in Fig. 9.5 are detailed below:

Type I Direct contact approach

This approach is based on a one to one relationship and includes the supply of stand alone dedicated equipment such as CNC machines. The main characteristics of this type of relationship is the existence of a manufacturing/R&D base in the UK and strong supplier knowledge of the market place. This type only refers to products with a high degree of standardisation and communication processes based on simple contacts. Customer involvement in R&D activities tends to be minimal;

Type II Indirect contact approach

This is similar to the previous type and is based on supply of foreign built AMT innovation and characterised by the absence of manufacturing/R&D bases in the UK. It includes the supply of stand alone dedicated equipment such as injection moulding machinery and CNC machines. The role of subsidiaries is one of sales and support only.

Type III The co-operative approach

This type generally requires projects to be co-ordinated and usually involves more than one supplier. It was found to be predominant in the computer industry where suppliers of software systems tend to liaise closely with suppliers of hardware equipment. This type of customer-supplier chain is characterised by much more intense communication processes and more customer involvement in R&D activities. Manufacturing/R&D bases are often present.

Type IV Business systems – multi-supply source

This type was found to be applicable to complex AMT projects such as Flexible Manufacturing Systems (FMS). A major supplier is put in charge of the project

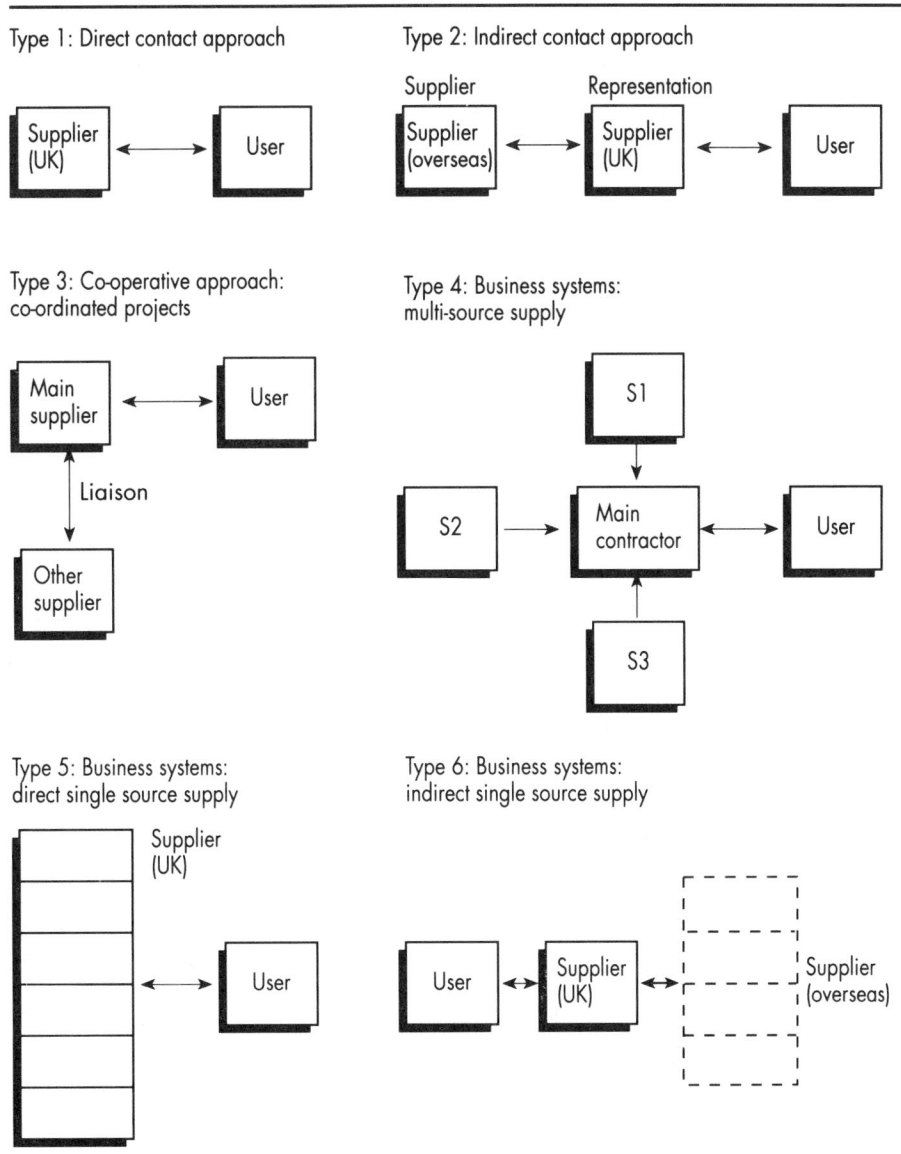

9.5 Patterns of AMT user-supplier relationships.

management activities and manages dealings with second tier suppliers on behalf of the customer. The main suppliers in this category tend to have their own manufacturing/R&D base in the UK. In addition to manufacturing their own products, they may manufacture other equipment under license. There is a high requirement for project management capability in this case and the communication processes tend to be complex. The customers concerned are involved throughout the various stages of the projects. These projects are based on revolutionary ideas/technologies. There is therefore low penetration in the market place and both suppliers and users have shared learning processes.

AMT implementation

E = effective
I = ineffective

AMT implementation columns:
- Need establishment strategy (E / I)
- Manufacturing strategy (E / I)
- Financial justification (E / I)
- Supplier appraisal strategy (E / I)
- Employee appraisal strategy (E / I)
- Project management (E / I)
- Supplier involvement (E / I)
- Communication strategy with suppliers (E / I)

AMT diffusion rows:

AMT diffusion	E / I
Customer need analysis	E / I
Idea generation/screening	E / I
Product development/manufacture	E / I
Customer involvement in R & D	E / I
Product diffusion	E / I
Information dissemination	E / I
Technical expertise	E / I
Project management capability	E / I
Level of support	E / I
Level of back-up	E / I
Customer education and training	E / I
Communication strategy with customers	E / I

9.6 An explanatory model on user/supplier interactions in the context of AMT.

Type V Business systems – direct single source supply

Similarly to the previous type, this pattern is applicable to complex projects such as FMS. The main feature here is the huge supplier capability in manufacturing a wide range of products to provide total turnkey projects using their own equipment, with limited utilisation of second tier suppliers.

Type VI Business systems – indirect single source supply

Similarly to the previous two patterns, this type deals with the implementation of complex AMT projects such as Automatic Guided Vehicle Systems (AGVs). Advanced Manufacturing Technology innovation is revolutionary and not based on previous technologies. The communication processes are highly complex and tend to be characterised by suppliers and users learning together. The suppliers concerned have strong manufacturing/R&D bases based overseas. The UK subsidiary assumes the role of project co-ordinator, with high technical expertise and plays a crucial role in liaising with the customers at various stages of the project implementation.

Based on the various patterns of customer-supplier chains in the context of AMT innovation, the author proposes a model which reflects key determinants in establishing bonds between customers and suppliers. The model suggests that there are three parts to the establishment of customer-supplier chains:

(i) **AMT implementation dimension:** This is based on criteria which were found to affect the user adoption process;
(ii) **AMT diffusion dimension:** This is based on criteria which were found to affect the supplier diffusion process;
(iii) **The interaction dimension:** This is based on the combination of variables in the adoption process with others from the diffusion process.

The model is represented in Fig. 9.6. The variables which are the building blocks have all been found to have some prominence in determining various climates of customer-supplier interactions.

The combination of the various interactions between variables pertaining to the diffusion and adoption processes determines the type of interaction process, Fig. 9.7.

Various interaction modes can be represented as a function of adoption and diffusion variables:

$$I = f(V1 \ldots V8; V1 \ldots V12)$$

Where: I = Interaction mode
f = Function of
V1 . . . V8 = Variables 1 to 8
(Implementation dimension)
V1 . . . V12 = Variables 1 to 12
(Diffusion dimension)

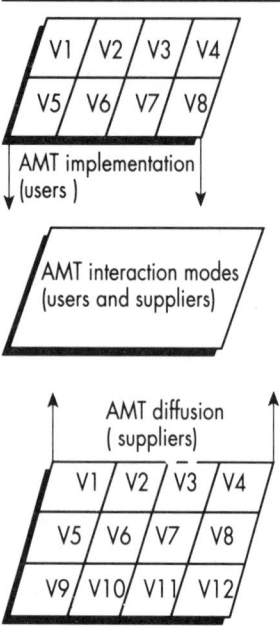

9.7 The effectiveness of AMT interaction processes.

CUSTOMER-SUPPLIER CHAINS: AN EXTENDED MODEL

One is urged to ask whether customer-supplier chains based on dealings with suppliers of technological processes and suppliers of components/raw materials are enough? They may be as long as the customer (OEM) can manage process cap: 'ility and carry on ensuring Zero Defect. What happens in reality however is that suppliers of technological processes carry on developing better designed and more capable processes which have gone through rigorous testing and where customers have been extensively involved. Suppliers of components/raw materials tend to carry on developing new products which have better performance characteristics and which may or may not cost the customer less money.

The two sets of efforts are however carried out independently. Suppliers of technological systems tend to test performance of their processes by using a range of materials/components known to them and which are available in the market place. This may inhibit process flexibility if they have not taken into account materials being developed in the future. On the other hand, suppliers of raw materials/components may use process equipment which may not be compatible with that of their customers or which may cease to become compatible if customers decide to upgrade their process equipment.

This has been reported many times, for example suppliers of plastics injection moulding machinery do not take into account the latest developed polymers or suppliers of toolings do not take into account the type of machine tools customers are using. The problems which can occur restrict the flexibility of the customer and may even limit process capability and mislead customers into investigating for random or systematic causes of variation, if they have not been made aware that the process equipment capability has not previously been tested for new raw materials/ components. There is therefore a missing link for the perfect customer-supplier chain, Fig. 9.8.

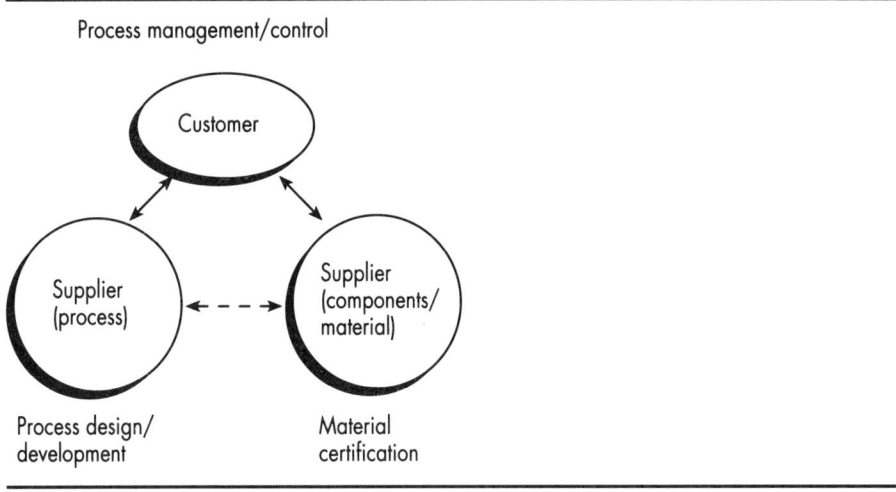

9.8 Customer-supplier chain – The missing link.

The extended customer-supplier model suggests that both suppliers of process equipment have to work much more closely together, if they have developed long term partnerships with the same customer. This is thought to be necessary if the concept of Zero Defect is to be achieved. Both types of suppliers can benefit from such a relationship. By gaining access to privileged information on future customer intentions in relation to capital investment, suppliers of process equipment may get involved as early as possible with the customer to design, manufacture, test and implement the equipment desired. Suppliers of raw materials/components on the other hand may decide to work closely with the supplier of technological equipment on existing and new products so that process capability is determined before the implementation programme starts.

Extended customer-supplier chains, Fig. 9.9, mean that total compatibility and synchronisation is achieved all the time with benefits to all parties concerned.

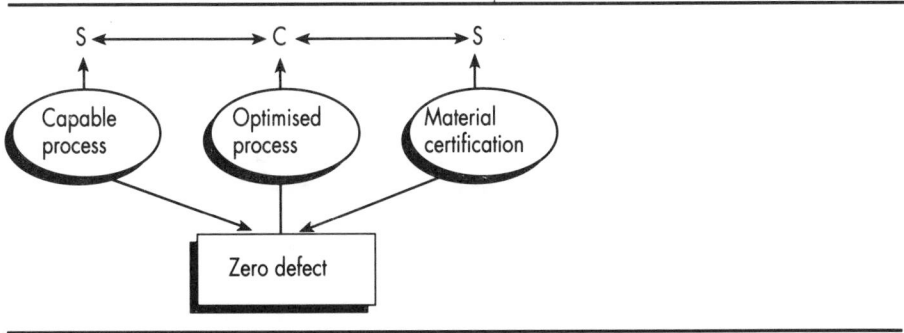

9.9 Extended customer-supplier chain.

10

ESSENTIALS OF TQM: CONTINUOUS IMPROVEMENT

CONTINUOUS IMPROVEMENT: WHAT IS IT?

Continuous improvement can be considered as the 'wheels' of the organisational vehicle. It is the effort produced by the wheels which will make the vehicle move forward. Organisations in the past have been concerned with doing 'more of the same'[24] with disregard for customer feedback and market demands. When performance decreases, organisations tend to double their efforts in 'doing more of the same'. Others called this approach 'Local Optimisation'[29] where different groups within one organisation focus on their own area of interest. This is thought to be due to lack of communication, lack of shared goals and lack of co-operation.

The traditional approach towards improvement lacked in consistency, in will and determination and in measurement of effort made, which are all necessary if superior performance is to be achieved in a modern business environment. Table 10.1 briefly summarises the traditional approach to continuous improvement and its limitations.[17]

Table 10.1 Traditional approach to continuous improvement

Type of approach	Limitations
Undertaking capital investment programmes to modernise factories plant and equipment	Planning and implementation timescales are usually extended
	Payback/benefits take much longer than predicted
	Valuable production and industrial engineering resources become heavily committed to project's life following commissioning
Localised improvement initiatives	Areas tackled may not be the ones that can provide biggest improvements for business performance
	Improvements made in one area may cause unanticipated problems elsewhere
	Day to day pressures mean that required resources for the project may not be consistently forthcoming

Various proposals have been put forward to explain what needs to be done to change the approach to continuous improvement.

1 Use of critical thinking skills for effective problem-solving:[4] The wealth of specialised knowledge in any business is far more important than any technological sophisticated innovation. More emphasis needs to be placed on people.
2 Continuous improvement is not a standard management practice:[8] Continuous improvement requires critical thinking and management techniques such as SPC.[4]
3 The customer is the next process in the chain. Customer feedback and input should not be regarded as a necessary evil but more as an opportunity for conducting improvement.[3]
4 Create a management system which will consider continuous improvement as a never-ending activity: Conway suggests the following:[11]

To improve all work processes we must know about all the work at all levels. We use our knowledge and understanding of these work processes to find the problems, errors, complexities and waste, and get rid of them. The company must improve internal and external processes, seeking to measure and improve quality with a customer focus. Customers define quality, and we continuously improve our processes to give them the quality services and products they require.'

5 Quality at the heart of business strategy: This point was raised by various gurus and champions of quality.[13] Juran for instance argued that what was missing in the West is a 'grand strategy' which puts quality into the business plan. He suggested the following six steps for establishing a strong continuous improvement programme.

● Providing leadership from the top;
● Establishing vision and policies;
● Establishing and deploying quality goals;
● Providing resources and training;
● Establishing measurements;
● Reviewing performance regularly;
● Rewarding the reward system.

The role of senior managers in instigating successful continuous improvement programmes has been argued by others. Kano for instance[13] debates that continuous improvement depends on the effort of a lot of people. This requires what Kano called 'crisis consciousness'. Kano concluded that crisis consciousness is what pushes people forward to make improvements.

6 Total optimisation: Using people's skills and knowledge so that they are no longer confined to a localised area but geared towards a total goal oriented organisation.[29] Optimisation can be achieved by providing people with the necessary tools and direction, by creating a supportive environment and by sharing results with everyone concerned.

To come to an acceptable definition of continuous improvement therefore one has to accept that major changes have to take place and the shift of emphasis has to be heavily biased towards people. In addition goals have to have a long term characteristic. Most of all and as suggested by Juran, a quality strategy has to be incorporated in the overall business plan to make continuous improvement a viable proposition.

Changes required for the introduction of continuous improvement do not necessarily mean more expenses to the companies concerned. As has been argued by Butlin[17] the introduction of continuous improvement has the following attractions:

- Continuous improvement can be implemented in a short period of time and functions on an ongoing basis;
- Implementation of continuous improvement can be carried out in a structured manner;
- The continuous improvement scheme is shopfloor based and uses minimal internal and external resources;
- It is an inexpensive approach to improving business overall performance.

The necessary changes required for the implementation of continuous improvement are more in terms of attitudes and beliefs rather than financial commitments. As Suzaki suggests:[29]

'We may grasp an idea intellectually, but our hearts may not be in it enough to put it into practice.'

Suzaki[29] strongly argues that the following seven points determine the successful criteria of continuous improvement programmes:

1 Challenging conventional beliefs;
2 Bias towards experimentation: This is the best means by which problems can be made visible;
3 Tolerance for failure: Continuous improvement comes from a learning cycle;
4 Trust;
5 Teamwork: Total as opposed to local optimisation;
6 Flexibility: Rigid structures will inhibit progress;
7 Discipline: Stick to set standards and conduct measurement wherever possible.

The above seven points reflect change in attitudes where commitment is reflected by what is in the heart rather than the magnitude of financial investment programmes. However changing people's attitudes for the introduction of continuous improvement may be a daunting task. The best description of continuous improvement is perhaps the one given by Kehrl[26] who argues that:

'Continuous improvement comes only when individuals are motivated to achieve regular improvements in all areas of their work. It is acceptance of the reality that people and their brain children – like their own children – require years of patient nurturing before they reach the potential that was there at birth. Technology is important, but equally important is what we do in the years after we get the new machine or process or system in place. With a continuous improvement approach, the benefit of a major step in technology is multiplied by the many small steps that follow. And that holds true whether you are dealing with improvements in quality, marketing, design, productivity, financial systems, or human development.'

CONTINUOUS IMPROVEMENT OR KAIZEN: WHAT IS THE DIFFERENCE?

Kaizen in Japan means ongoing improvement which involves everyone in the organisation. Kaizen affects all layers of management and workers. In fact the concept of Kaizen in Japan is deep rooted and applies to everyday life. Improvement in Japan concerns social life, personal life and working life. Kaizen is very much a customer-driven strategy and therefore efforts have to be sustained to maintain customer satisfaction.

The concept is made easily applicable because there is wide recognition that problems are existing everywhere in organisations and that those need to be tackled if companies are to progress. Profit margins in Japan are thin and organisations have to strive for excellence to achieve minimum profitability levels. The driving force in wanting to improve is not a management push but a general concern on the welfare of the employer organisations and the belief that continuous improvement will benefit the organisation and in turn will benefit the individual. This is facilitated by the existence of a positive climate and a culture which supports improvement.

Many writers in the West have suggested that the Japanese culture makes the concept of Kaizen much more easily applicable in Japan than in the West. This, however, is contested by Imai,[33] who wrote a book on Kaizen. Imai argues that:

'Many Japanese management practices succeed simply because they are good management practices. This success has little to do with cultural factors. And the lack of cultural bias means that these practices can be – and are – just as successfully employed elsewhere. Just as Japan has its plodding companies destined to fall by the wayside of progress, so does the United States have excellent companies setting new standards for product and service quality. The distinction is not one of nationality. It is one of mentality.'

These management practices can be translated in a variety of ways such as for example establishing a culture which treats problems as opportunities for improvement rather than blaming people. Fear removal and encouraging people to admit problems freely are important management tasks. In addition Japanese management systems place a lot of emphasis on collaboration, team effort and interfunctional activity. Reward systems are for overall effort rather than individual results. People are encouraged to own the processes they operate and control on an everyday basis and they are given modern tools and trained on new techniques to make improvement an easier target to achieve.

Kaizen is process-oriented rather than individual task oriented. This is different from the West where most emphasis is placed on individual performances and rewards according to results with disregard for the process and its capability. In the West results, because of their short term nature and their ease of quantification, tend to form the basis for decision making with disregard to the strength of the business for future competitiveness.

Continuous improvement in Japan means that the efforts have to be sustained, could be slow in making progress and may be invisible. This would not apply in the West where improvement means breakthroughs and major leaps. The returns have to be visibly quantifiable. Incremental improvements are often disregarded because their effect may be considered as insignificant in the short term and they may not be easily quantified in monetary terms.

Continuous improvement is usually represented in terms of Kaizen and innovation. In the West it is mainly via the efforts of technological innovation that improvement is determined. Huge capital expenditure programmes are carried out and various formulae for maximising the benefits and ensuring the returns are determined. The use of people is therefore to ensure that the returns are obtained. People do not drive this effort, they are merely a tool. In Japan however, the Kaizen element is very much people oriented and tends to play a much more important role than innovation. Japanese organisations maximise benefit from technological innovations by using people's knowledge, skills and determined effort to improve the process. Innovation in Japan is only introduced if severe limitations in the process have been encountered or if investment is part of a wider programme intended to meet customer requirements in a better way.

Efforts coming from the implementation of technological innovation are big leaps which are followed by a major slide. This is because standards tend to deteriorate, technology tends to be superseded, and market requirements change thus limiting flexibility of the innovation. The only way to progress is by sustaining huge capital investment programmes. Kaizen however is a reflection of cumulative positive efforts which ensure that organisations' competitiveness is positively progressed. Kaizen is a people-oriented approach to competitiveness whilst innovation is a technology-oriented approach to competitiveness.

Table 10.2 represents a comparison between the Japanese approach to competition (Kaizen) and the Western approach (innovation).[33]

Table 10.2 Kaizen versus innovation: Japanese versus Western approach to continuous improvement

	Kaizen	**Innovation**
Effect	Long term and long lasting but undramatic	Short term but dramatic
Pace	Small steps	Big steps
Timeframe	Continuous and incremental	Intermittent and non-incremental
Change	Gradual and constant	Abrupt and volatile
Involvement	Everybody	Select few 'champions'
Approach	Collectivism, group efforts, systems approach	Rugged individualism, individual ideas and efforts
Mode	Maintenance and improvement	Scrap and rebuild
Spark	Conventional know-how and state of the art	Technological breakthroughs, new inventions, new theories
Practical requirements	Requires little investment but great effort to maintain it	Requires large investment but little effort to maintain it
Effort orientation	People	Technology
Evaluation criteria	Process and efforts for better results	Results for profits
Advantage	Works well in slow-growth economy	Better suited to fast growing company

Total Quality Management seems to be the ideal opportunity for organisations to tackle the various obstacles to implementing continuous improvement based on a blend of Kaizen and innovation. It must be recognised that the following elements are essential if any continuous improvement initiative is to succeed:

1 Continuous improvement is a customer-driven effort. Targets can only be set and determined by customer requirements;
2 The use of knowledge work is required. Any continuous improvement initiative will depend on people's skills, knowledge, expertise and creative output;
3 Continuous improvement is about interfunctional problem-solving activity and

team work. Shared goals and objectives are the key to successful continuous improvement programmes;

4 Continuous improvement is about driving out fear and making problems an opportunity for improvement;

5 Continuous improvement focuses on the whole process (means and the ends) rather than the results only;

6 Improvement is about slow and gradual steps rather than single shots or big leaps. It is about the long term health of the business rather than the short term profitability;

7 Continuous improvement requires positive management systems which create a positive climate for improvement and supportive management teams;

8 Management systems include the use of tools and techniques to understand processes, measure existing performance, identify problems and implement the solutions;

9 Continuous improvement has to be based on Deming's PDCA cycle.

LEADERSHIP FOR CONTINUOUS IMPROVEMENT

The role of leadership as an essential part of TQM has been thoroughly discussed in Chapter 8. It has already been emphasised that continuous improvement requires strong involvement from the top. Juran for instance insists on the formation of a quality council represented by a senior management team. The role of leaders in continuous improvement has been described in a variety of ways by many writers.

Senior management have to look for 'golden nuggets' on the shopfloor by listening to and involving their employees.[25] This is perhaps a useful approach in creating an employee relations climate based on mutual co-operation and trust and therefore could be considered as a first step towards culture change. Others write that management commitment has to be translated in terms of not just clear understanding of quality concepts but taking the initiative to improve themselves, their leadership and their processes.[1] Leaders, it has been suggested, need to play a combined role of coach, cheerleader and captain of a team relay race in the context of continuous improvement.[1]

The role of the leader has to be reflected in the whole PDCA cycle. In continuous improvement the role of leaders can be represented as follows:

Plan Commitment to plan and implement change intended to meet customer requirements in a better way;

Do Communicate effectively through teamwork and better employee involvement;

Check Investigate processes using analytical tools and techniques to eliminate waste and streamline operations through planned actions and a commitment to improvement;

Act Conduct measurement of results and performance so that continuous improvement of the process and output is achieved.

Other writers have suggested that the role of leaders in the context of continuous improvement revolves round their interaction with people.[32] For example, it has been suggested that leaders have first of all to gain their subordinates and bosses' trust. Secondly a leader has to be more of a facilitator and decision maker than a problem solver. Thirdly leaders are expected to be good and effective communicators. Leaders have also got to be good at time management, they must take good care of people they are in charge of, must provide vision for the organisation they represent, must be highly visible and approachable, must be firm and effective in their decision making, reliable, open-minded and exude integrity.[32] Leaders have to be part of all aspects of the continuous improvement process. Their involvement should be in the planning, implementation, measurement and the championing of the whole effort so that it becomes a never ending quest for improvement and progress.

Sahney[30] proposes ten key roles for leaders for effective implementation of a continuous improvement programme as follows:

1 Top management leadership;
2 Corporate framework for quality;
3 Transformation of corporate culture;
4 Customer focus;
5 Continuous improvement in quality;
6 Process improvement;
7 Quality education and training;
8 Measurement and use of statistical concepts;
9 Employee recognition and involvement;
10 Integration with management practice.

These various roles are the necessary requirements for establishing a climate in which continuous improvement can prosper and become part of everyday working life. Although these various roles appear to be very demanding, the initial challenge for leaders is to get everybody on the same side and everyone's contribution towards the common goal. Once a culture of common beliefs, principles, objectives and concerns has been established, people will manage their own tasks and will take voluntary responsibility to improve processes which they own.

THE ROLE OF TEAMS IN CONTINUOUS IMPROVEMENT

Teams are an integral part of continuous improvement. Indeed with teams, a level of synergy can be created which would lead to the achievement of superior performance based on creative output, high quality standards, enthusiasm, common goals and good understanding of employer organisation's mission and goals. The importance of team work has always been recognised. However, since the focal point in organisations has been results, teams were not thought of at the strategic level and always considered to be capable of self-management at the bottom levels.

It has always been assumed for example that people are capable of organising themselves without the interference of management and that they can solve quality and productivity problems on their own. Additionally, it has always been assumed that teams are well equipped in terms of skill, knowledge and guidance on how to solve problems. Management have always assumed that by providing information and by improving communication channels people will perform better. Is this why Quality Circles (QC) have failed in the West?

Quality Circles: Their role in continuous improvement

Quality Circles which have been successful in Japan have met with a lot of resistance in the West and in many cases have proved to be complete failures. Various reasons have been suggested, some of them are summarised in Table 10.3.

The table carries two messages which are key determinants to successful implementation of QCs. First, QCs have to be an integral part of a much wider quality improvement programme which is based on a quality policy. Secondly, without

Table 10.3 Quality Circles: Why they have failed in the West?

Reference	Reasons
6	Lack of participatory management
	Job insecurity
	Low worker skill levels
	Unions
9	The conceptual approach: In Japan, QCs are viewed as an extension to a wider quality improvement programme, by managerial means. This is not the case in the West
	Prior training of managers: In Japan, managers were given extensive training on how to manage quality. In the West this was not the case. In the West the task of managing quality was delegated to facilitators or consultants
	Co-ordination and guidance: Plenty of guidance on training and other issues in Japan, not the case in the West
10	Organisational climate: management style, employee attitudes, etc
	Structure
19	Commitment and teamwork are synonymous words in Japan, this is not the case in the West
	In Japan there is – A well established senior-junior system – Continuous training and re-training both 'in house' and 'on the job' – The formation of other small groups, (management improvement groups) in all areas of the company – A widely practised system of job rotation – Company-specific knowledge is extensive within the group – Backed up by accumulated practices of other groups All the above points are lacking in the West
27	Unwillingness of middle managers and first-line supervisors to involve themselves in QC activities
	Top management considers QC to be the responsibility of workers only
23	In Japan there is the following: – Narrowly defined chains of command – Consensual decision making at least at higher levels – Intensive cross-skill training in conjunction with career development programmes – Extraordinary focus on quality/effectiveness

management commitment and involvement, QCs are doomed to fail. The latter point was emphasised by many writers. It has been concluded that management style and commitment are the most important determinants of quality circle usage and effectiveness.[15]

Quality Circles are characterised by their voluntarism and the encouragement of workers own initiative to solve problems which surround their work environments. In a way QCs are a means of participation and employee involvement to bring about change by a bottom-up approach. This aspect of team work is different from Continuous Improvement Teams which are led by management who have the task of selecting problems and then recruiting members of the organisation who have the necessary skill, knowledge and know-how in contributing to their solutions.

Figure 10.1 represents a pyramid of how the continuous improvement process is usually conducted.[22] The bottom-up approach is represented by voluntary teams who form their own circles to tackle common problems encountered in their work environment. Quality Improvement Teams (QITs) however are teams represented by management members representing different functions and having a wide pool of knowledge and expertise.

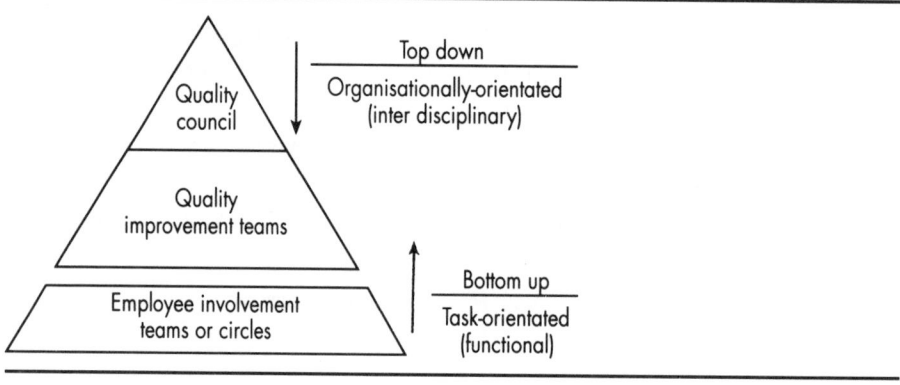

10.1 The quality improved process based on a team approach.

The role of the quality council is in formulating a quality policy, its planning and in providing a sense of direction for the policy to be implemented effectively. It is obvious that a starting point is to ensure that quality improvement is an integral part of the business mission and that there is full commitment from the top.

Teams: How do they work?

Much research has been carried out on establishing how teams tend to work innovatively. The Sheffield Innovation Research Group which was set up in 1985 has investigated factors which facilitate or inhibit innovation in a team, what distinguishes a highly innovative from a less innovative team, how the innovative process is being carried out and what measures could be taken to facilitate innovations in a team context.[12] The group have established that there are four key determinants which highlight group innovativeness as follows:

1 Vision: A shared idea of a valued outcome in the group;

2 Participative safety: High levels of participation lead to less resistance to change and therefore a greater likelihood to innovate;

3 Climate for excellence: Effort and determination to achieve high performance standards and the commitment to carry out necessary changes to achieve excellence;

4 Support for innovation: Management support has to be visible. It is often reported that support for innovation is articulated but not enacted.

The Sheffield Innovation Group[12] have concluded by providing a check list which can be used by various teams to assess the degree of their effectiveness in each of the four key determinants, Table 10.4.

Table 10.4 Team innovation checklist

Vision	Climate for excellence
Does the team have a clearly articulated vision, mission or set of objectives?	Is excellent task performance of central importance to the team?
Is the vision (set of objectives) shared by all team members?	What procedures and methods are used to monitor and improve performance levels?
Is the mission or set of objectives clearly stated?	Are all team members committed to excellent standards?
Was the vision (set of objectives) originally developed and negotiated by the whole team?	Are team members prepared to discuss opposing ideas fully
Is this vision (set of objectives) attainable?	

Participative safety	Support for innovation
Do team members share information fully with each other?	Do team members support new ideas?
Do all team members participate in decision making?	Do team members give time, co-operation and resources to help each other implement new ideas?
Are team members ready to propose new ideas which challenge existing ways of doing things?	Does the team leader support and encourage new ideas?
Do team members discuss each other's work related anxieties and successes?	Does the team leader offer practical help and resources for the development of new ideas?
Is there a climate of trust and warmth within the group?	

Whilst senior managers play a major role in setting up the teams, allocating resources, providing information, guidance and support, the checklist in Table 10.4 shows that teams have to manage themselves and run themselves autonomously. Teams have to be open with each other, members have to be encouraged to express their feelings openly, they have to trust each other, develop objectives for the benefit of all the team and not a few members, solve conflicts, promote high commitment and develop a consensus in decision making amongst others.[20]

There are however barriers to team building[20] which have to be recognised and avoided at any cost. The major obstacles can be classified into two areas:

1 **The problem with non-conformists:** Senior management may tend to encourage, support and listen to the ideas coming from the conformist members and not those who do not conform. The latter group tend to develop what has been termed as 'natural conservatism'. They are not encouraged to express their true feelings. In many cases, the non-conformists are the more creative people in their group but their ideas are not widely welcomed by the group.

2 **The problem of over-conformity:** This problem has been labelled as 'groupthink' and has the following characteristics:[20]

● Shared stereotypes about people or groups outside;
● Mind guarding, or protecting the leader against information that conflicts with the group's aims or values;
● Belief in the inherent morality of the work of the group;
● Illusion of invulnerability – that nothing can threaten the group;
● Self-censorship – members hold back from saying things that might conflict with commonly held views;
● Illusion and unanimity – a belief that everyone is in agreement;
● Rationalising information conflicting with group views.

The dangers from both non- and over-conformity is that individuals (non-conformists) will always remain detached from group norms and values and will never contribute effectively. In the case of over-conformity, the teams can become so obsessed with their norms and values that they spend most time trying to protect their ideas and justify their actions without appreciating the fact that great changes are taking place in the environment surrounding them.

Teams therefore, to be effective, have to protect the individual's interests and channel everyone's effort through effectively towards the common destiny and objectives. This can be achieved by creating a climate in which individuals can freely express their feelings and where they can voice their support as much as their disagreement. In addition, the team has to be flexible in its approach and be prepared to review its mission, values and objectives if changes in the external environment make it necessary. Managers can play a crucial role in the building of effective teams. They can create a climate where non-conformism is not seen as a negative development but an opportunity to ask why individuals tend to disagree with the rest of the group. Conversely there should not be a need for over-conformism. People should not be too protective of management systems, ideas and plans, and should be encouraged to challenge them at any time so that continuous improvement can become a viable outcome.

THE IMPLEMENTATION OF CONTINUOUS IMPROVEMENT: HOW TO DO IT?

It is hard to pinpoint what exactly triggers off successful implementation of continuous improvement as a never ending activity. It is even harder to be inspired by championing organisations in the West since successful efforts at continuous improvement have to be sustained for a long period of time. This also makes it harder to try and prescribe how the process of continuous improvement can be introduced and managed since organisations are at different levels of the competitive spectrum and are also characterised by various cultures, management systems, resources, skills, etc.

One can however pinpoint very accurately why major moves to implement continuous improvement fail.[14]

- It has been reported for instance that if quality is ill defined or merely confined to meeting technical specifications, this effort will be doomed to fail. Quality has to be appreciated for its more pervasive role in transforming parameters of competitiveness and enabling workers and managers alike to raise work standards for excellence.
- Management commitment once again keeps appearing as a prerequisite for making continuous improvement programmes successful. There are no compromises in this area. Any half hearted effort will lead to failure in continuous improvement initiatives.
- Continuous improvement cannot be treated as another fad or a management exercise for a specific purpose. It is only when quality is accepted as a new way of working and doing business which is essential for companies' survival, that continuous improvement efforts are likely to succeed.
- Lack of appreciation of the need to change organisational culture. It is vital that an organisational transformation takes place in order to reap the benefits from continuous improvement activities.
- Continuous improvement cannot be based on use of statistical tools and techniques alone. Improvement does not happen by using control charts and collecting data statistically. Processes have to be owned, well understood, investigated and continuously improved.

Perhaps a starting point for the introduction of continuous improvement programmes is to ensure management understanding of the potential benefits which can be obtained from the implementation of quality, and to ensure their total commitment. Management commitment has to pervade down to the bottom layers of the organisations concerned, to get everyone on board and everybody appreciating the need to compete on quality and the need to improve overall performance. This is perhaps the first step towards conducting a cultural change. This could take a long time to achieve and management have to be patient to give people time to re-adjust and be convinced of the need to embark on a major quality improvement process.

Besides structuring the pyramid for continuous improvement and allocating responsibilities, management have to ensure that people are adequately trained and provided with modern tools and techniques to be used for continuous improvement programmes. Various changes have to take place such as management systems, communication systems, structural changes, reward systems, decision making processes and performance measurement criteria (not result-based but process-based).

Juran suggests that for a quality improvement process to start bringing about benefits will take many years.[13] He estimated that:

- Choice of strategy will take one year;
- Improvements at a test site, plus evaluation of results will take one year;
- Scaling up to companywide improvement, including strategic quality management at test site will take two years;
- Scaling up to strategic quality management will take up to two years.

Various ways of introducing continuous improvement have been suggested. Some guidelines have been summed up in Table 10.5 from different literature. The various propositions are all valid, based on practical examples and will all have many common approaches.

Table 10.5 Some guidelines for implementing continuous improvement

Reference	Suggested factors
14	A context that shapes the expression of all work – its vitality, creativity, and quality
	Empowering people with the information, resources and support they need to fully express their capabilities
	Intense and pervasive communication about direction, co-operation, problems and results
	Constant discovery and elimination of barriers to people's performance
7	A set of core concepts that provide common terminology and ideas about quality and its meaning and application to everyone's work
	A systematic and common process that everyone uses for identifying and working quality issues through to effective prevention or corrective action
	A set of managing elements that define the areas for change in an effective organisational change process
5	Familiarisation (ongoing)
	Development of a team network
	Training
	Introduction of measurement techniques
	Strategic planning (ongoing)
18	Create constancy of purpose for improvement of product and service
	Adopt the new philosophy
	Cease dependence on mass inspection
	End the practice of awarding business on the basis of price tag alone
	Improve constantly and forever the system of production and service
	Institute training
	Adopt and institute leadership
	Drive out fear
	Break down barriers between staff areas
	Eliminate slogans, exhortations, and targets for the workforce
	Eliminate numerical quotas for the workforce
	Eliminate numerical goals for people in management
	Remove barriers that rob people of pride of workmanship
	Encourage education and self-improvement for everyone
	Take action to accomplish the transformation

Table 10.5 Some guidelines for implementing continuous improvement (*cont.*)

Reference	Suggested factors
16	Recognition and articulation of the quality problem
	Gaining senior management's commitment and increasing quality awareness within the organisation
	Formulating a company-wide quality management system
	Using a series of short-term achievable proposals for quality improvement
21	Support, involvement and legitimisation from the appropriate level of top management
	A critical mass of 'masters' who have the theoretical and experiential foundation to make the effort work
	Well-thought through and evolving improvement plans that integrate with other strategic plans
	Application of the appropriate tools and techniques
	Mechanisms to offset entropy. The improvement process must be managed with the same level of discipline given to managing budgets and technology
	Patient impatience. Real change and the impact of that change takes time
	Tremendous amounts of integration, co-ordination, communication and conflict management
	A supportive infrastructure

Towards a culture of never ending improvement: A tentative model

The model which is illustrated in Fig. 10.2 reflects two phases of the implementation of continuous improvement.

Phase 1: This phase represents the introduction of the continuous improvement initiative. It is dependent on the existence of four main criteria which include:

● Management commitment;
● A positive climate for improvement;
● Resource allocation;
● Help and support.

The implementation stages are reflected by a period of explaining the philosophy of continuous improvement (getting people on board), group establishment, group cohesion, training on problem solving techniques, presentation skills and the implementation of endorsed solutions for the first problems solved.

This phase is basically a learning curve and the problems solved are incremental in their impact. This phase can be seen as occupying negative time as it is time which does not add value.

Phase 2: This phase marks team independence, and their confidence in managing their own problem solving activities. It therefore means that there is much less reliance on consultants, great reduction in management time and since problem

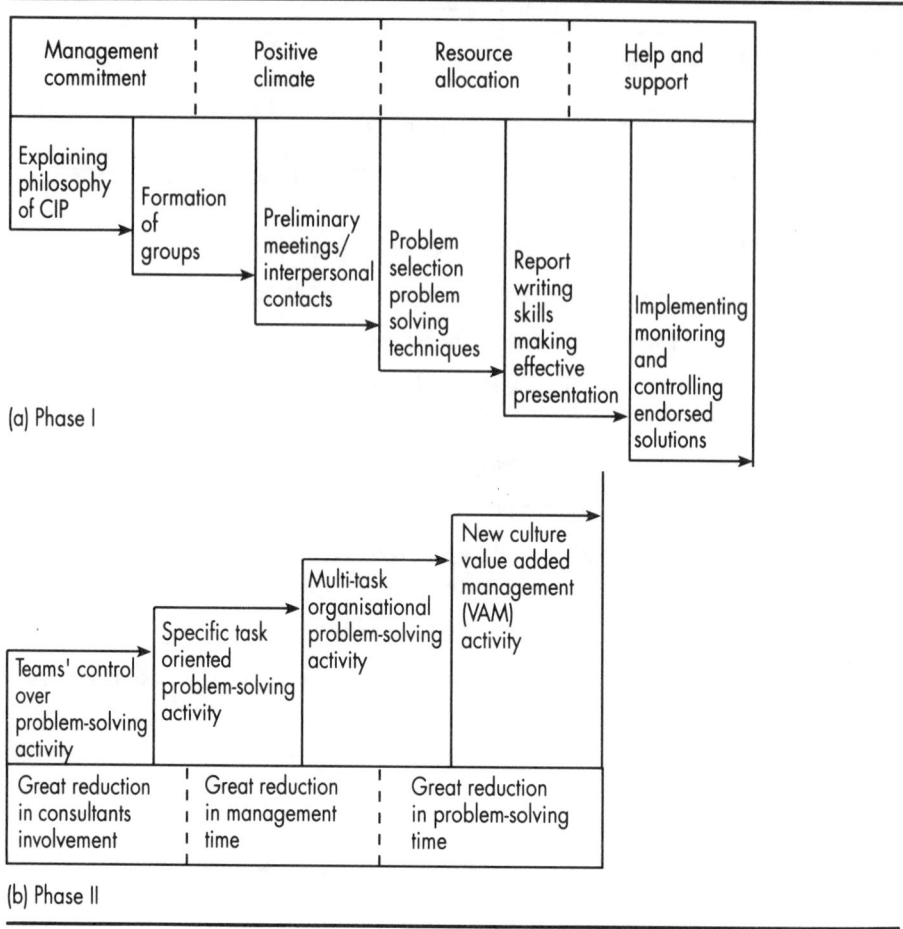

Management commitment	Positive climate	Resource allocation	Help and support

Explaining philosophy of CIP → Formation of groups → Preliminary meetings/ interpersonal contacts → Problem selection problem solving techniques → Report writing skills making effective presentation → Implementing monitoring and controlling endorsed solutions

(a) Phase I

Teams' control over problem-solving activity → Specific task oriented problem-solving activity → Multi-task organisational problem-solving activity → New culture value added management (VAM) activity

Great reduction in consultants involvement	Great reduction in management time	Great reduction in problem-solving time

(b) Phase II

10.2 Towards a culture of never ending improvement.

solving techniques are familiar to all members, problem solving time is greatly reduced.

This phase represents a positive evolution in time where there is a gradual shift from specific task oriented activity to a multi-task (organisational) problem solving activity. Eventually, as the exercises repeat themselves, a culture of never ending improvement is established.

Continuous improvement will succeed if it is based on a committed will to improve from both workers and managers; if it has total organisational involvement; if it is customer-oriented and relies on visible measurements. The point which one can make is that there are no losers in the implementation of continuous improvement. Every organisation which approaches this endeavour will benefit in some form or another. The level of benefits will depend on the effort put in. The time of reaping the benefits will vary according to the type of transformational changes which need to be carried out.

Continuous improvement is the best vehicle in the quest for progress and excellence. Total Quality Management is about continuous improvement for doing things right first time and everytime and doing the right things externally. Since economic viability is a major consideration in the TQM philosophy, continuous improvement becomes the means by which waste of any kind is identified and removed and where limitations are identified and removed so that processes can be optimised to reflect strength, fitness for competitiveness and excellence in performance.

11

CONCLUDING REMARKS: IMPLEMENTATION, COSTING AND MEASUREMENT ISSUES

THE ROAD TO EXCELLENCE

This book has covered TQM from a macro perspective without attempt to scrutinise any particular aspect. This general approach, it is hoped, is intended to highlight to the student/practitioner in the engineering field, that TQM is not a highly focused activity but represents a broad philosophy which embraces every aspect of businesses and which determines parameters for modern competitiveness.

The book has not therefore tackled questions such as how to implement TQM, how quality is costed or how performance is presented based on quality criteria. Instead, the book has attempted to answer questions such as – What is the relevance of quality to engineers? What is it? Where did it come from? What does it involve? What are its building blocks?

This chapter attempts to answer the above questions albeit very briefly. Total Quality implementation is necessary for establishing a culture of continuous improvement, using the PDCA cycle to identify waste and eliminate it, aiming for a Zero Defect objective. This is the internal objective of refining the business and making everything visible. At a later stage, TQM implementation of the 'newly changed' and rejuvenated organisation will be looking for the establishment of best practice with an external focus on competitors, Fig. 11.1.

Implementation of TQM therefore goes through a stage of understanding its impact, adopting its methods and measuring its impact. At various levels, quality costing in all processes needs to be conducted to support the achievement of superior performance.

Implementation in the organisation which has radically changed its culture, and where competitiveness is based on quality criteria, is characterised by an optimisation of internal and external operations in pursuit of excellence. This is supported by a process of benchmarking continuously and throughout the whole organisation, Fig. 11.2

TQM IMPLEMENTATION

Most organisations get inspired by the teachings of one of the main gurus of TQM, discussed in Chapter 2, such as Crosby, Juran or Deming. Whilst this is highly

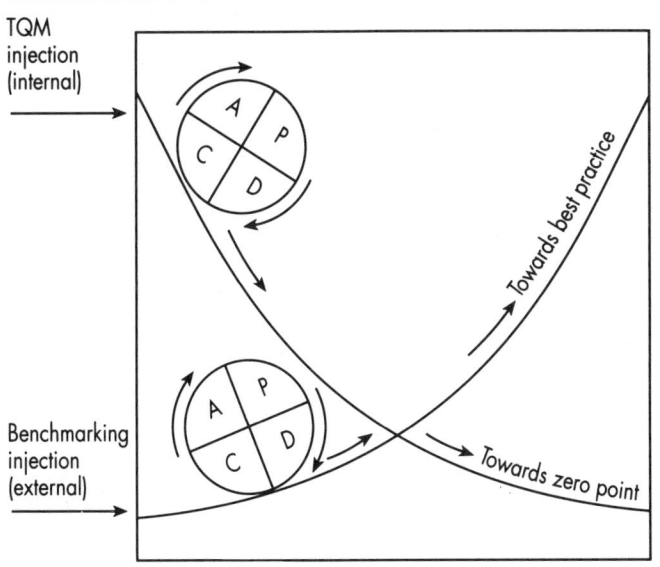

11.1 The road to excellence.

desirable, following too closely the views of one single guru may have limitations. Some gurus place too much emphasis on technical processes and some concentrate more on people/management issues. For example Crosby's approach is based on the four absolutes of quality management (conformance to requirements, the system for causing quality is prevention not appraisal, the performance standard is Zero

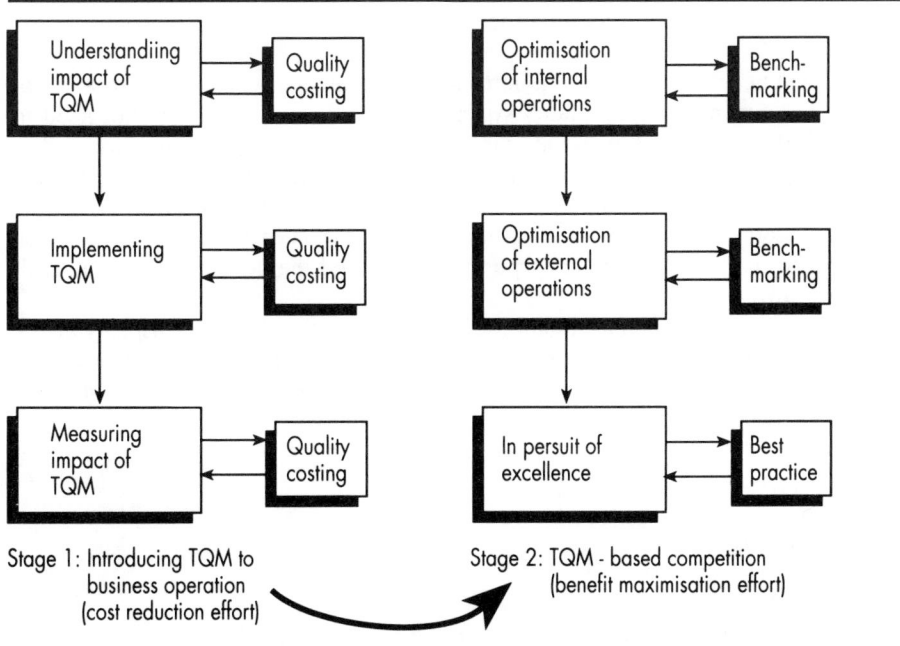

11.2 TQM implementation: cost reduction/benefit maximisation effort.

Defect, the measurement of quality is the price of non-conformance). Crosby insists that there has to be a clear policy, through training of the workforce and management and commitment through what he calls 'executive witness'.

Deming and Juran however place more emphasis on the process. They believe that Zero Defect can only be achieved by continuous improvement as a never-ending activity. They argue that Zero Defect as a slogan can demotivate people, particularly if they are not provided with explanations on how to achieve it. The Crosby approach does not explain how to achieve Zero Defect. Some people argue that the Deming and Juran approaches, because of their keen interest on the process and the obtainment of the hard facts, are too cold and do not necessarily motivate people to adopt TQM practice.

The truth is that quality cannot be purchased as a package. The implementation of TQM is a unique experience to individual organisations and the ideas of individual gurus will not necessarily be enough by themselves to solve all the problems or bring about the necessary changes. It is more beneficial perhaps to adopt a strategy based on a mixture of ideas from the various gurus. This has been widely supported by various people. Total Quality Management has been referred to as a 'self-learning process'[1] where organisations have to purpose build their own requirements, by picking ideas and mixing them without having to follow closely the teachings of any guru in particular.

A practical model of TQM implementation which contains a mixture of ideas supported by the various gurus was developed by Oakland.[11] This model has been successfully introduced by a wide variety of organisations both in manufacturing and service industries.

The Oakland model (represented in Fig. 3.4) is characterised by hard necessities, soft outcomes and prerequisites.

At the heart of the model is the establishment of customer-supplier chains where the interplay of supplier and customer processes determines the strategy for continuous improvement, through process feedback and customer feedback.

- The hard necessities include the introduction of quality teams, the utilisation of tools and techniques and quality systems. These three elements do not need to be introduced in any sequential manner. They are however essential for under-standing processes, identifying problem areas, collecting data and implementing solutions so that continuous improvement becomes a visible objective.
- Soft outcomes result from the introduction of the hard building blocks which mark the start of a change in corporate culture and the facilitation of communi-cation processes.
- The prerequisite is management commitment. Unlike the other aspects of the model, management commitment cannot be built-in or instigated. It has to be inherent within the beliefs of senior managers who are responsible for the implementation of TQM.

There are thirteen steps in the Oakland approach to TQM implementation as follows:

- Understanding quality;
- Commitment to quality;
- Policy on quality;
- Organisation for quality;
- Measurement costs of quality;
- Planning for quality;

– Design for quality;
– System for quality;
– Capability for quality;
– Control for quality;
– Team work for quality;
– Training for quality;
– Implementation of TQM.

The thirteen stages represent a gradual progression towards implementing a TQM based culture.

QUALITY COSTING

Quality costing is not an exercise which is going to solve organisational problems or have an impact on performance. Quality costing can be considered as a means to an end, to help improve quality[3] and help companies reach their quality targets. Quality costing is a process-related exercise rather than for product control. The intention of quality costing is to spur some positive action as has been stated:[9]

'Quality cost systems are used as an aid in setting priorities for quality improvement projects, studying cost trends to re-allocated resources, focusing multistep operations, measuring performance, and balancing efforts in reducing variation in design versus manufacturing. Measurements don't solve problems but can spur beneficial action.'

There are two approaches to quality costing:

(i) **The traditional model or PAF model where the pattern of quality costing includes Prevention, Appraisal and Failure:** These tend to decrease as quality improvement becomes more and more an integral part of business operations. PAF costs include the following:[6, 2, 9]

   Prevention costs: Costs of quality systems, quality training and education;

   Appraisal costs: Costs of performing quality inspection and audits in-house as well as audits of suppliers;

   Failure costs (external): Costs associated with failures discovered outside the plant. These affect both cost and reputation;

   Failure costs (internal): Costs associated with failures discovered inside the plant.

(ii) **Process-based costing:** A more radical approach to costing is one which considers the Cost of Quality (COQ) to be made up of two distinct components:
   – the price of conformance (Prevention and Appraisal) and the price of non-conformance (Failure cost).[10]

Process modelling leads to a good understanding of how a process functions in its present state. By identifying different variables, costs can be placed under categories such as people, equipment, materials and environment. The costs are allocated according to whether they enable the process to be 100% effective (Cost of

Conformance = COC) or whether the cost is linked to an attributable variable that is causing the process to be ineffective (Cost of Non-Conformance = CONC).

This exercise of allocating COC and CONC costs is extremely valuable, since it provides an opportunity for improvement. Based on information provided, management can take decisions on what kind of improvement programmes need to be implemented to render the process 100% effective and eliminate all the costs of non-conformance.

Process effectiveness is however not constant and can be improved upon. Opportunities for improvement depend on process capability studies and information provided by process costing.

Process modelling for costing purposes is compatible with the ethos of TQM, which places emphasis on process ownership, understanding, control and improvement.

QUALITY MEASUREMENT

Unlike quality costing, quality measurement relates to the ends in terms of overall business performance. Quality measurement has to adopt a process-based approach which looks at Value Added Management activity throughout the whole organisation.

The problem with measurement is similar to costing. Questions such as what to measure? Why measure? How to measure? and Where to measure? have to be raised. In relation to these issues, Sink[12] writes:

> '"Measurement is a mystery". Most people who attack the task of developing measurement systems eventually come to this conclusion. Even those who are considered experts readily admit that measurement is complex and still an unresolved mystery. Measurement is complex, frustrating, difficult, challenging, important, abused and misused. Measurement at the individual, group, and organisational levels has tremendous problems and opportunities associated with it.'

Total Quality Management has an impact on every aspect of a business. The approach to its implementation will determine how effective the measurement exercise is going to be.

There are two possible approaches to TQM implementation, Fig. 11.3 and 11.4, a bolt-on approach and an integrated approach. The impact of TQM implementation as a bolt on component is characterised as:

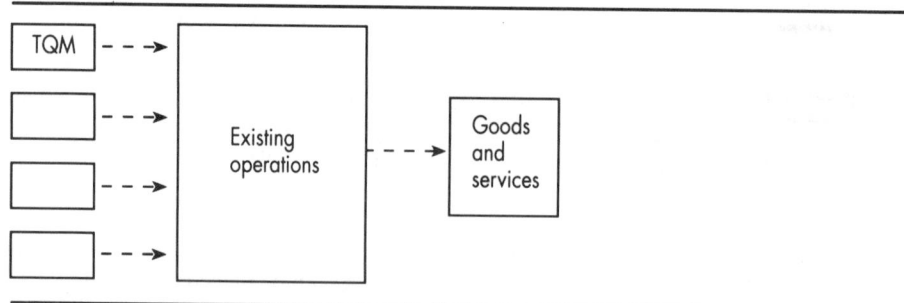

11.3 TQM as a bolt on activity to existing business operations.

- Diluted;
- Difficult to assess;
- Brings little/no change.

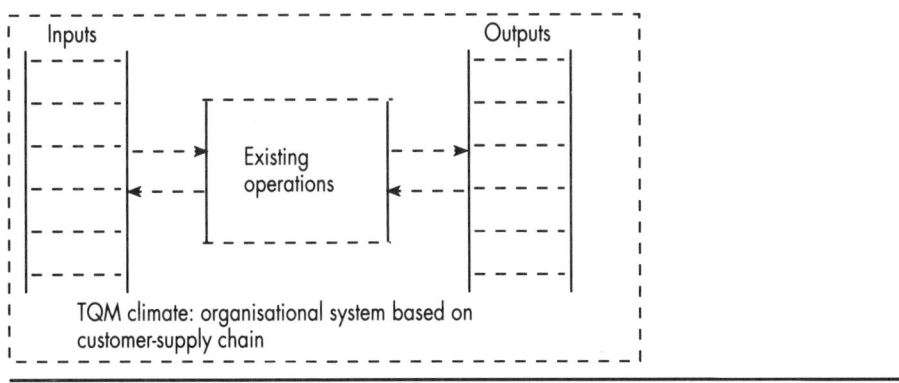

11.4 TQM as an integrated model.

The impact of TQM as an integrated model is characterised by:

- Synergy;
- A knock-on effect;
- Easy to assess;
- Brings big changes.

The measurement process in the context of TQM refers to the integrated model. The measurement of TQM effectiveness takes place at the human, technical and business levels of the organisation, Fig. 11.5.

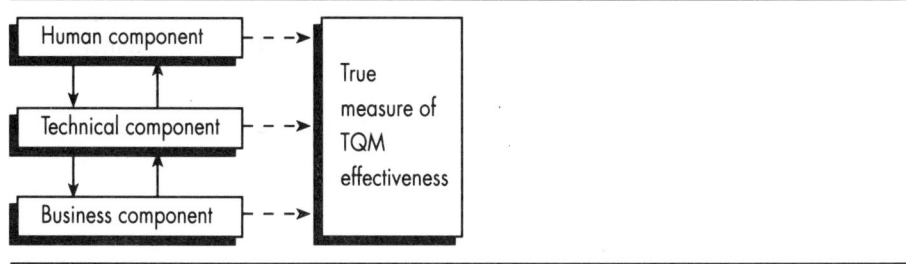

11.5 Measuring the effectiveness of TQM.

Sink[12] suggests that the organisational system comprises of providers, inputs, value adding processes, outputs and customers. The performance of the total organisational system can be characterised by seven inter-related criteria:

1 Effectiveness;
2 Efficiency;
3 'Total quality';
4 Productivity;
5 Quality of working life;
6 Innovation;
7 Financial performance.

It is suggested that the seven criteria embrace every aspect of business behaviour and therefore provide the basis for incremental measurements which are inter-related and which reflect overall business performance in the market place.

There is no doubt that, in the near future, issues on quality costing and quality measurement will become much more prominent, particularly for organisations which will be at an advanced stage of TQM implementation and who will have started to reap some of the real benefits of TQM.

BIBLIOGRAPHY

CHAPTER 1

1 Lake M (1988), 'Re-examining the role for industrial engineering', Proceedings of IIE Integrated Systems Conference, October 30–November 2, St Louis, USA.

2 McManus K R (1988) 'Changing the IE's role for a participative environment', Proceedings of IIE Integrated Systems Conference, October 30–November 2, St Louis, USA.

3 McGinnis L F (1989), 'IEs must maintain and strengthen empirical base – role and identity of profession are at stake', Industrial Engineering, Volume 21, No 3, pp 36–40.

4 Pesavento A I R (1989), IEs role has changed radically at Square D', Industrial Engineering. Volume 21, No 3, pp 40–42.

5 Seifert L (1989), 'The Industrial Engineer's new role in manufacturing?', Industrial Engineering, Volume 21, No 4, pp 40–41.

6 Tomkins J A (1989), 'Industrial Engineering and manufacturing design: IEs urged to step forward and claim design turf', Industrial Engineering, Volume 21, No 6, pp 44–45.

7 Engwall R L (1989), 'The expanding role of IEs in manufacturing', Industrial Engineering, Volume 21, No 6, pp 52–53.

8 Edosomwan J A (1987), 'Industrial engineers' roles are numerous and varied in high technology environment', Industrial Engineering, (December), pp 36–36.

9 Beuret G and Webb A (1983), 'Goals of Engineering Education (GEEP): Engineers – servants or saviours' , a DES/CNAA report, CNAA Development Services Publication 2, London: Council for National Academic Awards.

10 Burns N D (1988), 'Fitting the engineer to changing technologies', Chartered Mechanical Engineer, (February), pp 36–37.

11 Paton B (1988), 'Industrial Engineers at Frito-Lay follow non-traditional career with broad responsibilities', Industrial Engineering, (May), pp 20–23.

12 Seifert D J and Settles F S (1989), 'Are Industrial Engineers working on the right things in manufacturing?', Industrial Engineering, (February), pp 46–47.

13 Badiru A B (1987), 'Training the IE for a management role', Industrial Engineering, (December), pp 18–23.

14 Parnaby J (1988), 'Creating a competitive manufacturing strategy', Production Engineer, (July/August), pp 24–28.

15 Parnaby J (1986), 'The design of competitive manufacturing systems', International Journal of Technology Management, Vol 1, No 3.

16 Parnaby J (1987), 'A systems' engineering approach to fundamental changes in manufacturing', 9th Industrial Engineering Managers Conference, New Orleans, 9–11 March, IIE: USA.

17 Parnaby J (1986), 'Competitiveness through systems engineering', Cambridge Manufacturing Forum Proceedings – Winning in 1990, (July), IMechE: London.

18 Parnaby J (1986), 'Education and training in manufacturing systems engineering', PEP '86 Conference, (July), IProdE: London.

19 Parnaby J (1987), 'Education and training in manufacturing systems engineering', Proc IEE, Vol 134, PEA, No 10, (December), pp 816–824.

20 Lorriman J (1986), 'Ichiban – the Japanese approach to engineering education', Electronics and Power, (August), pp 573–577.

21 Wild R (1985), 'The education and training of engineers and managers for manufacture', Industrial and Commercial Training, (September/October), pp 17–19.

22 Horn C A (1983), 'The development of management in engineering', Electronics and Power, (January), pp 82–85.

23 Industrial Engineering Terminology, Industrial Engineering Management Press, Norcross: USA.

CHAPTER 2

1 Managing into the '90s – The Deming philosophy, The Enterprise Initiative, London: The Department of Trade and Industry.

2 Quality Management – A guide for chief executives, London: The Department of Trade and Industry.

3 Knight M (1988), 'Deming – a prophet with new honour', Production Engineer, (April), pp 58–59.

4 Deming W E (1982), Quality, productivity and competitive position, Cambridge, Massachusetts: MIT Centre for Advanced Engineering Study.

5 Crosby P (1979), 'Quality is Free – the art of making quality certain', New York: McGraw Hill.

6 Kacker R N (1987), 'Taguchi's quality philosophy: analysis and commentary', Quality Assurance, Vol 13, No 3, (September), pp 65–71.

7 Juran J M (1986), 'The quality trilogy', Quality Progress, (August), pp 21.

8 Garving D A (1987), 'Competing on the eight dimensions of quality', Harvard Business Review, (November-December), pp 101–109.

9 Bendell T (1988), 'Taguchi comes to Europe', Professional Engineering, (September), pp 80–81.

10 Taguchi G and Clausing D (1990), 'Robust quality', Harvard Business Review, (January–February), pp 65–75.

11 Taguchi G, El-Sayed E A, Hsiang T (1989), 'Quality engineering in production systems', USA: McGraw Hill International Editions.

12 Feingenbaum A V (1983), 'Total Quality Control', New York: McGraw Hill.

13 Cole G S (1988), 'The changing relationships between original equipment manufacturers and their suppliers', International Journal of Technology Management, Vol 3, No 3, pp 299–324.

14 Deming W E (1982), 'Quality, productivity and competitive position', Centre for Advanced Engineering Study, Cambridge: MIT Press.

15 Hodgson A (1987), 'Deming's never-ending road to quality', Personnel Management, (July) pp 40–44.

16 Box G et al (1988), 'An explanation and critique of Taguchi's contributions to quality engineering', Quality and Reliability Engineering International, Vol 4, pp 123–131.

17 Cullen J (1987), 'An introduction to Taguchi methods', Quality Today, (September), pp 43–46.

18 Trevor M (1986), 'Quality Control – learning from the Japanese', Long Range Planning, Vol 19, No 5, pp 46–53.

19 Drucker P F (1990), 'The emerging theory of manufacturing', Harvard Business Review, (May-June), pp 94–102.

20 Castle D R (1989), 'An IE perspective on Deming's 14 points', Industrial Engineering, Vol 21, No 9, (September), pp 23–28.

21 Garvin D A (1988), Managing Quality, New York: The Free Press.

22 Sepehri M (1987) (Editor), Quest for Quality, Norcross , Georgia: Industrial Engineering and Management Press.

23 Dingus V R (1988), 'Industrial Engineers meet Dr Deming: A matter of corporate survival', in Dingus R and Golomski W A (Editors): 'A quality revolution in manufacturing', Norcross, Georgia: Industrial Engineering and Management Press.

24 Schonberger R J and Knod E M jr (1988), 'Operations management – servicing the customer', 3rd Ed, Plano, Texas: Business Publications, Inc.

25 Oakland J S (1989), 'Total Quality Management', Oxford: Heinemann Professional Publishing.

26 Dale B G and Plunkett J J (1990), 'Managing quality', London: Philip Alan.

27 Tijunelis D and McKee K E (1987) (Editors), 'Manufacturing high technology handbook', New York: Marcel Dekker, Inc.

28 Juran J M (1988), 'Juran on planning for quality', New York: The Free Press – A division of McMillan, Inc.

29 Deming W E (1986), 'Out of crisis', Cambridge, USA: Cambridge University Press.

30 Ouchi (1981), 'Theory Z: How American business can meet the Japanese challenge', Reading, Mass: Addison-Wesley Publishing.

CHAPTER 3

1 Pfau L D (1989), 'Total Quality Management gives companies a way to enhance position in global marketplace', Industrial Engineering, (April), pp 17–21.

2 Shetty Y K (1987), 'Product quality and competitive strategy', Business Horizon, (May-June), pp 46–52.

3 Badiru A B (1990), 'A systems approach to Total Quality Management', Industrial Engineering, (March), pp 33–36.

4 Gettings M (1990), 'A computer-aided approach to manufacturing quality', Industrial Engineering, (March), pp 18–21.

5 Derrick F W, Desai H B, O'Brien W R (1990), 'Survey shows employees at

different organizational levels define quality differently', Industrial Engineering, (April), pp 22–27.

6 Farsad B, Elshennawy A K (1989), 'Defining service quality is difficult for service and manufacturing firms', Industrial Engineering, (March), pp 17–19.

7 Hammons C, Maddux GA (1990), 'Total Quality Management in the public sector', Management Decision, Vol 28, No 4, pp 15–19.

8 Handfield R (1989), 'Quality management in Japan versus the United States: An overview', Production and Inventory Management Journal, second quarter, pp 79–85.

9 Takeuchi H, Quelch J A (1983), 'Quality is more than making a good product', Harvard Business review, (July-August), pp 139–145.

10 Summer L T (1987), 'Design quality needs quality management', Chartered Mechanical Engineer, (January), pp 33–34.

11 Hohner G (1988), 'JIT/TQC: Integrating product design with shopfloor effectiveness', Industrial Engineering, pp 42–48.

12 Dingus V R (1988), 'Quality is exceeding customer expectations', Industrial Engineering, pp 24–25.

13 Sohal A S, Tay G S, Wirth A (1989), 'Total Quality Control in an Asian division of a multinational corporation', International Journal of Quality and Reliability Management, Vol 6, No 6, pp 60–74.

14 'Building a quality focus in government', Proceedings of Quality and Productivity Improvement Conference, June 1–2, Vienna, Virginia: USA.

15 Sarazen J S (1988), 'Quality plan development: A key stop towards customer enthusiasm', Quality Progress, (October), pp 72–74.

16 Fortuna R M (1988), 'Beyond quality: Taking SPC upstream', Quality Progress, Vol 21, No 6, pp 23–28.

17 Foster M, Whittle S (1989), 'The quality management maze', TQM Magazine, Vol 1, No 3, pp 143–148.

18 Tilley B G (1988), 'Achieving business quality improvement', Quality Assurance, Vol 14, No 4, pp 166–172.

19 Garvin D A (1987), 'Competing on the eight dimensions of quality', Harvard Business Review, (November-December), pp 101–109.

20 Brache A P, Rummler G A (1988), 'The three levels of quality', Quality Progress, (October) pp 46–51.

21 Chase R L (1988) (Editor), 'Total Quality Management', IFS (Publications)/ Springer-Verlag, UK.

22 Sepehri M (1987) (Editor), 'Quest for quality – Managing the total system', Industrial Engineering and Management press, Norcross, Georgia: USA.

23 Garvin D A (1987), 'What does "product quality" really mean?', in Sepehri M (Editor): 'Quest for quality – managing the total system', Industrial Engineering and Management Press, Norcross, Georgia: USA.

24 Freund R A (1987), 'Definitions and basic quality concepts', in Sepehri M (Editor): 'Quest for quality – managing the total system', Industrial Engineering and Management Press, Norcross, Georgia: USA.

25 Johnson M M (1987), 'An investigation of the effects of quality determinants', in Sepehri, M (Editor): 'Quest for quality – managing the total system', Industrial Engineering and Management Press, Norcross, Georgia: USA.

26 Besterfield D H (1986), 'Quality Control', Prentice Hall International Editions, USA.

27 Dale B G, Plunkett J J (1990) (Editors): Managing quality, Philip Allan, London.

28 Tijunelis D, McKee K E (1987) (Editors), 'Manufacturing high technology handbook', Marcell Dekker, Inc, New York: USA.

29 Garvin D A (1988), 'Managing Quality', The Free Press – A division of MacMillan Inc, New York.

30 Oakland J S (1989), 'Total Quality Management', Heinemann Professional Publishing, UK.

31 Gitlow H et al (1989), 'Tools and methods for the improvement of quality', Richard D Irwin, Inc, Boston: USA.

32 Collard R (1989), 'Total Quality – success through people', Institute of Personnel Management, London, IPM.

33 Wagel W H et al (1988), 'Quality – the bottom line', Personnel, Vol 65, No 7, pp 28–43.

34 Van Gigch J P (1977), 'Quality – producers and consumers views', Quality Progress, ASQC, (April).

35 Higgins J M, Vincze J W (1986), 'Strategic management and organisational policy – text and cases', The Dryden Press – CBS Publishing, Japan Ltd: Chicago.

36 Zairi M, Fitzmaurice C (1987), 'The management of quality: A behavioural question', Proceedings of Qualitaetskontrolle '87 Conference, 15–17 Sept 1987, Stuttgart, W Germany: TCM Expositions Ltd.

37 New C C, Myers A (1986), 'Managing manufacturing operations in the UK 1975–1985', British Institute of Management, UK.

38 'Productivity and Quality Today – A current evaluation of P&QI', Institute of Industrial Engineers, Norcross, Georgia: USA.

39 Ross J E, Shetty Y K (1985), 'Making quality a fundamental part of strategy', Long Range Planning, Vol 18, No 1, pp 53–58.

40 Wheelwright S C (1981), 'Japan where operations are strategic', Harvard Business Review, (July-August), pp 67–74.

41 Shetty Y K (1987), 'Product quality and competitive strategy', Business Horizons, (May-June), pp 46–52.

42 Wilcock D (1984), 'Just what is AMT and how can it be implemented?', The Production Engineer, (June), pp 10–12.

43 Tiernan T (1987), 'A potent arsenal of weapons', British Manufacturing Technology , (April), pp 6–11.

44 Goldhar J D (1986), 'In the factory of the future innovation is productivity', Research Management, (March-April), pp 26–33.

45 Weaver L J (1987), 'New chairman urges application of AMT', Application of Computers to Manufacturing Engineering (ACME) Newsletter, Issue No 4, (March), London: Science Engineering Research Council.

46 Committee on the Effective Implementation of Advanced Manufacturing technology (1986), Human Resource Practices for Implementing Advanced Manufacturing technology; Commission on Engineering and Technical Systems, Washington DC: National Academy Press.

47 Edwards C (1985), 'Why AMT?', Advanced Manufacturing Technology – Boardroom Report, (July), pp 5–8.

48 Donaldson W M (1986), 'AMT – selecting the most profitable option', CADCAM '86 Conference Proceedings, Birmingham: EMAP International, UK.

49 Advisory Council for Applied Research and Development (ACARD) (1983), 'New opportunities in manufacturing – the management of technology', London: HMSO.

50 NEDO (1985), 'Advanced Manufacturing Technology – the impact of new technology on engineering batch production', London: National Economic Development Office (NEDO).

51 Marshall P (1986), 'Advanced Manufacturing Technology – the route to industrial prosperity', 2nd National Conference on Production Research, (September), Edinburgh: Napier College of Technology.

CHAPTER 4

1 Willborn W (1988), 'Quality Management System – A planning and auditing guide', Industrial Press Inc, New York.

2 Duncan J, Thorpe B, Summer P (1990), 'Quality Assurance in construction, Gower, UK.

3 Chase R L (1989), 'Winning with quality – A practical approach to the development of a total quality strategy', IFS (Publications) Ltd, UK.

4 Stebbing L (1989), 'Quality assurance', John Wiley & Sons, Chichester: UK.

5 Zeller H J (Editor) (1988), 'The best on quality targets, improvements, systems'. International Academy for Quality, Carl Hanser Verlag: W Germany.

6 Schonberger R J and Knod E M (1988), 'Operations management – serving the customer', Business Publications, Inc, Plan, Texas: USA.

7 Wilborn W (1989), 'Dynamic auditing of quality assurance: Concept and method', International Journal of Quality and Reliability Management, Volume 7, No 3, pp 35–41.

8 Quality Systems BS 5750: Parts 1, 2 and 3. British Standards Institution, UK, 1979.

9 Quality Systems BS 5750: Parts O, 1, 2 and 3, British Standards Institution, UK, 1987.

10 International Organisation for Standardization: ISO Quality Systems 9000, 9001, 9002, 9003 and 9004.

11 Ford 101 Quality System standard, Ford Motor Company, Brentwood, Essex, 1987.

12 Stanford L (1990), 'Standards, quality and 1992', Professional Engineering, (March), pp 29–30.

13 Burn G R (1987), 'The philosophy behind BS 5750 – 1987', paper presented to the Institution of Production Engineers, Quality Management Group, (10th December), Birmingham.

14 Unknown, (1990) 'The chemistry of Quality Assurance', Automation, November, pp 37–38.

15 Aquino M A (1990), 'Improvement US compliance: A new look at auditing', Quality Progress, (October), pp 47–49.

16 Reynolds E A (1990), 'The science of quality audit and evaluation', Quality Progress, (July), pp 55–56.

17 Hashim M, Khan M (1990), 'Quality standards – past, present and future', Quality Progress, (June), pp 56–59.

18 Klock J J (1990), 'How to manage 3,500 (or fewer) supplier', Quality Progress, (June), pp 43–47.

19 Van Nuland Y (1990), 'The new common language for 12 countries', Quality Progress, (June), pp 40–41.

20 Kalinosky I S (1990), 'The total quality system – going beyond ISO 9000', Quality Progress, (June), pp 50–54.

21 Van Nuland Y (1990), 'Prerequisites to implementation', Quality Progress, (June), pp 36–39.

22 Burr J T (1990), 'The future necessity', Quality Progress, (June), pp 19–23.

23 Bochling W H (1990), 'Europe 1992: Its effect on international standards', Quality Progress, (June), pp. 29–32.

CHAPTER 5

1 Oakland J S (1989), 'Total quality management', Heinemann Publishers Inc, London.

2 Juran J M (1988), 'Juran on planning for quality', The Free Press, New York.

3 Wantuck K A (1989), 'Just In Time for America', The Forum Ltd, Milwaukee (USA).

4 Guy S (1987), 'SPC – its role in chemical analysis', Quality Today, (September), pp 16–23.

5 Burr A (1989), 'Quality by numbers', Industrial Computing, (May), pp 28–30.

6 Hodgson M (1987), 'TQC: A trivial pursuit or a step to the 90s', BPICS 22nd European Conference on Production & Inventory Control, 17–20 November, Blackpool, UK.

7 Kyde W C and Layden J (1988), 'Real time data acquisition using SPC', Manufacturing Engineering, (October), pp 64–66.

8 Krupp J A (1987), 'Process capability: One element of zero inventories', Production and Inventory Management, 3rd Quarter, 1987.

9 Whitehead R (1986), 'SPC – one way to "zero scrap" ', Production Engineer, (September), pp 37–41.

10 Stevick G E (1990), 'Preventing process problems', Quality Progress, September, pp 67–73.

11 Anderson L H (1990), 'Controlling process variation is key to manufacturing success', Quality Progress, (August), pp 91–93.

12 Shainin P D (1990), 'The tools of quality: Part III: Control charts', Quality Progress, August, pp 79–82.

13 Burr J T (1990), 'The tools of quality: Part I: Going with the flow(chart)', Quality Progress, (June), pp 64–67.

14 Sarazen J S (1990), 'The tools of quality part II; Cause and Effect diagrams', Quality Progress, July, pp 59–62.

15 Juran J M (Editor) (1989), 'Quality control handbook', 4th edition, McGraw Hill Book Co, USA.

16 Burr J T (1990), 'The tools of quality part VI: Pareto charts', Quality Progress, November, pp 59–61.

17 Nolan T W and Provost L P (1990), 'Understanding variation', Quality Progress, May, pp 70–78.

18 Coleman D E and Stein P G (1990), 'Improving measurements', Quality Progress, November, pp 35–39.

19 Skrabec Q R (1990), 'Ancient process control and its modern implications', Quality Progress, November, pp 49–52.

20 Modaress B and Ausari A (1989), 'Quality control techniques in US firms:

A survey', Production and Inventory Management Journal, 2nd Quarter, 1989.

21 Tribus M and Tsuda Y (1988), 'The quality imperative in the new economic era', in Dingus V R and Golomski W A (Eds): 'A quality revolution in manufacturing', Industrial Engineering and Management Press, Norcross, Georgia (USA).

22 Oakland J S and Followell R F (1990), 'Statistical Process Control, Heinemann Newness, London.

23 Shaw P and Dale B G (1990), 'Statistical process control', in Dale B G and Plunkett J J (Eds): 'Managing quality', Philip Allan, London.

24 Wantuck K A (1989), 'Just In Time for America', The Forum Ltd, Milwaukee, USA.

25 Gitlow H, Gitlow S, Oppenheim A, Oppenheim R (1989), 'Tools and methods for the improvement of quality', Richard D Irwin, Inc, Homewood: USA.

26 Schonberger R J and Knod E M (1988), 'Operations management', 3rd edition, Business Publications, Inc, Plano, Texas: USA.

27 Lucas J M (1987), 'Cumulative Sum (CUSUM) control schemes', in Sepehri M (Editor): 'Quest for quality', Industrial Engineering and Management Press, Norcross: USA.

28 Owen M (1989), 'SPC – an overview', in Dale B G (Editor): 'Tools and techniques for TQM', IFS (Publications) Ltd, Bedford: UK.

29 Barker R L (1989), 'The seven new QC tools', in Dale, B G (Editor): 'Tools and techniques for TQM, IFS (Publications) Ltd, Bedford: UK.

30 McCabe W J (1989), 'Examining processes improves operations', Quality Progress, July, pp 26–32.

31 Mohanty R P and Dahanayka N (1989), 'Process improvement: Evaluation of methods', Quality Progress, September, pp 45–48.

32 Propst A L (1989), 'In search of a new process', Quality Progress, June, pp 43–47.

33 Ralyea D B (1989), 'The simple power of Pareto', Quality Progress, May, pp 38–39.

34 Hahn G J and Boardman T J (1985), 'Statistical concepts for quality improvement: A new perspective', Quality Progress, November, pp 300–36.

35 Goh T N (1988), 'Statistical methodologies for quality and production improvement', Industrial Management and Data Systems (IMDS), September/October, pp 21–24.

36 Griffin T L (1985), 'A roadmap for SPC – Implementation plan keeps SPC efforts on track', Quality Progress, November, pp 69–71.

37 Moen R D and Nolan T W (1987), 'Process Improvement', Quality Progress, September, pp 62–68.

38 Ackerman R B, Plsek P E, Surette G J (1986), 'Quality tools: Meeting the needs of tomorrow's industry', Quality Progress, October, pp 61–65.

39 Burr J T (1990), 'The tools of Quality – part VII: Scatter diagrams', Quality Progress, December, pp 87–89.

40 Ranney G B (1990), 'The implications of variation', Quality Progress, December, pp 71–77.

41 Ishikawa K (1985), 'What is total quality control? the Japanese way', Translated by David J Lu, Englewood Cliffs, NJ: Prentice- Hall, USA.

42 Harrington H J and Revelle J B (1988), 'Total quality issues and activities in the defense industry', in Dingus V R and Golomski W A (Eds): 'A quality revolution in manufacturing, Industrial Engineering and Management Press, Norcross, Georgia: USA.

CHAPTER 6

1 Schonberger R J and Knod E M (1988), 'Operations Management – serving the customer', 3rd edition, Business Publications, Inc, Plano Texas.

2 Takatsuki R (1982), 'Productivity and quality innovation with TPM (Total productive Maintenance)', in Monden Y (Editor): 'Applying Just In Time: The American/Japanese Experience', Industrial Engineering and Management Press, Norcross, Georgia.

3 Bailey C L, Maggard B N, Moss, D W (1987), 'Total productive maintenance: A team implementation approach', in Proceedings of International Industrial Engineering Conference, May 22–25, 1988, Orlando: Industrial Engineering and Management Press.

4 Singh B B (1988), 'Maintenance patterns evaluation for electric plant equipment and facilities', In Proceedings of International Industrial Engineering Conference, May 22–25, 1988, Orlando, Industrial Engineering and Management Press.

5 Tombari H A (1982), 'Designing a maintenance management system', Production and Inventory Management, 4th Quarter, pp 139–147.

6 Priestley C (1983), 'Purchasing must push for planned maintenance', Purchasing, September 29th, p 29.

7 Tersine R J (1983), 'Preventive maintenance: A path to higher productivity', Society for Advancement of Management (S.A.M), Advanced Management Journal, Spring 1983, pp 39–44.

8 Sadler K (1988), 'Maintenance – the key to integration', BPICS 23rd European Conference on Production and Inventory Control, 2–4 November, Birmingham (UK).

9 Senker P (1986), 'Automation and maintenance training', Robotica (1986), Volume 4, pp 47–50.

10 Hutchins D (1990), 'Taking the medicine', Manufacturing Engineer, September, 20–22.

11 Willmott P (1990), 'Managing maintenance', Manufacturing Engineer, June, pp 28–30.

12 Willmott P (1990), 'Maintaining profitability', Manufacturing Engineer, May, pp 30–32.

13 Oliver S (1990), 'Beyond the oily rag', Manufacturing Engineer, October, pp 42–45.

14 Newman R (1985), 'MRP where M = Preventative Maintenance', Production and Inventory Management', Second Quarter, pp 21–28.

15 Gallimore K F, Penlesky R J (1988), 'A framework for developing maintenance strategies', Production and Inventory Management Journal, First Quarter, pp 16–21.

16 Burgess J A (1990), 'What price quality?', Professional Engineering, May, p 28.

17 Seddon G (1988), 'Maintenance matters', Industrial Computing, April, pp 29–34.

18 Brick J M, Michael J R and Morganstein D (1989), 'Using statistical thinking to solve maintenance problems', Quality Progress, May, pp 55–60.

19 Sadler K (1989), 'Maintenance – a vital element', December-January, pp 35–36.

20 Patton J D (1983), 'Preventative Maintenance', Instrument Society of America, USA.

21 Suzaki K (1987), 'The new manufacturing challenge – techniques for continuous improvement', The Free Press, New York.

CHAPTER 7

1 Jenkins J (1989), 'Corporate manslaughter – companies on trial', Director, (April), pp 124–127.

2 Rock S (1989), 'Can Boeing fly out of trouble?', Director, (July), pp 53–55.

3 Dobinson J (1991), 'Work can damage your health', Director, (February), p 72.

4 Denton, D K (1982), 'Safety management: Improving performance', New York, McGraw Hill Book Company.

5 Tye J (1988), 'Introduction to safety management', Modern Management, Summer 1988, pp 8–9.

6 Herbert E (1990), 'COSHH and the questions it has raised', Professional Engineering, January, pp 30–32.

7 Powley D (1989), 'Life under COSHH', Manufacturing Engineer, September, pp 29–30.

8 Simms, J (1983), 'Cost-effective safety training – the way forward', Training Officer, May, pp 142–144.

9 Barrett B N, Brown H, James P W (1988), 'Achieving health and safety at work: The problem of evaluating management effectiveness', PR, Vol 12, No 2, pp 16–20.

10 James P (1990), 'Holding managers to account on safety', Personnel Management, April, pp 54–58.

11 Rose M I (1988), 'Quality vs safety', Quality Progress, June, pp 70–71.

12 Boyle A (1981), 'Methodology and evaluation of accident investigation – Part I: Accident investigation as a skill and the background knowledge required', Safety Surveyor, July, pp 4–9.

13 Boyle A (1981), 'Methodology and evaluation of accident investigation, Part 2: The practical skills required for investigations', Safety Surveyor, September, pp 4–11.

14 Oram S A J (1981), 'How managers see their health and safety "responsibilities" ', Management Monitor, pp 3–6.

15 Warren B (1991), 'The trivial pursuit of Zero Risk', Best of Business International, Winter 1990–91, pp 32–37.

16 Evans J M (1986), 'Manufacturing mistakes', Proceedings of 3rd International Conference on Human Factors in Manufacturing, Bedford (UK), IFS (Conferences) Ltd, pp 221–228.

17 Botterill M (1990), 'Health and Safety at work', Management Services, April, pp 6–10.

18 Fitzmaurice C and Zairi M (1988), 'The automated environment: A challenge for the safety practitioner', Proceedings of International Conference on Ergonomics, Occupational Safety and Health and the Environment, October 24–28, Beijing (China), Vol 1, pp 195–204.

19 Fitzmaurice C and Zairi M (1987), 'The management of quality: A behavioural question', Proceedings of Qualitaetskontrolle '87 Conference, September 15–17, Stuttgart (West Germany), TCM Expositions Limited.

20 Carlsson J (1984), 'Robots accidents in Sweden, 1979 – 84', Solna (Information on arbetsskador 1984:2), 1984.

21 Nicholaisen P (1985), 'Industrial safety in the use of industrial robots', paper presented at Fellbach Congress on mechanisation, automation and the use of industrial robots in arc welding, 13–15 March 85, 95–98.

22 Smith M J, Cohen B F G, Stammerjohn L W, Happ A (1981), 'Health complaints

– potential health hazards of video display terminals', US Department of Health and Human Services, Cincinnati, 1981.

23 'VDUs: Health and Jobs', The Labour Research Department, London, 1985.

CHAPTER 8

1 Peters T, Austin N (1985), 'MBWA (managing by walking around)', California Management Review, Vol XXVIII, Fall 1985, No 1, pp 9–34.

2 Tunstall W B (1986), 'The break up of the bell system: A case study in cultural transformation', California Management Review, Volume XXVIII, Winter 1986, No 2, pp 110–124.

3 Isenberg D J (1984), 'How senior managers think', Harvard Business Review, November – December, pp 81–90.

4 Spicer H (1984), 'How to create commitment', Management Today, November, pp 94–98.

5 Lorsch J W (1986), 'Managing culture: The invisible barrier to change', California Management Review, Volume XXVIII, Winter, No 2, pp 95–109.

6 Martin P and Nicholls J (1985), 'How to manage', Management Today, April, pp 56–57, 107, 110–112.

7 Kennedy C (1989), 'Culture club – companies with a mission to change', Director, December, pp 40–44.

8 Hogg C (1989), 'Searching for the rare beast', Director, December, pp 62–67.

9 Lidstone J (1989), 'Projected image – making corporate identity work', Director, pp 88–90.

10 Kilmann R H, Saxton M J, Serpa R (1986), 'Issues in understanding and changing culture', California Management Review, Volume XXVIII, Winter 1986, No 2, pp 87–94.

11 Strauss N (1989), 'How to be leader of the grand', Director, June, p 49.

12 Ninomya J S (1988), 'Wagon masters and lesser managers', Harvard Business Review, March-April, pp 84–90.

13 Bartolome F, Laurent A (1986), 'The manager: master and servant of power', Harvard Business Review, Vol 64, No 6, November-December, pp 77–81.

14 Kotter J P (1990), 'What leaders really do', Harvard Business Review, May-June, pp 103–111.

15 Wynne B (1989), 'Leadership and excellence', Management Decision, Vol 28, No 1, pp 15–19.

16 Price F (1987), 'Out of Bedlam: The new philosophy of management by quality leadership', The International Journal of Quality and Reliability Management, Vol 4, No 2, pp 63–73.

17 Harris P R (1986), 'Management development for the new work culture', International Journal of Manpower, Vol 7, No 4, pp 23–27.

18 Denton D K (1989), 'Four steps to resolving conflicts', Quality Progress, Vol 22, No 4, pp 29–33.

19 Nadler D A, Tushman M L (1990), 'Beyond the charismatic leader: Leadership and organizational change', California Management Review, Winter 1990, pp 77–97.

20 Carroll D T (1981), 'Boards and managements: ten challenges and responses', Harvard Business Review, September-October, pp 62–66.

21 Patton A, Baker J C (1987), 'Why won't directors rock the boat', Harvard Business Review, November-December, pp 10–18.

22 Collier A T (1968), 'Business leadership and a creative society', Harvard Business Review, January-February.

23 Stayer R (1990), 'How I learned to let my workers lead', Harvard Business Review, November-December, pp 66–83.

24 Gilbert R J (1990), 'Are you committed or COMMITTED?', Quality Progress, May, pp 45–48.

25 Gibson T C (1990), 'Helping leaders accept leadership of Total Quality Management', Quality Progress, November, pp 45–47.

26 Peters T (1988), 'Facing up to the need for a management revolution', California Management Review, Vol XXX, No 2, Winter 1988, pp 7–38.

27 Drucker P F (1990), 'Managing the non-profit organization', Butterworth-Heinemann Ltd, Oxford, UK.

28 Hsieh T Y (1990), 'Leadership actions', The McKinsey Quarterly, No 4, pp 42–57.

29 Conger J A (1990), 'The dark side of leadership', Organizational Dynamics, pp 44–55.

30 Senge P M (1990), 'The leader's new work: building learning organizations', Sloan Management Review, Fall 1990, pp 7–23.

31 Campbell A (1991), 'A mission to succeed', Director, February, pp 66–68.

32 Strauss N (1989), 'Clarity begins at home', Director, May, p 47.

33 Margerison C (1990), 'The ways managers make their organisations succeed', Leadership & Organization Development Journal, Vol 11, No 4, pp 17–22.

34 Botterill M (1990), 'Changing corporate culture', Management Services, June, pp 14–18.

35 Lowe T A, McBean G M (1989), 'Honesty without fear', Quality Progress, November, pp 30–34.

36 Kono T (1990), 'Corporate culture and long range planning', Long Range Planning, Vol 23, No 4, pp 9–19.

37 Parker H (1990), 'The company chairman – his role and responsibilities', Long Range Planning, Vol 23, No 4, pp 35–43.

38 Anthony R D (1990), 'The paradox of the management culture or "he who leads is lost" ', Personnel Review, Vol 19, No 4, pp 3–8.

39 Schein E H (1985), 'Organizational power and leadership', Jossey Bass, San Francisco.

40 Adamson F B (1989), 'Cultivating a charismatic quality leader', Quality Progress, July, pp 56–57.

41 Linkow P (1989), 'Is your culture ready for total quality?', Quality Progress, November, pp 69–71.

42 Peters T (1988), 'Leadership excellence in the 1990s: Learning to love change', Journal of Management Development, Vol 7, No 5, pp 5–9.

43 Dimma W A (1989), 'On leadership', Business Quarterly, Winter, pp 17–20.

44 Germain R, Cooper M B (1990), 'How a customer mission statement affects company performance', Industrial Marketing Management, Vol 19, pp 47–54.

45 Oeh R, Kleiner B H (1990), 'Lessons from business leaders of today', Industrial Management, January/February, pp 31–32.

46 Higginson T J, Waxler R P (1989), 'Developing a trust culture: to survive in the 1990s', Industrial Management, November/December, pp 27–28, 32.

47 Kouzes J M, Posner B Z (1989), 'The leadership challenge', Josey-Bass, San Francisco.

48 Ishizuna Y (1990), 'The transformation of Nissan – the reform of corporate culture', Long Range Planning, Vol 23, No 3, pp 9–15.

49 Bavly D, Bavly H (1986), 'What is the board of directors good for?', Long Range Planning, Vol 19, No 3, pp 20–26.

50 Pinnell B (1986), 'The role of the board in corporate planning', Long Range Planning, Vol 19, No 5, pp 27–32.

51 Kotter J (1982), 'The general managers', New York, Free Press.

52 Townsend R (1984), 'Further up the organization', New York, Knopf.

53 Drucker P F (1985), 'Changing the world of the executive', London, Heinemann.

54 Daniel D R (1961), 'Management information crisis', Harvard Business Review, Vol 39, No 5, September-October, pp 111–121.

55 Martin P, Nichols J (1984), 'How to create commitment', Management Today, November, pp 94–98.

56 Conger J A (1985), 'Charismatic leadership in business: An exploratory study', Ann Arbor, MI: University Microfilms International.

CHAPTER 9

1 Patterson J W, Engelkemeyer S (1989), 'A company cannot live by its quality alone', Quality Progress, August, pp 25–27.

2 Lyons T F, Krachenberg A R, Henke J W (1990), 'Mixed motive marriages: What's next for buyer-supplier relations?', Sloan Management Review, Spring 1990, pp 29–36.

3 Narus J A, Anderson J C (1988), 'Strengthen distributor performance through channel positioning', Sloan Management Review, Winter 1988, pp 31–40.

4 Waddock S A (1988), 'Building successful social partnerships', Sloan Management Review, Summer 1988, pp 17–23.

5 Ulrich D (1989), 'Tie the corporate knot: Gaining complete customer commitment', Sloan Management Review, Summer 1989, pp 19–27.

6 Cohen M A, Lee H L (1990), 'Out of touch with customer needs? Spare parts and faster sales service', Sloan Management Review, Winter 1990, pp 55–66.

7 Henderson J C (1990), 'Plugging into strategic partnerships: the critical IS connection', Sloan Management Review, Spring 1990, pp 7–18.

8 Stevens G C (1988), 'Successful supply-chain management', Management Decision, Vol 28, No 8, pp 25–30.

9 Yaus L P (1988), 'The global search for quality', Quality Progress, August, pp 51–53.

10 Shapiro B P, Rangan V K, Moriarty R T, Ross E B (1987), 'Manage customers for profits (not just for sales)', Harvard Business Review, September-October, pp 101–108.

11 Connor A I, Macedo N M, Wright A M (1989), 'The impact of Just-In-Time on buyer/seller relationships: An interaction approach', Proceedings of MEG '89 Conference, Glasgow School of Business, Scotland.

12 Robins F D (1989), 'Expectations Management', Proceedings of MEG '89 Conference, Glasgow Business School, Scotland.

13 Fulmer W E, Goodwin J (1988), 'Differentiation: begin with the customer', Business Horizons, September-October, pp 55–62.

14 Spekman R E (1988), 'Strategic supplier selection: Understanding long term buyer relationships', Business Horizons, July-August, pp 75–81.

15 MacBeth D K, Baxter L F, Neil G C (1988), 'Buyer-vendor relationships with Just In Time: Lessons from US multinationals', Industrial Engineering, September, pp 38–41.

16 Lee S M, Ebrahimpour M (1987), 'Just In Time', Management Decision, Vol 25, No 6, pp 50–54.

17 Blenkhorn D L, Noori A H (1990), 'What it takes to supply Japanese OEMs, Industrial Marketing Management, Vol 19, pp 21–30.

18 Bernard P (1989), 'Managing vendor performance', Production and Inventory Management Journal, First Quarter, pp 1–9.

19 Newman R G (1988), 'The buyer – supplier relationship under Just In Time', Production and Inventory Management Journal, Third Quarter, pp 45–50.

20 Burt D N (1989), 'Managing suppliers up to speed', Harvard Business Review, July-August, pp 127–135.

21 Burton T T (1988), 'JIT/repetitive sourcing strategies: "Tying the knot" with your suppliers', Production and Inventory Management Journal, Fourth Quarter, pp 38–42.

22 Salmond D, Spekman R (1986), 'Collaboration as a mode of managing long term buyer-supplier relationships', AMA Educators Conference Proceedings, IL: AMA, Chicago, 1986, pp 205–211.

23 Willis T H, Huston C R, Aby C D (1989), 'Just In Time purchasing from the suppliers' point of view', Industrial Management, November/December, pp 23–26.

24 Gitlow H S, Wiesner D A (1988), 'Vendor relations: An important piece of the quality puzzle', Quality Progress, January, pp 19–23.

25 Mcdermott, L C, Emerson M (1991), 'Quality and service for internal customers', Training and Development Journal, January, pp 61–64.

26 Klock J J (1990), 'How to manage 3,500 (or fewer) suppliers', Quality Progress, June, pp 43–46.

27 Houlihan J B S (1984), 'Supply chain management', BPICS 19th European Conference on Production and Inventory Control, 15–17 Nov 1984, Birmingham.

28 Kalff R J (1984), 'Supplier/customer relations', BPICS 19th European Conference on Production and Inventory Control, 15–17 Nov 1984, Birmingham.

29 Jackson B B (1985), 'Build customer relationships that last', Harvard Business Review, November-December, pp 120–128.

30 Reichheld F F, Sasser W E (1990), 'Zero Defections: Quality comes to services', Harvard Business Review, September-October, pp 105–111.

31 Myer R (1989), 'Suppliers – manage your customers', Harvard Business Review, November-December, pp 160–168.

32 MacBeth D, Ferguson N, Neil G C, Baxter L F (1989), 'Not purchasing but supply chain management', Purchasing and Supply Management, November, pp 30–32.

33 Abraham Y, Holt T, Kathawala Y (1989), 'Just In Time: Supplier-side strategic implications', Industrial Management & Data Systems, Vol 90, No 3, pp 12–17.

34 Sullivan L P (1986), 'Quality function deployment', Quality Progress, June, pp 39–50.

35 Broeker E J (1989), 'Build a better supplier-customer relationship', Quality Progress, September, pp 67–68.

36 Lamming R (1986), 'For better or for worse – technical change and buyer-supplier relationships in the UK automobile component industry', in Voss C A (Editor): 'Managing Advanced Manufacturing Technology', UK: IFS (Publications) Ltd.

37 Parkinson S T (1980), 'User-supplier interaction in new product development', PhD thesis, University of Strathclyde, Glasgow: Department of Marketing.

38 Webster F E jr (1984), 'Industrial Marketing Strategy', 2nd Edition, John Wiley, New York.

39 Hall R I (1980), 'Survival strategies in a hostile environment', Harvard Business Review, (September-October), pp 75–85.

40 Tornatzky L G et al (1983), 'The process of technological innovation: Reviewing the literature', USA: National Science Foundation.

41 Webster F E jr (1979), 'Industrial Marketing Strategy', New York: John Wiley & Sons.

42 Ettlie J E and Rubenstein A H (1981), 'Stimulating the flow of innovations to the US automation industry', Technology Forecasting and Social Change, Vol 19, pp 33–55.

43 Abernathy W J (1978), 'The productivity dilemma: Roadblocks to innovation in the automobile industry', Baltimore: John Hopkins University Press.

44 Campbell N (1983), 'Interaction strategies for the management of buyer/seller relationships in industrial markets'. PhD thesis, Faculty of Technology, University of Manchester: Department of Management Studies.

45 Cunningham M T and Homse E (1984), 'The roles of personal contacts in supplier-customer relationships', Occasional paper No 8410, University of Manchester Institute of Science and Technology (UMIST), Department of Management Sciences.

46 Zairi M (1989), 'The management of advanced Manufacturing technology: A study of user-supplier networks', PhD thesis, Stafforshire Polytechnic, The Management Centre.

47 Brand G (1972), 'The industrial buying decision', London: Cassell.

48 Luffman G (1974), 'The processing of information by industrial buyers', Industrial Marketing Management, Vol 3, No 6, pp 363–375.

49 Hakansson H (editor) (1982), 'International Marketing and purchasing of industrial goods: An interaction approach, USA: John Wiley & Sons.

CHAPTER 10

1 Wall S J, Zeynel S C (1991), 'The senior manager's role in quality improvement', Quality Progress, January, pp 66–68.

2 Gitlow H S, Gitlow S, Oppenheim A, Oppenheim R (1990), 'Telling the quality story', Quality Progress, September, pp 41–46.

3 Schobert F G, Brown C L (1990), 'A strategy for continuous improvement', Quality Progress, October, pp 69–71.

4 Robert M, Racine B, Bowers C (1990), 'A workers' mind is a terrible thing to waste', Quality Progress, October, pp 59–61.

5 Roth W (1990), 'Dos and don'ts of quality improvement', Quality Progress, August, pp 85–87.

6 Drago R (1988), 'Quality circle survival: An exploratory analysis', Industrial Relations, Vol 27, No 3, Fall 1988, pp 336–351.

7 Harwood C C, Pieters G R (1990), 'How to manage quality improvement', Quality Progress, March, pp 45–48.

8 Pettersson M (1989), 'Continual improvement for competitive advantage', Industrial Management & Data Systems, Vol 90, No 1, pp 4–10.

9 Juran J M (1987), 'QC Circles in the West', Quality Progress, September, pp 60–61.

10 Bagwell T C (1987), 'Quality circles: two keys to success', Quality Progress, September, pp 57–59.

11 Conway W E (1988), 'The right way to manage', Quality Progress, January, pp 14–15.

12 Hardy G, West M (1990), 'Innovative teams at work', Personnel Management, September, pp 48–53.

13 Karabatsos N (1989), 'Continuous improvement – the challenge for the nineties', Quality Progress, August, pp 17–20.

14 Hoernschemeyer D (1989), 'The four cornerstones of excellence', Quality Progress, August, pp 37–40.

15 O'Donnell M, O'Donnell R J (1984), 'Quality circles – the latest fad or a real winner?', Business Horizons, May-June, pp 58–62.

16 Instone, F J, Dale B G (1988), 'A case study of the typical issues involved in quality improvement', International Journal of Operations and Production Management, Vol 9, No 1, pp 15–26.

17 Butlin C (1989), 'Continuous improvement', BPICS Annual Conference, 4–6 December 1989, Birmingham, pp 319–330.

18 Hammons C, Maddax G A (1989), 'An obligation to improve', Management Decision, Vol 27, No 6, pp 5–8.

19 Perman D C (1989), 'Training, problem-solving and quality improvement – some forgotten lessons from Japan', International Journal of Quality and Reliability Management, Vol. 6, No 6, pp 18–23.

20 Jacobs R C, Everett J G (1988), 'The importance of team building in a high-tech environment', European Industrial Training, Vol 12, No 4, pp 10–16.

21 Rossier P E, Sink D S (1990), 'What's ahead for productivity and quality improvement?', Industrial Engineering, March, pp 25–31.

22 Heath P M (1989), 'The path to quality achievement through teamwork plus commitment', International Journal of Quality and Reliability Management, Vol 6, No 2, pp 51–59.

23 Wolff P J (1987), 'Western problems – Eastern solutions: Mixed promise of quality circles', Journal of Managerial Psychology, Vol 2, No 2, pp 3–8.

24 Ashton D, Dooney J (1990), 'Lasting improvement', Total Quality Management, April, pp 91–95.

25 Imberman W (1986), 'The golden nuggets on the factory floor', Business Horizons/ July-August, pp 63–69.

26 Kehrl H (1988), 'Continuous improvement: How to get it, MIT Management: Sloan School of Management, Massachusetts Institute of Technology.

27 Persico J (1989), 'Team up for quality improvement', Quality Progress, Vol 22, No 1, January, pp 33–37.

28 Ward K, Willis T H (1989), 'Managing change in an operations system', Management Decision, Volume 28, No 7, pp 17–21.

29 Suzaki K (1987), 'The new manufacturing challenge – techniques for continuous improvement', New York, The Free Press

30 Sahney V K (1990), 'The role of management in implementing the quality improvement process', Proceedings of International Industrial Engineering Conference, Atlanta, Georgia: Industrial Engineering & Management Press.

31 Kulikowski J (1990), 'Employee involvement for quality and productivity

improvement', Proceedings of International Industrial Engineering Conference, Atlanta, Georgia: Industrial Engineering & Management Press.

32 Gartman J B, Fargher J S W (1990), 'Productivity and quality improvement: The leadership dimension', Proceedings of International Industrial Engineering Conference, Atlanta, Georgia: Industrial Engineering & Management Press.

33 Imai M (1986), KAIZEN – The key to Japan's competitive success, New York: Random House Business Division.

CHAPTER 11

1 Jackson S (1990), 'Calling the gurus', Director, October, pp 95–101.

2 Camppanella J, Corcoran F J (1983), 'Principles of quality costs', Quality Progress, April, pp 16–22.

3 Sullivan E (1983), 'Quality costs: current ideas', Quality Progress, April, pp 24–25.

4 Schneiderman A M (1986), 'Optimum quality costs and Zero Defects: Are they contradictory concepts?', Quality Progress, November, pp 28–31.

5 Israeli A, Fisher B (1991), 'Cutting quality costs', Quality Progress, January, pp 46–48.

6 British Standard 6143 (1990), 'Guide to the economics of quality, Part 2: Prevention, appraisal and failure model', British Standard Institution, London 1990.

7 British Standard guide to the economics of quality (draft) in preparation for the production of part 1: Process cost control, BSI, London 1990.

8 Quality costs, National Quality Campaign, Department of Trade and Industry, London 1989.

9 Golomski W A (1988), 'Applications of quality cost concepts', in Dingus, V R & Golomski W A (Eds): 'A quality revolution in manufacturing', Industrial Engineering & Management Press, Norcross, Atlanta: IIE.

INDEX